Ralph Waldo Emerson, Charles Sumner, Harriet Beecher Stowe, John Brown, Theodore Parker, John Greenleaf Whittier, Wendell Phillips

The anti-slavery struggle

Ralph Waldo Emerson, Charles Sumner, Harriet Beecher Stowe, John Brown, Theodore Parker, John Greenleaf Whittier, Wendell Phillips

The anti-slavery struggle

ISBN/EAN: 9783744737111

Printed in Europe, USA, Canada, Australia, Japan

Cover: Foto ©ninafisch / pixelio.de

More available books at **www.hansebooks.com**

THE
OLD SOUTH LEAFLETS.

FIFTEENTH SERIES.

1897.

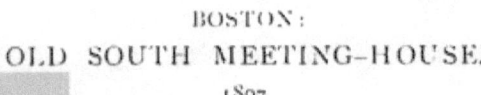

BOSTON:
OLD SOUTH MEETING-HOUSE.
1897.

INTRODUCTION.

The Old South Leaflets were prepared primarily for circulation among the attendants upon the Old South Lectures for Young People. The subjects of the Leaflets are immediately related to the subjects of the lectures, and they are intended to supplement the lectures and stimulate historical interest and inquiry among the young people. They are made up, for the most part, from original papers of the periods treated in the lectures, in the hope to make the men and the public life of the periods more clear and real.

The Old South Lectures for Young People were instituted in the summer of 1883, as a means of promoting a more serious and intelligent attention to historical studies, especially studies in American history among the young people of Boston. The success of the lectures has been so great as to warrant the hope that such courses may be sustained in many other cities of the country.

The Old South Lectures for 1883, intended to be strictly upon subjects in early Massachusetts History, but by certain necessities somewhat modified, were as follows: "Governor Bradford and Governor Winthrop," by Edwin D. Mead. "Plymouth," by Mrs. A. M. Diaz. "Concord," by Frank B. Sanborn. "The Town-meeting," by Prof. James K. Hosmer. "Franklin, the Boston Boy," by George M. Towle. "How to study American History," by Prof. G. Stanley Hall. "The Year 1777," by John Fiske. "History in the Boston Streets," by Edward Everett Hale. The Leaflets prepared in connection with these lectures consisted of (1) Cotton Mather's account of Governor Bradford, from the "Magnalia"; (2) the account of the arrival of the Pilgrims at Cape Cod, from Bradford's Journal; (3) an extract from Emerson's Concord Address in 1835; (4) extracts from Emerson, Samuel Adams, De Tocqueville, and others, upon the Town-meeting; (5) a portion of Franklin's Autobiography; (6) Carlyle on the Study of History; (7) an extract from Charles Sumner's oration upon Lafayette, etc.; (8) Emerson's poem, "Boston."

The lectures for 1884 were devoted to men representative of certain epochs or ideas in the history of Boston, as follows: "Sir Harry Vane, in New England and in Old England," by Edward Everett Hale, Jr. "John Harvard, and the Founding of Harvard College," by Edward Channing, Ph.D. "The Mather Family, and the Old Boston Ministers," by Rev. Samuel J. Barrows. "Simon Bradstreet, and the Struggle for the Charter," by Prof. Marshall S. Snow. "Samuel Adams, and the Beginning of the Revolution," by Prof. James K. Hosmer. "Josiah Quincy, the Great Mayor," by Charles W. Slack. "Daniel Webster, the Defender of the Constitution," by Charles C. Coffin. "John A. Andrew, the Great War Governor," by Col. T. W. Higginson. The Leaflets prepared in connection with the second course were as follows: (1) Selections from Forster's essay on Vane, etc.; (2) an extract from Cotton Mather's "Sal Gentium"; (3) Increase Mather's "Narrative of the Miseries of New England"; (4) an original account of "The Revolution in New England" in 1689; (5) a letter from Samuel Adams to John Adams, on Republican Government; (6) extracts from Josiah Quincy's

Boston Address of 1830; (7) Words of Webster; (8) a portion of Governor Andrew's Address to the Massachusetts Legislature in January, 1861.

The lectures for 1885 were upon "The War for the Union," as follows: "Slavery," by WILLIAM LLOYD GARRISON, JR. "The Fall of Sumter," by COL. T. W. HIGGINSON. "The Monitor and the Merrimac," by CHARLES C. COFFIN. "The Battle of Gettysburg," by COL. THEODORE A. DODGE. "Sherman's March to the Sea," by GEN. WILLIAM COGSWELL. "The Sanitary Commission," by MRS. MARY A. LIVERMORE. "Abraham Lincoln," by HON. JOHN D. LONG. "General Grant," by CHARLES C. COFFIN. The Leaflets accompanying these lectures were as follows: (1) Lowell's "Present Crisis," and Garrison's Salutatory in the *Liberator* of January 1, 1831; (2) extract from Henry Ward Beecher's oration at Fort Sumter in 1865; (3) contemporary newspaper accounts of the engagement between the Monitor and the Merrimac; (4) extract from Edward Everett's address at the consecration of the National Cemetery at Gettysburg, with President Lincoln's address; (5) extract from General Sherman's account of the March to the Sea, in his Memoirs; (6) Lowell's "Commemoration Ode"; (7) extract from Lincoln's First Inaugural Address, the Emancipation Proclamation, and the Second Inaugural Address; (8) account of the service in memory of General Grant, in Westminster Abbey, with Archdeacon Farrar's address.

The lectures for 1886 were upon "The War for Independence," as follows: "Samuel Adams and Patrick Henry," by EDWIN D. MEAD. "Bunker Hill, and the News in England," by JOHN FISKE. "The Declaration of Independence," by JAMES MACALLISTER. "The Times that tried Men's Souls," by ALBERT B. HART, PH.D. "Lafayette, and Help from France," by PROF. MARSHALL S. SNOW. "The Women of the Revolution," by MRS. MARY A. LIVERMORE. "Washington and his Generals," by GEORGE M. TOWLE. "The Lessons of the Revolution for these Times," by REV. BROOKE HERFORD. The Leaflets were as follows: (1) Words of Patrick Henry; (2) Lord Chatham's Speech, urging the removal of the British troops from Boston; (3) extract from Webster's oration on Adams and Jefferson; (4) Thomas Paine's "Crisis," No. 1; (5) extract from Edward Everett's eulogy on Lafayette; (6) selections from the Letters of Abigail Adams; (7) Lowell's "Under the Old Elm"; (8) extract from Whipple's essay on "Washington and the Principles of the Revolution."

The course for the summer of 1887 was upon "The Birth of the Nation," as follows: "How the Men of the English Commonwealth planned Constitutions," by PROF. JAMES K. HOSMER. "How the American Colonies grew together," by JOHN FISKE. "The Confusion after the Revolution, by DAVIS R. DEWEY, PH.D. "The Convention and the Constitution," by HON. JOHN D. LONG. "James Madison and his Journal," by PROF. E. B. ANDREWS. "How Patrick Henry opposed the Constitution," by HENRY L. SOUTHWICK. "Alexander Hamilton and the *Federalist*." "Washington's Part and the Nation's First Years," by EDWARD EVERETT HALE. The Leaflets prepared for these lectures were as follows: (1) Extract from Edward Everett Hale's lecture on "Puritan Politics in England and New England"; (2) "The English Colonies in America," extract from De Tocqueville's "Democracy in America"; (3) Washington's Circular Letter to the Governors of the States, on Disbanding the Army; (4) the Constitution of the United States; (5) "The Last Day of the Constitutional Convention," from Madison's Journal; (6) Patrick Henry's First Speech against the Constitution, in the Virginia Convention; (7) the *Federalist*, No. IX.; (8) Washington's First Inaugural Address.

The course for the summer of 1888 had the general title of "The Story of the Centuries," the several lectures being as follows: "The Great Schools after the Dark Ages," by EPHRAIM EMERTON, Professor of History in Harvard University. "Richard the Lion-hearted and the Crusades," by MISS NINA MOORE, author of "Pilgrims and Puritans." "The World which Dante knew," by SHATTUCK O. HARTWELL, Old South first prize essayist, 1883. "The Morning Star of the Reformation," by REV. PHILIP S. MOXOM. "Copernicus and Columbus, or the New Heaven and the New Earth," by PROF. EDWARD S. MORSE. "The People for whom Shakespeare wrote," by CHARLES DUDLEY WARNER. "The Puritans and the English Revolution," by CHARLES H. LEVERMORE, Professor of History in the Massachusetts Institute of Technology. "Lafayette and the Two Revolutions which he saw," by GEORGE MAKEPEACE TOWLE.

The Old South Lectures are devoted primarily to American history. But it is a constant aim to impress upon the young people the relations of our own history to English and general European history. It was hoped that the glance at some striking chapters in the history of the last eight centuries afforded by these lectures would be a good preparation for the great anniversaries of 1889, and give the young people a truer feeling of the continuity of history. In connection with the lectures the young people were requested to fix in mind the following dates, observing that in most instances the date comes about a decade before the close of the century. An effort was made in the Leaflets for the year to make dates, which are so often dull and useless to young people, interesting, significant, and useful.— 11th Century: Lanfranc, the great mediæval scholar, who studied law at Bologna, was prior of the monastery of Bec, the most famous school in France in the 11th century, and archbishop of Canterbury under William the Conqueror, died, **1089**. 12th Cent.: Richard I. crowned, **1189**. 13th Cent.: Dante at the battle of Campaldino, the final overthrow of the Ghibellines in Italy, **1289**. 14th Cent.: Wyclif died, **1384**. 15th Cent.: America discovered, **1492**. 16th Cent.: Spanish Armada, **1588**. 17th Cent.: William of Orange lands in England, **1688**. 18th Cent.: Washington inaugurated, and the Bastile fell, **1789**. The Old South Leaflets for 1888, corresponding with the several lectures, were as follows: (1) "The Early History of Oxford," from Green's "History of the English People"; (2) "Richard Cœur de Lion and the Third Crusade," from the Chronicle of Geoffrey de Vinsauf; (3) "The Universal Empire," passages from Dante's *De Monarchia;* (4) "The Sermon on the Mount," Wyclif's translation; (5) "Copernicus and the Ancient Astronomers," from Humboldt's "Cosmos"; (6) "The Defeat of the Spanish Armada," from Camden's "Annals"; (7) "The Bill of Rights," 1689; (8) "The Eve of the French Revolution," from Carlyle. The selections are accompanied by very full historical and bibliographical notes, and it is hoped that the series will prove of much service to students and teachers engaged in the general survey of modern history.

The year 1889 being the centennial both of the beginning of our own Federal Government and of the French Revolution, the lectures for the year, under the general title of "America and France," were devoted entirely to subjects in which the history of America is related to that of France, as follows: "Champlain, the Founder of Quebec," by CHARLES C. COFFIN. "La Salle and the French in the Great West," by REV. W. E. GRIFFIS. "The Jesuit Missionaries in America," by PROF. JAMES K. HOSMER. "Wolfe and Montcalm: The Struggle of England and France for the Continent," by JOHN FISKE. "Franklin in France," by GEORGE M. TOWLE. "The Friendship of Washington and Lafayette," by MRS. ABBA GOOLD WOOLSON. "Thomas Jefferson and the Louisiana Purchase," by ROBERT MORSS LOVETT, Old South prize essayist, 1888. "The Year 1789," by REV. EDWARD EVERETT HALE. The Leaflets for the year were as follows: (1) Verrazzano's account of his Voyage to America; (2) Marquette's account of his Discovery of the Mississippi; (3) Mr. Parkman's Histories; (4) the Capture of Quebec, from Parkman's "Conspiracy of Pontiac"; (5) selections from Franklin's Letters from France; (6) Letters of Washington and Lafayette; (7) the Declaration of Independence; (8) the French Declaration of the Rights of Man, 1789.

The lectures for the summer of 1890 were on "The American Indians," as follows: "The Mound Builders," by PROF. GEORGE H. PERKINS. "The Indians whom our Fathers Found," by GEN. H. B. CARRINGTON. "John Eliot and his Indian Bible," by REV. EDWARD G. PORTER. "King Philip's War," by MISS CAROLINE C. STECKER, Old South prize essayist, 1889. "The Conspiracy of Pontiac," by CHARLES A. EASTMAN, M.D., of the Sioux nation. "A Century of Dishonor," by HERBERT WELSH. "Among the Zuñis," by J. WALTER FEWKES, PH.D. "The Indian at School," by GEN. S. C. ARMSTRONG. The Leaflets were as follows: (1) extract from address by William Henry Harrison on the Mound Builders of the Ohio Valley; (2) extract from Morton's "New English Canaan" on the Manners and Customs of the Indians; (3) John Eliot's "Brief Narrative of the Progress of the Gospel among the Indians of New England," 1670; (4) extract from Hubbard's "Narrative of the Troubles with the Indians" (1677) on the Beginning of King Philip's War; (5) the Speech of Pontiac at the Council at the River Ecorces, from Parkman's "Conspiracy of Pontiac"; (6) extract from Black Hawk's autobiography, on the Cause of the Black Hawk War; (7) Coronado's Letter to Mendoza (1540) on his Explorations in New Mexico; (8) Eleazar Wheelock's Narrative (1762) of the Rise and Progress of the Indian School at Lebanon, Conn.

The lectures for 1891, under the general title of "The New Birth of the World," were devoted to the important movements in the age preceding the discovery of America, the several lectures being as follows: "The Results of the Crusades," by F. E. E. HAMILTON, Old South prize essayist, 1883. "The Revival of Learning," by PROF. ALBERT B. HART. "The Builders of the Cathedrals," by PROF. MARSHALL S. SNOW. "The Changes which Gunpowder made," by FRANK A. HILL. "The Decline of the Barons," by WILLIAM EVERETT. "The Invention of Printing," by REV. EDWARD G. PORTER. "When Michael Angelo was a Boy," by HAMLIN GARLAND. "The Discovery of America," by REV. E. E. HALE. The Leaflets were as follows: (1) "The Capture of Jerusalem by the Crusaders," from the Chronicle of William of Malmesbury; (2) extract from More's "Utopia"; (3) "The Founding of Westminster Abbey," from Dean Stanley's "Historical Memorials of Westminster Abbey"; (4) "The Siege of Constantinople," from Gibbon's "Decline and Fall of the Roman Empire"; (5) "Simon de Montfort," selections from Chronicles of the time; (6) "Caxton at Westminster," extract from Blade's Life of William Caxton; (7) "The Youth of Michael Angelo," from Vasari's "Lives of the Italian Painters"; (8) The Discovery of America," from Ferdinand Columbus's life of his father."

The lectures for 1892 were upon "The Discovery of America," as follows: "What Men knew of the World before Columbus," by PROF. EDWARD S. MORSE. "Leif Erikson and the Northmen," by REV. EDWARD A. HORTON. "Marco Polo and his Book," by MR. O. W. DIMMICK.

"The Story of Columbus," by Mrs. Mary A. Livermore. "Americus Vespucius and the Early Books about America," by Rev. E. G. Porter. "Cortes and Pizarro," by Prof. Chas. H. Levermore. "De Soto and Ponce de Leon," by Miss Ruth Ballou Whittemore, Old South prize essayist, 1891. "Spain, France, and England in America," by Mr. John Fiske. The Leaflets were as follows: (1) Strabo's Introduction to Geography; (2) the Voyages to Vinland, from the Saga of Eric the Red; (3) Marco Polo's account of Japan and Java; (4) Columbus's Letter to Gabriel Sanchez, describing his First Voyage; (5) Amerigo Vespucci's account of his First Voyage; (6) Cortes's account of the City of Mexico; (7) the Death of De Soto, from the "Narrative of a Gentleman of Elvas"; (8) Early Notices of the Voyages of the Cabots.

The lectures for 1893 were upon „The Opening of the Great West," as follows: "Spain and France in the Great West," by Rev. William Elliot Griffis. "The North-west Territory and the Ordinance of 1787," by John M. Merriam. "Washington's Work in Opening the West," by Edwin D. Mead. "Marietta and the Western Reserve," by Miss Lucy W. Warren, Old South prize essayist, 1892. "How the Great West was settled," by Charles C. Coffin. "Lewis and Clarke and the Explorers of the Rocky Mountains," by Rev. Thomas Van Ness. "California and Oregon," by Prof. Josiah Royce. "The Story of Chicago," by Mrs. Mary A. Livermore. The Leaflets were as follows: (1) De Vaca's account of his Journey to New Mexico, 1535; (2) Manasseh Cutler's Description of Ohio, 1787; (3) Washington's Journal of his Tour to the Ohio, 1770; (4) Garfield's Address on the North-west Territory and the Western Reserve; (5) George Rogers Clark's account of the Capture of Vincennes, 1779; (6) Jefferson's Life of Captain Meriwether Lewis; (7) Fremont's account of his Ascent of Fremont's Peak; (8) Father Marquette at Chicago, 1673.

The lectures for 1894 were upon "The Founders of New England," as follows: "William Brewster, the Elder of Plymouth," by Rev. Edward Everett Hale. "William Bradford, the Governor of Plymouth," by Rev. William Elliot Griffis. "John Winthrop, the Governor of Massachusetts," by Hon. Frederic T. Greenhalge. "John Harvard, and the Founding of Harvard College," by Mr. William R. Thayer. "John Eliot, the Apostle to the Indians," by Rev. James De Normandie. "John Cotton, the Minister of Boston," by Rev. John Cotton Brooks. "Roger Williams, the Founder of Rhode Island," by President E. Benjamin Andrews. "Thomas Hooker, the Founder of Connecticut," by Rev. Joseph H. Twichell. The Leaflets were as follows: (1) Bradford's Memoir of Elder Brewster; (2) Bradford's First Dialogue; (3) Winthrop's Conclusions for the Plantation in New England; (4) New England's First Fruits, 1643; (5) John Eliot's Indian Grammar Begun; (6) John Cotton's "God's Promise to his Plantation"; (7) Letters of Roger Williams to Winthrop; (8) Thomas Hooker's "Way of the Churches of New England."

The lectures for 1895 were upon "The Puritans in Old England," as follows: "John Hooper, the First Puritan," by Edwin D. Mead; "Cambridge, the Puritan University," by William Everett; "Sir John Eliot and the House of Commons," by Prof. Albert B. Hart; "John Hampden and the Ship Money," by Rev. F. W. Gunsaulus; "John Pym and the Grand Remonstrance," by Rev. John Cuckson; "Oliver Cromwell and the Commonwealth," by Rev. Edward Everett Hale; "John Milton, the Puritan Poet," by John Fiske; "Henry Vane in Old England

and New England," by PROF. JAMES K. HOSMER. The Leaflets were as follows: (1) The English Bible, selections from the various versions; (2) Hooper's Letters to Bullinger; (3) Sir John Eliot's "Apology for Socrates"; (4) Ship-money Papers; (5) Pym's Speech against Strafford; (6) Cromwell's Second Speech; (7) Milton's "Free Commonwealth"; (8) Sir Henry Vane's Defence.

The lectures for 1896 were upon "The American Historians," as follows: "Bradford and Winthrop and their Journals," by MR. EDWIN D. MEAD; "Cotton Mather and his 'Magnalia,'" by PROF. BARRETT WENDELL; "Governor Hutchinson and his History of Massachusetts," by PROF. CHARLES H. LEVERMORE; "Washington Irving and his Services for American History," by MR. RICHARD BURTON; "Bancroft and his History of the United States," by PRES. AUSTIN SCOTT; "Prescott and his Spanish Histories," by HON. ROGER WOLCOTT; "Motley and his History of the Dutch Republic," by REV. WILLIAM ELLIOT GRIFFIS; "Parkman and his Works on France in America," by MR. JOHN FISKE. The Leaflets were as follows: (1) Winthrop's "Little Speech" on Liberty; (2) Cotton Mather's "Bostonian Ebenezer," from the "Magnalia"; (3) Governor Hutchinson's Account of the Boston Tea Party; (4) Adrian Van der Donck's Description of the New Netherlands in 1655; (5) The Debate in the Constitutional Convention on the Rules of Suffrage in Congress; (6) Columbus's Memorial to Ferdinand and Isabella, on his Second Voyage; (7) The Dutch Declaration of Independence in 1581; (8) Captain John Knox's Account of the Battle of Quebec. The last five of these eight Leaflets illustrate the original material in which Irving, Bancroft, Prescott, Motley, and Parkman worked in the preparation of their histories.

The lectures for 1897 were upon "The Anti-slavery Struggle," as follows: "William Lloyd Garrison or Anti-slavery in the Newspaper," by WILLIAM LLOYD GARRISON, JR.; "Wendell Phillips or Anti-slavery on the Platform," by WENDELL PHILLIPS STAFFORD; "Theodore Parker or Anti-slavery in the Pulpit," by REV. EDWARD EVERETT HALE; "John G. Whittier or Anti-slavery in the Poem," by MRS. ALICE FREEMAN PALMER; "Harriet Beecher Stowe or Anti-slavery in the Story," by MISS MARIA L. BALDWIN; "Charles Sumner or Anti-slavery in the Senate," by MOORFIELD STOREY; "John Brown or Anti-slavery on the Scaffold," by FRANK B. SANBORN; "Abraham Lincoln or Anti-slavery Triumphant," by HON. JOHN D. LONG. The Leaflets were as follows: (1) The First Number of *The Liberator*; (2) Wendell Phillips's Eulogy of Garrison; (3) Theodore Parker's Address on the Dangers from Slavery; (4) Whittier's Account of the Anti-slavery Convention of 1833; (5) Mrs. Stowe's Story of "Uncle Tom's Cabin"; (6) Sumner's Speech on the Crime against Kansas; (7) Words of John Brown; (8) The First Lincoln and Douglas Debate.

The Leaflets for 1883 are now mostly out of print. Those of 1884 and subsequent years, bound in paper covers, may be procured for thirty-five cents per volume. Address *Directors of Old South Work*, Old South Meeting-house, Boston.

The Old South Leaflets, which have been published during the last fifteen years, in connection with these annual courses of historical lectures at the Old South Meeting-house, have attracted so much attention and proved of so much service that the Directors have entered upon the publication of the Leaflets for general circulation, with the needs of schools, colleges, private clubs, and classes especially in mind. The Leaflets are prepared by Mr. Edwin D. Mead. They are largely reproductions of important original papers, accompanied by useful historical and bibliographical notes. They consist, on an average, of sixteen pages, and are sold at the low price of five cents a copy, or four dollars per hundred. The aim is to bring them within easy reach of everybody. The Old South Work, founded by Mrs. Mary Hemenway, and still sustained by provision of her will, is a work for the education of the people, and especially the education of our young people, in American history and politics; and its promoters believe that few things can contribute better to this end than the wide circulation of such leaflets as those now undertaken. It is hoped that professors in our colleges and teachers everywhere will welcome them for use in their classes, and that they may meet the needs of the societies of young men and women now happily being organized in so many places for historical and political studies. Some idea of the character of these Old South Leaflets may be gained from the following list of the subjects of the first eighty-five numbers, which are now ready. It will be noticed that most of the later numbers are the same as certain numbers in the annual series. Since 1890 they are essentially the same, and persons ordering the Leaflets need simply observe the following numbers.

No. **1.** The Constitution of the United States. **2.** The Articles of Confederation. **3.** The Declaration of Independence. **4.** Washington's Farewell Address. **5.** Magna Charta. **6.** Vane's "Healing Question." **7.** Charter of Massachusetts Bay, 1629. **8.** Fundamental Orders of Connecticut, 1638. **9.** Franklin's Plan of Union, 1754. **10.** Washington's Inaugurals. **11.** Lincoln's Inaugurals and Emancipation Proclamation. **12.** The Federalist, Nos. 1 and 2. **13.** The Ordinance of 1787. **14.** The Constitution of Ohio. **15.** Washington's Circular Letter to the Governors of the States, 1783. **16.** Washington's Letter to Benjamin Harrison, 1784. **17.** Verrazzano's Voyage, 1524. **18.** The Constitution of Switzerland. **19.** The Bill of Rights, 1689. **20.** Coronado's Letter to Mendoza, 1540. **21.** Eliot's Brief Narrative of the Progress of the Gospel among the Indians, 1670. **22.** Wheelock's Narrative of the Rise of the Indian School at Lebanon, Conn., 1762. **23.** The Petition of Rights, 1628. **24.** The Grand Remonstrance. **25.** The Scottish National Covenants. **26.** The Agreement of the People. **27.** The Instrument of Government. **28.** Cromwell's First Speech to his Parliament. **29.** The Discovery of America, from the Life of Columbus by his son, Ferdinand Columbus. **30.** Strabo's Introduction to Geography. **31.** The Voyages to Vinland, from the Saga of Eric the Red. **32.** Marco Polo's Account of Japan and Java. **33.** Columbus's Letter to Gabriel Sanchez, describing the First Voyage and Discovery. **34.** Amerigo Vespucci's Account of his First Voyage. **35.** Cortes's Account of the City of Mexico. **36.** The Death of De Soto, from the "Narrative of a Gentleman of Elvas." **37.** Early Notices of the Voyages of the Cabots. **38.** Henry Lee's Funeral Oration on Washington. **39.** De Vaca's Account of his Journey to New Mexico, 1535. **40.** Manasseh Cutler's Description of Ohio, 1787. **41.** Washington's Journal of his Tour to the Ohio, 1770. **42.** Garfield's Address on the North-west Territory and the Western Reserve. **43.** George Rogers Clark's Account of the Capture of Vincennes, 1779. **44.** Jefferson's Life of Captain Meriwether Lewis. **45.** Fremont's Account of his Ascent of Fremont's Peak. **46.** Father Marquette at Chicago, 1673. **47.** Washington's Account of the Army at Cambridge, 1775. **48.** Bradford's Memoir of Elder Brewster. **49.** Bradford's First Dialogue. **50.** Winthrop's "Conclusions for the Plantation in New England." **51.** "New England's First Fruits," 1643. **52.** John Eliot's "Indian Grammar Begun." **53.** John Cotton's "God's Promise to his Plantation." **54.** Letters of Roger Williams to Winthrop. **55.** Thomas Hooker's "Way of the Churches of New England." **56.** The Monroe Doctrine: President Monroe's Message of 1823. **57.** The English Bible, selections from the various versions. **58.** Hooper's Letters to Bullinger. **59.** Sir John Eliot's "Apology for Socrates." **60.** Ship-money Papers. **61.** Pym's Speech against Strafford. **62.** Cromwell's Second Speech. **63.** Milton's "A Free Commonwealth." **64.** Sir Henry Vane's Defence. **65.** Washington's Addresses to the Churches. **66.** Winthrop's "Little Speech" on Liberty. **67.** Cotton Mather's "Bostonian Ebenezer," from the "Magnalia." **68.** Governor Hutchinson's Account of the Boston Tea Party. **69.** Adrian Van der Donck's Description of New Netherlands in 1655. **70.** The Debate in the Constitutional Convention on the Rules of Suffrage in Congress. **71.** Columbus's Memorial to Ferdinand and Isabella, on his Second Voyage. **72.** The Dutch Declaration of Independence in 1581. **73.** Captain John Knox's Account of the Battle of Quebec. **74.** Hamilton's Report on the Coinage. **75.** William Penn's Plan for the Peace of Europe. **76.** Washington's Words on a National University. **77.** Cotton Mather's Lives of Bradford and Winthrop. **78.** The First Number of *The Liberator*. **79.** Wendell Phillips's Eulogy of Garrison. **80.** Theodore Parker's Address on the Dangers from Slavery. **81.** Whittier's Account of the Antislavery Convention of 1833. **82.** Mrs. Stowe's Story of "Uncle Tom's Cabin." **83.** Sumner's Speech on the Crime against Kansas. **84.** The Words of John Brown. **85.** The First Lincoln and Douglas Debate.

The leaflets are also furnished in bound volumes, each volume containing twenty-five leaflets: Vol. i., Nos. 1–25; Vol. ii., 26–50; Vol. iii., 51–75. Price per volume, $1.50. Title-pages with table of contents will be furnished to all purchasers of the leaflets who wish to bind them for themselves. Address *Directors of the Old South Work*, Old South Meetinghouse, Boston.

It is hoped that this list of Old South Lectures and Leaflets will meet the needs of many clubs and classes engaged in the study of history, as well as the needs of individual students, serving as a table of topics. The subjects of the lectures in the various courses will be found to have a logical sequence; and the leaflets accompanying the several lectures can be used profitably in connection, containing as they do full historical notes and references to the best literature on the subjects of the lectures.

Old South Leaflets.
No. 78.

The Liberator.
Vol. I.   No 1.

WILLIAM LLOYD GARRISON and
ISAAC KNAPP, *Publishers.*

BOSTON, MASSACHUSETTS.— Saturday, January 1, 1831.

Our Country is the World — Our Countrymen are Mankind.

THE SALUTATION.

To date my being from the opening year,
I come, a stranger in this busy sphere,
Where some I meet perchance may pause and ask,
What is my name, my purpose, or my task?

My name is 'LIBERATOR'! I propose
To hurl my shafts at freedom's deadliest foes!
My task is hard — for I am charged to save
Man from his brother! — to redeem the slave!

Ye who may hear, and yet condemn my cause,
Say, shall the best of Nature's holy laws
Be trodden down? and shall her open veins
Flow but for cement to her offspring's chains?

Art thou a parent? shall thy children be
Rent from thy breast, like branches from the tree,
And doom'd to servitude, in helplessness,
On other shores, and thou ask no redress?

Thou, in whose bosom glows the sacred flame
Of filial love, say, if the tyrant came,
To force thy parent shrieking from thy sight,
Would thy heart bleed — *because thy face is white?*

Art thou a brother? shall thy sister twine
Her feeble arm in agony on thine,
And thou not lift the heel, nor aim the blow
At him who bears her off to life-long wo?

THE LIBERATOR is published weekly at No. 6 Merchants' Hall. WM. L. GARRISON, *Editor.*
STEPHEN FOSTER, *Printer.* Terms, two dollars per annum, payable in advance.

Art thou a sister? will no desp'rate cry
Awake thy sleeping brother, while thine eye
Beholds the fetters locking on the limb
Stretched out in rest, which hence, must end, for him?

Art thou a lover? — no! naught e'er was found
In lover's breast, save cords of love, that bound
Man to his kind! then, thy profession save!
Forswear affection, or release thy slave!

Thou who art kneeling at thy Maker's shrine,
Ask if Heaven takes such offerings as thine!
If in thy bonds the son of Afric sighs,
Far higher than thy prayer his groan will rise!

God is a God of mercy, and would see
The prison-doors unbarr'd — the bondmen free!
He is a God of truth, with purer eyes
Than to behold the oppressor's sacrifice!

Avarice, thy cry and thine insatiate thirst
Make man consent to see his brother cursed!
Tears, sweat and blood thou drink'st, but in their turn,
They shall cry 'more!' while vengeance bids thee burn.

The Lord hath said it! — who shall him gainsay?
He says, 'the wicked, they shall go away' —
Who are the wicked? — Contradict who can,
They are the oppressors of their fellow man!

Aid me, NEW ENGLAND! 'tis my hope in you
Which gives me strength my purpose to pursue!
Do you not hear your sister States resound
With Afric's cries to have her sons unbound?

* * *

TO THE PUBLIC.

In the month of August, I issued proposals for publishing 'THE LIBERATOR' in Washington city; but the enterprise, though hailed in different sections of the country, was palsied by public indifference. Since that time, the removal of the Genius of Universal Emancipation to the Seat of Government has rendered less imperious the establishment of a similar periodical in that quarter.

During my recent tour for the purpose of exciting the minds of the people by a series of discourses on the subject of slavery, every place that I visited gave fresh evidence of the fact, that a greater revolution in public sentiment was to be effected in the free states — *and particularly in New-England* — than at the south. I found contempt more bitter, opposition more active, detraction more relentless, prejudice more stubborn, and apathy more frozen, than among slave owners themselves. Of course, there were individual exceptions to the contrary. This state of things afflicted, but did not dishearten me. I determined, at every hazard, to lift up the standard of emancipation in the eyes of the nation, *within sight of Bunker Hill and in the birth place of liberty.* That standard is now unfurled; and long may it float, unhurt by the spoliations of time or the missiles of a desperate foe — yea, till every chain be broken, and every bondman set free! Let southern oppressors tremble — let their secret abettors tremble — let their northern apologists tremble — let all the enemies of the persecuted blacks tremble.

I deem the publication of my original Prospectus * unnecessary, as it has obtained a wide circulation. The principles therein inculcated will be steadily pursued in this paper, excepting that I shall not array myself as the political partisan of any man. In defending the great cause of human rights, I wish to derive the assistance of all religions and of all parties.

Assenting to the 'self-evident truth' maintained in the American Declaration of Independence, 'that all men are created equal, and endowed by their Creator with certain inalienable rights — among which are life, liberty and the pursuit of happiness,' I shall strenuously contend for the immediate enfranchisement of our slave population. In Park-street Church, on the Fourth of July, 1829, in an address on slavery, I unreflectingly assented to the popular but pernicious doctrine of *gradual* abolition. I seize this opportunity to make a full and unequivocal recantation, and thus publicly to ask pardon of my God, of my country, and of my brethren the poor slaves, for having uttered a sentiment so full of timidity, injustice and absurdity. A similar recantation, from my pen, was published in the Genius of Universal Emancipation at Baltimore, in September, 1829. My conscience is now satisfied.

I am aware, that many object to the severity of my language; but is there not cause for severity? I *will be* as harsh as truth, and as uncompromising as justice. On this subject, I do not wish to think, or speak, or write, with moderation. No! no! Tell a man whose house is on fire, to give a moder-

* I would here offer my grateful acknowledgments to those editors who so promptly and generously inserted my Proposals. They must give me an available opportunity to repay their liberality.

ate alarm; tell him to moderately rescue his wife from the hands of the ravisher; tell the mother to gradually extricate her babe from the fire into which it has fallen;—but urge me not to use moderation in a cause like the present. I am in earnest—I will not equivocate—I will not excuse—I will not retreat a single inch—AND I WILL BE HEARD. The apathy of the people is enough to make every statue leap from its pedestal, and to hasten the resurrection of the dead.

It is pretended, that I am retarding the cause of emancipation by the coarseness of my invective, and the precipitancy of my measures. *The charge is not true.* On this question my influence,—humble as it is,—is felt at this moment to a considerable extent, and shall be felt in coming years—not perniciously, but beneficially—not as a curse, but as a blessing; and posterity will bear testimony that I was right. I desire to thank God, that he enables me to disregard 'the fear of man which bringeth a snare,' and to speak his truth in its simplicity and power.

And here I close with this fresh dedication:

> 'Oppression! I have seen thee, face to face,
> And met thy cruel eye and cloudy brow;
> But thy soul-withering glance I fear not now—
> For dread to prouder feelings doth give place
> Of deep abhorrence! Scorning the disgrace
> Of slavish knees that at thy footstool bow,
> I also kneel—but with far other bow
> Do hail thee and thy herd of hirelings base:—
> I swear, while life-blood warms my throbbing veins,
> Still to oppose and thwart, with heart and hand,
> Thy brutalizing sway—till Afric's chains
> Are burst, and Freedom rules the rescued land,—
> Trampling Oppression and his iron rod:
> *Such is the vow I take*—SO HELP ME GOD!'

WILLIAM LLOYD GARRISON.

BOSTON, January 1, 1831.

DISTRICT OF COLUMBIA.

What do many of the professed enemies of slavery mean, by heaping all their reproaches upon the south, and asserting that the crime of oppression is not national? What power but Congress—and Congress by the authority of the American people—has jurisdiction over the District of Columbia? That

District is rotten with the plague, and stinks in the nostrils of the world. Though it is the Seat of our National Government, — open to the daily inspection of foreign ambassadors, — and ostensibly opulent with the congregated wisdom, virtue and intelligence of the land, — yet a fouler spot scarcely exists on earth. In it the worst features of slavery are exhibited; and as a mart for slave traders, it is unequalled. These facts are well known to our two or three hundred representatives, but no remedy is proposed; they are known, if not minutely at least generally, to our whole population, — but who calls for redress?

Hitherto, a few straggling petitions, relative to this subject, have gone into Congress; but they have been too few to denote much public anxiety, or to command a deferential notice. It is certainly time that a vigorous and systematic effort should be made, from one end of the country to the other, to pull down that national monument of oppression which towers up in the District. We do hope that the 'earthquake voice' of the people will this session shake the black fabric to its foundation.

The following petition is now circulating in this city, and has obtained several valuable signatures. A copy may be found at the Bookstore of LINCOLN & EDMANDS, No. 59 Washington-street, for a few days longer, where all the friends of the cause are earnestly invited to go and subscribe.

Petition to Congress for the Abolition of Slavery in the District of Columbia.

To the Honorable Senate and House of Representatives of the United States of America in Congress assembled, the petition of the undersigned citizens of Boston in Massachusetts and its vicinity respectfully represents—

That your petitioners are deeply impressed with the evils arising from the existence of slavery in the District of Columbia. While our Declaration of Independence boldly proclaims as self-evident truths, 'that all men are created equal, that they are endowed by their Creator with certain inalienable rights, that among these are life, liberty, and the pursuit of happiness,' — at the very seat of government human beings are born, almost daily, whom the laws pronounce to be from their birth, not *equal* to other men, and who are, for life, deprived of *liberty* and the free *pursuit of happiness*. The inconsistency of the conduct of our nation with its political creed, has brought down upon it the just and severe reprehension of foreign nations.

In addition to the other evils flowing from slavery, both moral and political, which it is needless to specify, circumstances have rendered this District a common resort for traders in human flesh, who bring into it their captives in chains, and lodge them in places of confinement, previously to their being carried to the markets of the south and west.

From the small number of slaves in the District of Columbia, and the moderate proportion which they bear to the free population there, the difficulties, which in most of the slaveholding states oppose the restoration of this degraded class of men to their natural rights, do not exist.

Your petitioners therefore pray that Congress will, without delay, take such measures for the immediate or gradual abolition of Slavery in the District of Columbia, and for preventing the bringing of slaves into that District for purposes of traffic, in such mode, as may be thought advisable; and that suitable provision be made for the education of all free blacks and colored children in the District, thus to preserve them from continuing, even as free men, an unenlightened and degraded caste.

If any individual should be unmoved, either by the petition or the introductory remarks, the following article will startle his apathy, unless he be morally dead — dead — dead. Read it — read it! The language of the editor is remarkable for its energy, considering the quarter whence it emanates. After all, we are not the only fanatics in the land!

[From the Washington Spectator, of Dec. 1.]

THE SLAVE TRADE IN THE CAPITAL.

"The tender ties of father, husband, friend,
All bonds of nature in that moment end,
And each endures, while yet he draws his breath,
A stroke as fatal as the scythe of death:
They lose in tears, the far receding shore,
But not the thought that they must meet no more."

It is well, perhaps, the American people should know, that while we reiterate our boasts of liberty in the ears of the nations, and send back across the Atlantic our shouts of joy at the triumph of liberty in France, we ourselves are busily engaged in the work of oppression. Yes, let it be known to the citizens of America, that at the very time when the procession which contained the President of the United States and his Cabinet was marching in triumph to the Capitol, to celebrate the victory of the French people over their oppressors, another kind of procession was marching another way, and that consisted of colored human beings, handcuffed in pairs, and driven along by what had the appearance of a man on a horse! A similar scene was repeated on Saturday last; a *drove* consisting of males and females chained in couples, starting from Roby's tavern on foot, for Alexandria, where, with others, they are to embark on board a slave-ship in waiting to convey them to the

South. While we are writing, a colored man enters our room, and begs us to inform him if we can point out any person who will redeem his friend now immured in Alexandria jail, in a state of distress amounting almost to distraction.* He has been a faithful servant of a revolutionary officer who recently died — has been sold at auction — parted from affectionate parents — and from decent and mourning friends. Our own servant, with others, of whom we can speak in commendatory terms, went down to Alexandria to bid him farewell, but they were refused admission to his cell, as was said 'the sight of his friends made him feel so.' He bears the reputation of a pious man. It is but a few weeks since we saw a ship with her cargo of slaves in the port of Norfolk, Va.; on passing up the river, saw another ship off Alexandria, swarming with the victims of human cupidity. Such are the scenes enacting in the heart of the American nation. Oh patriotism! where is thy indignation? Oh philanthropy! where is thy grief? OH SHAME, WHERE IS THY BLUSH? Well may the generous and noble minded O'Connell say of the American citizen, '*I tell him he is a hypocrite. Look at the stain in your star-spangled standard that was never struck down in battle. I turn from the Declaration of American Independence, and I tell him that he has declared to God and man a lie, and before God and man I arraign him as a hypocrite.*' Yes, thou soul of fire, glorious O'Connell, if thou could but witness the spectacles in Washington that make the genius of liberty droop her head in shame, and weep her tears away in deep silence and undissembled sorrow, you would lift your voice even to tones of thunder, but you would make yourself heard. Where is the O'Connell of this republic that will plead for the EMANCIPATION OF THE DISTRICT OF COLUMBIA? These shocking scenes must cease from amongst us, or we must cease to call ourselves free; ay, and we must cease to expect the mercy of God — we must prepare for the coming judgment of Him who, as our charter acknowledges, made all men '*free and equal!*'

When a premium of Fifty Dollars is offered for the best theatrical poem, our newspapers advertise the fact with great unanimity. The following is incomparably more important.

* At the same time this man was sold, another — a husband — was knocked off. The tears and agonies of his wife made such an impression on the mind of a generous spectator, that he bought him back.

PREMIUM.

A Premium of Fifty Dollars, the Donation of a benevolent individual in the State of Maine, and now deposited with the Treasurer of the Pennsylvania Society for promoting the Abolition of Slavery, &c. is offered to the author of the best Treatise on the following subject: 'The Duties of Ministers and Churches of all denominations to avoid the stain of Slavery, and to make the holding of Slaves a barrier to communion and church membership.'

The composition to be directed (post paid) to either of the subscribers — the name of the author in a separate sealed paper, which will be destroyed if his work shall be rejected.

Six months from this date are allowed for the purpose of receiving the Essays.

The publication and circulation of the preferred Tract will be regulated by the Pennsylvania Society above mentioned.

W. RAWLE,
J. PRESTON,   } *Committee.*
THOMAS SHIPLEY,

Philadelphia, Oct. 11.

MY SECOND BALTIMORE TRIAL.

I have delayed making any public strictures upon this mock trial, for various considerations; and, in consequence of the length of the following report of it, (which, I will here barely remark, is as rich in embellishments as the ingenuity of a servile reporter could make it,) I am unable, in the present number, to give my defence. Next week, however, it shall come; in which, due notice shall be taken of Capt. Nicholas Brown's remarkable affidavit. To screen his employer from merited reprehension, he has chosen to invoke upon himself the guilt of the wicked transaction. Let him take the consequences.

Is the inquiry made, how do I bear up under my adversities? I answer — like the oak — like the Alps — unshaken, stormproof. Opposition, and abuse, and slander, and prejudice, and judicial tyranny, are like oil to the flame of my zeal. I am not discouraged; I am not dismayed; but bolder and more confident than ever. I say to my persecutors,—'I bid you defiance.' Let the courts condemn me to fine and imprisonment for denouncing oppression: Am I to be frightened by dungeons and chains? can they humble my spirit? do I not remember that I am an American citizen, and, as a citizen, a freeman, and what is more, a being accountable to God, I will not hold my peace on the subject of African oppression. If need be, who would not die a martyr to such a cause?

> 'Eternal spirit of the chainless mind!
>   Brightest in dungeons, Liberty! thou art,
>   For there thy habitation is the heart,—
> The heart which love of thee alone can bind;
> And when thy sons to fetters are consigned,—
> To fetters, and the damp vault's dayless gloom,
> Their country conquers with their martyrdom,
> And Freedom's fame finds wings on every wind.'

[From the Baltimore Gazette.]

BALTIMORE COUNTY COURT,

OCTOBER TERM, 1830.

Francis Todd, } Action on the case
vs. } for a libel.
William Lloyd Garrison. }

This cause was tried at the present term, before Archer, Chief Judge; the evidence on the trial was in substance as follows:

In October, 1829, the ship Francis, belonging to the plaintiff, who is a resident merchant at Newburyport, Massachusetts, on her voyage from Baltimore to New Orleans, took on board at Herring Bay in the Chesapeak, as passengers, about eighty negroes, purchased by Mr. George B. Milligan, formerly of the State of Delaware, but for some years a Planter in Louisiana, from two gentlemen in Calvert County, for his own use. The agreement for the transportation of these people was made by Mr. Milligan, with Captain Brown who commanded the vessel, and Mr. Henry Thompson, to whom she was consigned in Baltimore. The Plaintiff, the owner, was not consulted nor apprised of the destination or employment of the ship, until she was about to sail. By the agreement, these people were to be found in provisions by the Captain; but, solicitous for their comfort, Mr. Milligan had directed, before the vessel left Baltimore, that certain extra articles should be purchased for their use, such as blankets, shoes, hats, whiskey, sugar, tea, and a quantity of cotton shirting to be made up by the women during the passage, for themselves and children, with needles, thread, &c. amounting to $400. The provisions on board were all of the best quality:—for instance, prime Pork, which cost $12, and Mess Beef, which cost $11 per barrel.

Accompanied by Mr. Milligan, these people came on board cheerfully and willingly. Their former proprietors having been compelled to part with them, they rejoiced at the prospect of still living together, instead of being separated, as they would have been if otherwise disposed of. During the voyage there was not a single instance of complaint or discontent among them,—their accommodations on board were the same as those of the steerage passengers;—no restraint was imposed on them—no confinement resorted to, no fetters used. They arrived safely at their new home, about twenty miles below New Orleans, and when Captain Brown visited the Plantation, shortly before his return to Baltimore, he found them perfectly contented.

On the 20th November, some weeks after the ship had left Baltimore, the following article appeared in a newspaper printed in this city, 'edited and published by Benjamin Lundy and William Lloyd Garrison,' called 'Genius of Universal Emancipation.'

BLACK LIST.

HORRIBLE NEWS—DOMESTIC AND FOREIGN.

THE SHIP FRANCIS.

This ship, as I mentioned in our last number, sailed a few weeks since from this port with a cargo of slaves for the New Orleans market. I do not repeat the fact because it is a rare instance of domestic piracy, or because the case was attended with extraordinary circumstances; for the horrible traffic is briskly carried on, and the transportation was effected in the ordinary manner. I merely wish to illustrate New England humanity and morality. I am resolved to cover with thick infamy all who are concerned in this nefarious business.

I have stated that the ship Francis hails from my native place, Newburyport (Massachusetts,) is commanded by a yankee captain, and owned by a townsman named

FRANCIS TODD

Of Captain Nicholas Brown I should have expected better conduct. It is no worse to fit out piratical cruisers, or to engage in the foreign slave trade, than to pursue a similar trade along our coasts; and the men who have the wickedness to participate therein, for the purpose of heaping up wealth, should be SENTENCED TO SOLITARY CONFINEMENT FOR LIFE; *they are the enemies of their own species — highway robbers and murderers;* and their final doom will be, unless they speedily repent, *to occupy the lowest depths of perdition.* I know that our laws make a distinction in this matter. I know that the man who is allowed to freight his vessel with slaves at home, for a distant market, would be thought worthy of death if he should take a similar freight on the coast of Africa; but I know, too, that this distinction is absurd, and at war with the common sense of mankind, and that God and good men regard it with abhorrence.

I recollect that it was always a mystery in Newburyport how Mr. Todd contrived to make profitable voyages to New Orleans and other places, when other merchants, with as fair an opportunity to make money, and sending at the same ports at the same time, invariably made fewer successful speculations. The mystery seems to be unravelled. Any man can gather up riches, if he does not care by what means they are obtained.

The Francis carried off *seventy-five* slaves, chained in a narrow space between decks. Captain Brown originally intended to take *one hundred and fifty* of these unfortunate creatures; but another hard-hearted shipmaster underbid him in the price of passage for the remaining moiety. Captain B., we believe, is a *mason*. Where was his charity or brotherly kindness?

I respectfully request the editor of the Newburyport Herald to copy this article, or publish a statement of the facts contained herein — not for the purpose of giving information to Mr. Todd, for I shall send him a copy of this number, but in order to enlighten the public mind in that quarter.
—G.

At the succeeding February term of Baltimore City Court, the Grand Jury presented this publication as a 'gross and malicious libel.' They afterwards found an Indictment against both the Editors, which was at the same term tried against Garrison alone — Lundy being out of the State. The Jury, without hesitation, found a verdict of guilty; and after an ineffectual attempt to arrest the judgment, upon technical objections, the Court imposed a fine of $50. This the Defendant was either unable or unwilling to pay, and he was therefore committed, and remained in jail for some time, till it was satisfied.

A private action for this libel had been instituted by Mr. Todd against both the Editors; but in consequence of Lundy's absence, the process was served only on Garrison, who was in fact the writer of the article. After his conviction in the City Court, he was distinctly informed through his Counsel, that as Mr. Todd had no vindictive feelings to gratify, the suit would be withdrawn, if a proper apology, and recantation of the calumny were put upon record. This offer Mr. Garrison not only refused, but while in confinement, published a pamphlet containing, with *his* report of the trial, a republication of the libel, and a number of gross insinuations against the Chief Judge of the Court.

At the trial of the civil suit, the publication having been proved, Mr. Jones, the Pilot of the Francis, testified that the negroes were taken on board at Herring Bay, and that the ship then proceeded to Annapolis to obtain the necessary Custom House papers: — that they came on board cheerfully and willingly — and that while he remained with them, which was until he left the Capes, they appeared to be contented and happy. That unusual attention seemed to have been given to their comfort and accommodation; — their births were commodious, the women and children being separated from the men; — their provisions abundant and of good quality; — extra stores provided for them, which were distributed daily to them by Captain Brown, and that the clothing which had been furnished by Mr. Milligan, was amply sufficient for their wants. He further deposed that they were treated with kindness by Captain Brown; — that they were under no restraint, but were permitted to go about the ship by day and night, as other passengers, and that no chains, hand-cuffs, or other fetters, were used in any instance, nor did he believe that there were any on board the vessel.

The deposition of Capt. Nicholas Brown was then read by consent, in which he stated —

That about the middle of the month of September, 1829, he came on to Baltimore, to take charge of the ship Francis, of Newburyport, belonging to Francis Todd, merchant of that place, the said ship being consigned for freight or otherwise to Henry Thompson, merchant of this city — That in the month of October following, Mr. Thompson and himself engaged to carry to New Orleans on board the ship Francis, from seventy-five to one hundred black people, for account of Mr. Milligan, a very respectable planter on the banks of the Mississippi; and that they made this engagement without consulting the owner of the ship, neither could he have known it, until about the time of her sailing from Baltimore — That Mr. Thompson and himself were the Agents of the Francis in Baltimore — That he sailed from the port of Baltimore with the said ship about the 20th of October, having no slaves on board, and proceeded down the Chesapeak Bay as far as Herring Cove, where he received on board of the Francis eighty-eight black passengers in families, all brought up together on two estates in Calvert County; and that they were all perfectly willing to come on board the ship — nor was any one required to compel them, they having a perfect understanding with their new master, Milligan, who was present at the time of their embarkation, that they were not to be sold again at New Orleans — but that he intended them all for his own estate. That Mr. Thompson and Deponent provided for them on board the ship, previous to her departure from Baltimore, the best provisions; in addition to which, by request of Mr. Milligan, Mr. Thompson put on board, expressly for their use, tea, coffee, sugar, molasses, whiskey, tobacco, &c. &c. with every kind of convenience for using the same, and clothing of every description to make them comfortable, which was dealt out to them day after day, while on the passage, at my discretion; that they all expressed much satisfaction at their treatment while on board the ship; that they had their perfect liberty on board; that their conduct was good at all times; that they needed not chains nor confinement, nor was any one of them put in chains or confined during the whole passage. That after Deponent took them on board, he returned up the Bay as far as Annapolis, where they were all examined by an officer of the Customs, and regularly cleared from that port for New Orleans. That about the middle of November, he landed them all in good health and spirits, on the plantation for which they were intended, belonging to Mr. Milligan, 17 or 20 miles below the city of New Orleans. That their quarters on board the ship Francis were large *and not narrow*, that all of them had good comfortable sleeping places or berths, and that they were well provided with a plenty of blankets, &c. &c.—that the ship's hatches were never closed on them during the whole passage for any other purpose than to protect them from rough and wet weather and make them comfortable. Finally, from the very high opinion Deponent has of the honor and integrity of Mr. Milligan, their owner, he considers his act in carrying these people away as one of the best of his life.

Let it be remembered, that he was not the cause of their bondage, but that he has actually relieved their condition in some degree by carrying them to a climate much more congenial to their nature. Mr Francis Todd and Deponent were brought up together at Newburyport, from children, and he has known both him and his business up to this time, and never knew him to carry slaves in any of his vessels; and he verily and conscientiously believes he never had a slave or slaves carried in any vessel of his to any part of the world, except in the solitary instance of the ship Francis aforesaid; and he knows he never owned a slave in his life.

NICHOLAS BROWN.

Sworn and subscribed to before SAMUEL PICKERING,

A Justice of the Peace of the State of Maryland, for the City of Baltimore, on the 9th of September, 1830.

Here the case closed on the part of the Plaintiff. The defendant did not attempt any justification of the truth of the matters published ;—he examined no witnesses, and the cause having been submitted to the Jury, they returned a verdict for the Plaintiff, with damages of *One Thousand Dollars.*

A late Convention of the Manumission Society of North Carolina unanimously adopted the following report of a Committee appointed to investigate the subject. Coming from a slave state, it is doubly gratifying to my feelings.

'The Committee to whom was referred the communication from the Chair, report,

1. That it is the opinion of your committee that nothing libellous was contained in the article for which William L. Garrison was indicted and convicted.

2. That Mr. Garrison did not surpass that liberty which is guaranteed to the press by the constitution of the United States.

3. Your committee recommend that the Association enter their protest against the illegal and unconstitutional decision in Garrison's case.

4. That the communication entire be published in the Greensborough Patriot.'

The following commentary upon the trial was published in the Journal and Tribune of this city, some weeks since ; and, emanating from the pen of the editor of that paper — a lawyer — is entitled to much consideration.

We have read a report of the case of Francis Todd, of Newburyport, *vs.* W. L. Garrison, late editor of a Baltimore anti-slavery paper, for a libel, and we cannot but think the verdict of the jury doubtful in law, or if legal, unreasonable in point of damages. Mr Garrison edited a paper, devoted, we believe, from the best motives to the best of purposes. The charge that he made against Mr Todd, was, that he transported in his vessel a cargo of slaves from Maryland to Louisiana, there to be sold in the market, and that they, or a part of them, were in irons, or were put in irons during the passage, and were otherwise treated harshly. For this, Mr Garrison declared that he would cover Mr Todd 'with thick infamy.' Mr G. also *inferred* that Mr T. had made his property by carrying such freights.

We presume that the main fact of freighting a ship with negroes from one port of the United States to another, would be no libel, even if *false,* because this is a legal and usual business, with which it is no more libellous to charge a man, than to say he had caught a freight of fish and carried them to market.—The main fact, however, was admitted to be true ; but it was denied that the slaves were carried *to be sold,* they being already sold to a humane master [Mr Milligan.] It was also denied that the slaves were ironed or otherwise harshly treated. These denials not having been rejoined to by the defendant, and having in fact been supported by the evidence of the captain, and one or two others, must be taken as correct, and Mr Garrison's statements as erroneous, in the subordinate particulars of the irons, the harsh treatment, and intended sale at New Orleans.

It does seem to us, that to say a man puts a slave in irons, whips him or sells him, is not, *prima facie* a libel, even though false; because these are lawful acts for slave-owners to do, and they are done every day. If the writing state that such acts were done without cause, or to an unreasonable extent where there was cause, such writing, if untrue, might be a libel.

At all events, it was and is evident that Mr Garrison's intent and aim was to direct the force of public opinion against the sale and bondage of human beings 'born free and equal' (as a *certain Declaration* says,) and against all persons, *particularly Yankees*, who in any way co-operate in it, or profit by it. In so doing, he attacked the *laws* more than he did Mr. Todd, or at least equally with him, for he charged Mr T. with nothing which the laws of any State or of the United States do not allow under certain circumstances, and no circumstances whatsoever were stated; thus leaving the case open for the reader and the court to suppose justifiable as readily as unjustifiable cause. Here the maxim, that every thing is to be construed in the *milder sense*, was applicable. Mr Garrison had a perfect right, and in our opinion deserves praise for 'covering with infamy,' as 'thick' as he could, any slave dealer, slave owner, (*voluntarily* becoming or remaining such) or slave agent or driver in the world. All the infamy which he could heap upon them on the general grounds of violating the laws of God and nature, and justice and humanity, in trading in human flesh, or putting men in bondage, or holding them there longer than is absolutely necessary, was and is just, lawful, praiseworthy and profitable to the Commonwealth, and no libel at all; and we doubt very much whether the particular allegation of *putting in irons, treating harshly*, and *carrying to market*, are in themselves libellous, though false.

UNIVERSAL EMANCIPATION.

Though distant be the hour, yet come it must —
  Oh! hasten it, *in mercy*, righteous Heaven!
When Afric's sons, uprising from the dust,
  Shall stand erect — their galling fetters riven;
  When from his throne Oppression shall be driven,
An exiled monster, powerless through all time;
  When freedom — glorious freedom, shall be given
To every race, complexion, caste, and clime,
And nature's sable hue shall cease to be a crime!

Wo if it come with storm, and blood, and fire,
  When midnight darkness veils the earth and sky!
Wo to the innocent babe — the guilty sire —
  Mother and daughter — friends of kindred tie!
  Stranger and citizen alike shall die!
Red-handed Slaughter his revenge shall feed,
  And Havoc yell his ominous death-cry,
And wild Despair in vain for mercy plead —
While hell itself shall shrink, and sicken at the deed!

Thou who avengest blood! long-suffering Lord!
　My guilty country from destruction save!
Let Justice sheathe his sharp and terrible sword,
　And Mercy rescue, e'en as from the grave!
O for the sake of those who firmly brave
The lust of power — the tyranny of law —
　To bring redemption to the perishing slave —
Fearless though few — Thy presence ne'er withdraw,
　But quench the kindling flames of hot, rebellious war!

And ye — sad victims of base avarice!
　Hunted like beasts — and trodden like the earth;
Bought and sold daily, at a paltry price —
　The scorn of tyrants, and of fools the mirth —
Your souls debased from their immortal birth!
Bear meekly — as ye've born — your cruel woes;
　Ease follows pain — light, darkness — plenty, dearth:
So time shall give you freedom and repose,
And high exalt your heads above your bitter foes!

Not by the sword shall your deliverance be;
　Not by the shedding of your masters' blood;
Not by rebellion — or foul treachery,
　Up-springing suddenly, like swelling flood:
Revenge and rapine ne'er did bring forth good.
God's *time is best!* — nor will it long delay:
　Even now your barren cause begins to bud,
And glorious shall the fruit be! — Watch and pray,
For, lo! the kindling dawn, that ushers in the day!

G—n.

JOURNAL OF THE TIMES.

TO-DAY.

Another New Year is born, and, after the similitude of man's inevitable fate, in a little space must die. Brief as it will prove, how various and important will be its history — to individuals, as well as to nations! How many thrones may it not shake, or fetters sever, or revolutions witness! The crisis of the world has not yet come: scarcely the preface of its eventful history is writ. Empires are to be refashioned, and a large portion of the earth reclaimed from superstition and barbarism, from oppression and idolatry. We talk of the march of mind; we marvel at the age of creation; — but does knowledge keep pace with ignorance, or virtue with vice, or benevolence with suffering, or liberty with tyranny, among mankind? Most evidently not. How long will it take to regenerate and disenthral benighted Africa? how long to christianize Asia? how long to reform republican America? how long to redeem the world? Surely time is in its infancy. Strange that men predict a millennium at so early a day.

The past has been an eventful year; the present will probably be yet more troublous. Europe has just begun to feel the upheavings of the earthquake which is to overthrow its strong towers, and the heat of a fire which is to melt every chain. There are signs in the political firmament of Great Britain which portend sudden and disastrous convulsions: but known only to God are the hidden things of time.

In this country, of those who hailed the opening of the past year, there have died at least *three hundred thousand*. More than a million mourners have 'gone about the streets.' How frail is man! Who and how many must die the present year? Perhaps half a million. Of this number, how many shall we or our friends make? O Life! O Death! O Eternity!

In this free and christian republic, too, be it remembered, there were kidnapped during the past year, and reduced to remediless bondage, MORE THAN FIFTY THOUSAND INFANTS, the offspring of slave parents!!! *A greater number, this year, is to meet a similar doom!* Have we no reason to fear the judgments of Heaven upon our guilty land?

CORRESPONDENCE.

The following is an extract of a letter from one of the most distinguished reformers of the age. It contains some hints to ministers of the gospel, which ought to be given publicly for their benefit:

'The cause in which you are engaged, will certainly prevail, and so will mine;* but when? It is not for us to ask. God will accomplish it in his own time; and perhaps by our means. We ought to be content to be His instruments, without aspiring to direct Him. Slavery and war will be abolished throughout all Christendom, and the abolition of them depends on public opinion; and public opinion is directed by the pulpit and the press — by speaking and writing; and there is no other way. Unfortunately many of our ministers are too much under 'the fear of man which bringeth a snare,' and they therefore 'shun to declare the whole counsel of God.' Many who entertain correct sentiments about war and slavery, have not the moral courage to declare them. How they will answer it at the bar of God, I know not. Many seem to fear to examine these subjects, lest they should bring upon themselves greater responsibilities than they are willing to bear; not reflecting that duties neglected bring as great condemnation as crimes committed. *But all ministers are not so;* there are noble examples to the

* The cause of Peace.

contrary; and when the pulpit shall unite with the press, war and slavery will cease to pollute the Lord's vineyard.

Extract of a letter from a gentleman in Vermont.

'DEAR SIR — One of my neighbors has just had the reading of your proposals for the Liberator, &c. He says it is professedly *the very thing* that is wanted. If you steadfastly pursue your object, you will in the end be crowned with the honors of the greatest victory ever won by mortal power. He would assure you, that you need fear no overthrow in the contest — for the moral power of the nation is on your side; (1) and if you fail, you lose nothing — as, in that case, it will be evidenced that but little will have been left worth preserving.

'You will please forward me a copy of your paper, which will be paid for when received. And believe me a friend to Liberty, Peace, Temperance and Christian Morality; yet purified from licentiousness, violence, enthusiasm, (2) and fanaticism.'

(1) It may be; but at present it has no efficacy, being struck with a fearful paralysis. Still we confidently rely upon its awakened energy to redeem the land from the curse and crime of slavery.

(2) 'Enthusiasm'? In all great reformations, a generous and ever blazing enthusiasm is necessary to quicken the dormant, and to inspirit the heart of the reformer. But licentiousness, and violence, and fanaticism — these are traits which do not belong to truth or justice.

Extract of a letter from a gentleman in Mount-Vernon, N.H.

'DEAR SIR: — I have recently read your proposals for publishing the 'Liberator,' and I think that no American, who makes any pretensions to philanthropy, patriotism, morality or Christianity, can do less than wish you "God speed." You will please to add my name to your list of subscribers.'

WORKING MEN.

An attempt has been made — it is still making — we regret to say, with considerable success — to inflame the minds of our working classes against the more opulent, and to persuade them that they are contemned and oppressed by a wealthy aristocracy. That public grievances exist, is unquestionably true; but they are not confined to any one class of society. Every profession is interested in their removal — the rich as well as the poor. It is in the highest degree criminal, therefore, to exasperate our mechanics to deeds of violence, or to array them under a party banner; for it is not true, that, at any time, they have been the objects of reproach. Labor is not dishonorable. The industrious artisan, in a government like ours, will always be held in better estimation than the wealthy idler.

Our limits will not allow us to enlarge on this subject: we may return to it another time. We are the friends of reform; but that is not reform, which, in curing one evil, threatens to inflict a thousand others.

For 'THE SALUTATION' of the Liberator on our first page, we are indebted to a lady, who sustains a high reputation for poetical merit, and whose soul is overflowing with philanthropic emotion. Will the public help us to secure her constant services?

It will be our endeavor to diversify the contents of the Liberator, so as to give an edge to curiosity, and relieve the eye and mind of the reader. One page will be devoted to foreign and domestic transactions; another, to literary, miscellaneous and moral subjects.

Lord Erskine when at the bar, was always remarkable for the fearlessness with which he contended against the Bench. In a contest he had with Lord Kenyon, he explained the rule of his conduct at the Bar in the following terms:—

'It was,' said he, 'the first command and counsel of my youth, always to do what my conscience told me to be my duty, and to leave the consequences to God. I shall carry with me the memory, and I trust the practice, of this paternal lesson to the grave — I have hitherto followed it, and have no reason to complain that any obedience to it has been even a temporal sacrifice — I have found it, on the contrary, the road to prosperity and wealth, and I shall point it out as such to my children.'

The following individuals formed the jury which brought in a verdict of One Thousand Dollars, at Baltimore, in favor of Mr. Francis Todd. It will doutless gratify them to see their names 'in print.' More anon.

Daniel W. Crocker,
Samuel D. Walker,
William H. Beatty,
John Franciscus,
George M'Dowell,
G. A. Vonspreckelson,

Stewart Brown,
George A. Hughes,
Andrew Crawford,
Robert Hewitt,
James W. Collins.
John Walsh.

The trial of Judge Peck continues to occupy the attention of Congress, to the exclusion of almost all other business.

OUR APPEAL.

For the successful prosecution of our labors, we appeal to the following classes of our fellow countrymen, and we presume they are sufficiently numerous to fulfil our expectations:

To the religious — who profess to walk in the footsteps of their Divine Master, and to be actuated by a love which 'worketh no ill' to others. To whom, if not to them, shall we turn for encouragement?

To the philanthropic — who show their sincerity by their works, whose good deeds are more numerous than their professions, who not only pity but relieve.

To the patriotic — who love their country better than themselves, and would avert its impending ruin.

To the ignorant, the cold-hearted, the base, THE TYRANNICAL — who need to be instructed, and quickened, and reclaimed, and humanized.

TO OUR FREE COLORED BRETHREN.

Your moral and intellectual elevation, the advancement of your rights, and the defence of your character, will be a leading object of our paper. We know that you are now struggling against wind and tide, and that adversity 'has marked you for his own:' yet among three hundred thousand of your number, some patronage may be given. We ask, and expect, but little: that little may save the life of 'The Liberator.' Our enemies are numerous, active and inveterate; and a great effort will undoubtedly be made to put us down.

WALKER'S PAMPHLET.

The Legislature of North Carolina has lately been sitting with closed doors, in consequence of a message from the Governor relative to the above pamphlet. The south may reasonably be alarmed at the circulation of Mr. Walker's Appeal; for a better promoter of insurrection was never sent forth to an oppressed people. In a future number, we propose to examine it, as also various editorial comments thereon — it being one of the most remarkable productions of the age. We have already publicly deprecated its spirit.

The Publishers of the Liberator have formed their co-partnership with a determination to print the paper as long as they can subsist upon bread and water, or their hands obtain employment. The friends of the cause may, therefore, take courage; its enemies — may surrender at discretion.

GENIUS OF UNIVERSAL EMANCIPATION.

We congratulate our friend Lundy on the removal of his paper to Washington city. The Lord bless him abundantly in his new situation! What zeal has he not evinced, what suffering not felt, what sacrifice not made, in the noble cause to which he has devoted his life! Friends of bleeding humanity, uphold his arms, encourage his heart, patronize his work.

Editors who are willing to exchange sheets with the Liberator are requested to be prompt in their reciprocity.

The Cherokee Delegation to Congress have publicly denied the reports that their brethren were ready to make a treaty to emigrate, if reservations are granted certain Chiefs. They are determined to hold their ground, unless driven off by force.

The number of children between the ages of four and sixteen, in the common schools of Ohio, is believed to be not less than 350,000. The militia of the State comprises 116,000 men.

Last October, a plot for an insurrection, in which were 100 negroes engaged, some of whom were free, was discovered at Plaquemines, Louisiana. So say the papers.

FIFTH CENSUS OF MASSACHUSETTS.

Counties.	Males.	Females.	Colored.	Total.
Plymouth	20905	21678	410	42993
Suffolk	28586	31693	1883	62162
Nantucket	3339	3584	279	7202
Hampshire	14990	14995	225	30210
Bristol	23366	25178	930	49474
Middlesex	38107	39348	513	77968
Norfolk	20436	21296	169	41901
Barnstable	13997	14363	165	28525
Worcester	41545	42449	371	84365
Hampden	15288	16003	349	31640
Franklin	14447	14765	132	29344
Dukes	1702	1768	48	3518
Berkshire	18310	18510	1005	37825
Essex	39451	42929	527	82887
Totals	294449	308559	7006	610014

Free Colored Population.

Males under ten years of age,	804
of ten and under twenty four,	886
of twenty four and under thirty six,	726
of thirty six and under fifty five,	635
of fifty five and under one hundred,	321
of one hundred and upwards,	5
	3,377
Females under ten years of age,	823
of ten and under twenty four,	956
of twenty four and under thirty six,	810
of thirty six and under fifty five,	651
of fifty five and under one hundred,	385
of one hundred and upwards,	4
	3,629
Colored males,	3,377
Total number of free colored persons,	7,006

Population of Rhode-Island, in 1830, 97,212; in 1820, 83,059; increase 14,153.

Population of Connecticut, in 1830, 297,726; in 1820, 275,238; increase 22,488.

Population of Delaware, in 1830, 76,739; in 1820, 72,749; increase, 3,990.

Population of New York, in 1830, 1,934,496; in 1820, 1,372,812; increase 561,684.

Virginia.— In 45 counties of Virginia, which by the census of 1820 had a population of 438,165, the present population is found to be 506,516, making an increase of 68,351, or nearly 16 per cent. The increase in the number of whites is 41,468, or 17 per cent; of slaves 20,635, or 12 per cent.; and of free blacks 6,248, or 40 per cent. The increase of slaves heretofore has always been in greater ratio than that of whites. There is now a greater increase of whites.

[For the Liberator.]

TO AN INFANT.

Fair bud of being,— blossoming like the rose,
  Leaf upon leaf unfolding to the eye,
  In fragrance rich, and spotless purity,—
Which hourly dost some latent charm disclose;—
O may the dews and gentle rains of heaven
  Give to thy root immortal sustenance;
  So thou in matchless beauty shalt advance,
Nor by the storms of life be rudely driven.

But if, oh envious Death! this little flower
  Thou from its tender stem untimely break,
  An angel shall the drooping victim take,
And so transplant it to a heavenly bower;
Where it shall flourish in eternal spring,
Nurtured beneath the eye of a paternal King.

G—n.

A NOBLE SENTIMENT.

I have ever had in my mind, that when God should cast me into such a condition, as that I cannot save my life but by doing an indecent thing, he shows me the time is come wherein I should resign it; and when I cannot live in my own country but by such means as are worse than dying in it, I think he shows me, I ought to keep myself out of it.—*Algernon Sidney.*

[For the Liberator.]

NEW YEAR'S DAY.

Brightest, merriest of days!
Welcomed in a thousand lays!
Not a heart but leaps for gladness,
Not a brow that's veiled in sadness,
Not an eye that beams not brighter,
Not a step that is not lighter!
Day of joyful hopes and wishes,
Prodigal of gifts and kisses;
Want, with all his pining brood,
Leaps and sings for gratitude;
Nakedness — a shivering claimant —
Now obtains a seemly raiment;
Sorrow wipes her tears away,
On a happy New Year's Day;
All the forms of sharp distress,
Charity's fair hand doth bless!

  What awaits, O new-born Year!
On thy brief, untried career?
Pass not, till the world is free
From the yoke of tyranny;
Broken be th' oppressor's rod,
In the dust his throne be trod;—
Till the sea of human blood
Cease to roll its gory flood,
And the thundering tones of war
Echo not from lands afar;—
Till the scourge intemperance,
With its train, is banished hence;

Of the fall the deadliest fruit,
Sinking man below the brute;
Foulest of impurities,
Bloodiest of enemies,
Body-eater, soul-destroyer,
Universal plague — annoyer; —
Pass not, till, from sea to sea,
Christ shall gain supremacy;
Idols to the bats be given —
In their stead the Lord of heaven
Be consulted, loved, adored,
By a guilty race restored.

G—n.

The Life of William Lloyd Garrison, in four volumes, by his children, is an exhaustive work, not only a complete biography of the great reformer, but a history of the whole anti-slavery struggle. The eighth chapter of the first volume is devoted to the founding and early days of the *Liberator*, including a critical analysis of the first number. The first number was "a modest folio, of which the printed page of four columns measured fourteen inches by nine and a quarter." The contents of the first three pages of the first number, save a few unimportant news items not relating to the cause, are reprinted in the present leaflet, with two poems by Mr. Garrison from the fourth page. The balance of the fourth page was made up of brief general selections without significance. The poor little publication office was for some years in Merchants' Hall, a building burned in the great Boston fire of 1872. "The dingy walls, the small windows bespattered with printers' ink, the press standing in one corner, the composing stands opposite, the long editorial and mailing table covered with newspapers, the bed of the editor and publisher on the floor, — all these," says Oliver Johnson, "make a picture never to be forgotten." With the seventeenth number the plain heading gave way to an ornamental one with a rude cut representing a slave auction. A fac-simile of the first page of this number is given in the Life of Garrison, vol. i. p. 232. The paper was afterwards enlarged; and its publication was continued to the completion of its thirty-fifth volume, December, 1865.

Oliver Johnson's "William Lloyd Garrison and his Times" is a valuable work by one who knew Garrison well. There is a brief biography of Garrison by Archibald H. Grimke in the "American Reformers" series. The spirit and significance of Garrison's efforts, through the *Liberator*, are notably commemorated in Lowell's poem, "To William Lloyd Garrison."

PUBLISHED BY
THE DIRECTORS OF THE OLD SOUTH WORK,
Old South Meeting-house, Boston, Mass.

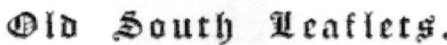

Old South Leaflets.

No. 79.

William Lloyd Garrison.

Eulogy by Wendell Phillips at the Funeral of Garrison, May 28, 1879.

It has been well said that we are not here to weep, and neither are we here to praise. No life closes without sadness. Death, after all, no matter what hope or what memories surround it, is terrible and a mystery. We never part hands that have been clasped lifelong in loving tenderness but the hour is sad. Still, we do not come here to weep. In other moments, elsewhere, we can offer tender and loving sympathy to those whose roof-tree is so sadly bereaved. But, in the spirit of the great life which we commemorate, this hour is for the utterance of a lesson: this hour is given to contemplate a grand example, a rich inheritance, a noble life worthily ended. You come together, not to pay tribute, even loving tribute, to the friend you have lost, whose features you will miss from daily life, but to remember the grand lesson of that career; to speak to each other, and to emphasize what that life teaches, — especially in the hearing of these young listeners, who did not see that marvellous career; in their hearing to construe the meaning of the great name which is borne world-wide, and tell them why on both sides the ocean the news of his death is a matter of interest to every lover of his race. As my friend said, we have no right to be silent. Those of us who stood near him, who witnessed the secret springs of his action, the consistent inward and outward life, have no right to be silent. The largest contribution that will ever be made by any single man's life to the knowledge of the working of our institutions will be the picture of his career. He sounded the depths of the weakness, he proved the ultimate strength, of republican institutions; he gave us to know the perils that confront us; he taught us to rally the strength that lies hid.

To my mind there are three remarkable elements in his career. One is rare even among great men. It was his own moral nature, unaided, uninfluenced from outside, that consecrated him to a great idea. Other men ripen gradually. The youngest of the great American names that will be compared with his was between thirty and forty when his first anti-slavery word was uttered. Luther was thirty-four years old when an infamous enterprise woke him to indignation, and it then took two years more to reveal to him the mission God designed for him. This man was in jail for his opinions when he was just twenty-four. He had confronted a nation in the very bloom of his youth. It could be said of him more than of any other American in our day, and more than of any great leader that I chance now to remember in any epoch, that he did not need circumstances, outside influence, some great pregnant event, to press him into service, to provoke him to thought, to kindle him into enthusiasm. His moral nature was as marvellous as was the intellect of Pascal. It seemed to be born fully equipped, "finely touched." Think of the mere dates; think that at some twenty-four years old, while Christianity and statesmanship, the experience, the genius of the land, were wandering in the desert, aghast, amazed, and confounded over a frightful evil, a great sin, this boy sounded, found, invented the talisman, "Immediate, unconditional emancipation on the soil." You may say he borrowed it — true enough — from the lips of a woman on the other side of the Atlantic; but he was the only American whose moral nature seemed, just on the edge of life, so perfectly open to duty and truth that it answered to the far-off bugle-note, and proclaimed it instantly as a complete solution of the problem.

Young men, you have no conception of the miracle of that insight; for it is not given to you to remember with any vividness the blackness of the darkness of ignorance and indifference which then brooded over what was called the moral and religious element of the American people. When I think of him, as Melancthon said of Luther, "day by day grows the wonder fresh" at the ripeness of the moral and intellectual life that God gave him at the very opening.

You hear that boy's lips announcing the statesmanlike

solution which startled politicians and angered church and people. A year afterwards, with equally single-hearted devotion, in words that have been so often quoted, with those dungeon doors behind him, he enters on his career. In January, 1831, then twenty-five years old, he starts the publication of "The Liberator," advocating the immediate abolition of slavery; and, with the sublime pledge: "I will be as harsh as truth and as uncompromising as justice. On this subject I do not wish to speak or write with moderation. I will not equivocate — I will not excuse — I will not retreat a single inch — AND I WILL BE HEARD."

Then began an agitation which for the marvel of its origin, the majesty of its purpose, the earnestness, unselfishness, and ability of its appeals, the vigor of its assault, the deep national convulsion it caused, the vast and beneficent changes it wrought, and its wide-spread, indirect influence on all kindred moral questions, is without a parallel in history since Luther. This boy created and marshalled it. His converts held it up and carried it on. Before this, all through the preceding century, there had been among us scattered and single abolitionists, earnest and able men; sometimes, like Wythe of Virginia, in high places. The Quakers and Covenanters had never intermitted their testimony against slavery. But Garrison was the first man to begin a *movement* designed to annihilate slavery. He announced the principle, arranged the method, gathered the forces, enkindled the zeal, started the argument, and finally marshalled the nation for and against the system in a conflict that came near rending the Union.

I marvel again at the instinctive sagacity which discerned the hidden forces fit for such a movement, called them forth, and wielded them to such prompt results. Archimedes said, "Give me a spot, and I will move the world." O'Connell leaned back on three millions of Irishmen, all on fire with sympathy. Cobden's hands were held up by the whole manufacturing interest of Great Britain. His treasury was the wealth of the middle classes of the country; and behind him also, in fair proportion, stood the religious convictions of England. Marvellous was their agitation. As you gaze upon it in its successive stages, and analyze it, you are astonished at what they invented for tools. But this boy stood alone,— utterly alone, at first. There was no sympathy anywhere; his hands were empty; one single penniless comrade was his only helper. Starving on bread and water, he could command the use of types, that was all. Trade endeavored to crush him; the intellectual life of America disowned him.

My friend Weld has said the Church was a thick bank of black cloud looming over him. Yes. But no sooner did the Church discern the impetuous boy's purpose than out of that dead, sluggish cloud thundered and lightened a malignity which could not find words to express its hate. The very pulpit where I stand saw this apostle of liberty and justice sore beset, always in great need, and often in deadly peril; yet it never gave him one word of approval or sympathy. During all this weary struggle Mr. Garrison felt its weight in the scale against him. In those years it led the sect which arrogates to itself the name of Liberal. If this was the bearing of so-called Liberals, what bitterness of opposition, judge ye, did not the others show? A mere boy confronts church, commerce, and college,— a boy with neither training nor experience! Almost at once the assault tells: the whole country is hotly interested. What created such life under those ribs of death? Whence came that instinctive knowledge? Where did he get that sound common sense? Whence did he summon that almost unerring sagacity which, starting agitation on an untried field, never committed an error, provoking year by year additional enthusiasm, gathering, as he advanced, helper after helper to his side? I marvel at the miraculous boy. He had no means. Where he got, whence he summoned, how he created, the elements which changed 1830 into 1835 — 1830 apathy, indifference, ignorance, icebergs, into 1835, every man intelligently hating him, and mobs assaulting him in every city — is a marvel which none but older men than I can adequately analyze and explain. He said to a friend who remonstrated with him on the heat and severity of his language, "Brother, I have need to be all on fire, for I have mountains of ice about me to melt." Well, that dungeon of 1830, that universal apathy, that deadness of soul, that contempt of what called itself intellect, in ten years he changed into the whole country aflame. He made every single home, press, pulpit, and senate-chamber a debating society, with *his* right and wrong for the subject. And, as was said of Luther, "God honored him by making all the worst men his enemies."

Fastened on that daily life was a malignant attention and

criticism such as no American has ever endured. I will not call it a criticism of hate: that word is not strong enough. Malignity searched him with candles from the moment he uttered that God-given solution of the problem to the moment when he took the hand of the nation and wrote out the statute which made it law. Malignity searched those forty years with candles; and yet even malignity has never lisped a suspicion, much less a charge,— never lisped a suspicion of anything mean, dishonorable, dishonest. No man, however mad with hate, however fierce in assault, ever dared to hint that there was anything low in motive, false in assertion, selfish in purpose, dishonest in method,— never a stain on the thought, the word, or the deed.

Now contemplate this boy entering such an arena, confronting a nation and all its forces, utterly poor, with no sympathy from any quarter, conducting an angry, wide-spread, and profound agitation for ten, twenty, forty years, amid the hate of everything strong in American life, and the contempt of everything influential, and no stain, not the slightest shadow of one, rests on his escutcheon! Summon me the public men, the men who have put their hands to the helm of the vessel of state since 1789, of whom that can be said, although love and admiration, which almost culminated in worship, attended the steps of some of them.

Then look at the work he did. My friends have spoken of his influence. What American ever held his hand so long and so powerfully on the helm of social, intellectual, and moral America? There have been giants in our day. Great men God has granted in widely different spheres,— earnest men, men whom public admiration lifted early into power. I shall venture to name some of them. Perhaps you will say it is not usual on an occasion like this; but long-waiting truth needs to be uttered in an hour when this great example is still absolutely indispensable to inspire the effort, to guide the steps, to cheer the hope, of the nation not yet arrived in the promised land. I want to show you the vast breadth and depth that this man's name signifies. We have had Webster in the Senate; we have had Lyman Beecher in the pulpit; we have had Calhoun at the head of a section; we have had a philosopher at Concord with his inspiration penetrating the young mind of the Northern States. They are the four men that history, perhaps, will mention somewhere near the great force whose closing in this scene we commemorate to-day. Remember now not merely the inadequate means at this man's control, not simply the bitter hate that he confronted, not the vast work that he must be allowed to have done,— surely vast, when measured by the opposition he encountered and the strength he held in his hands,— but dismissing all those considerations, measuring nothing but the breadth and depth of his hold, his grasp on American character, social change, and general progress, what man's signet has been set so deep, planted so forever on the thoughts of his epoch? Trace home intelligently, trace home to their sources, the changes, social, political, intellectual, and religious, that have come over us during the last fifty years,— the volcanic convulsions, the stormy waves which have tossed and rocked our generation,— and you will find close at the sources of the Mississippi this boy with his proclamation!

The great party that put on record the statute of freedom was made up of men whose conscience he quickened and whose intellect he inspired, and they long stood the tools of a public opinion that he created. The grandest name beside his in the America of our times is that of John Brown. Brown stood on the platform that Garrison built; and Mrs. Stowe herself charmed an audience that he gathered for her, with words which he inspired, from a heart that he kindled. Sitting at his feet were leaders born of "The Liberator," the guides of public sentiment. I know whereof I affirm. It was often a pleasant boast of Charles Sumner that he read "The Liberator" two years before I did; and, among the great men who followed his lead and held up his hands in Massachusetts, where is the intellect, where is the heart, that does not trace to this printer-boy the first pulse that bade him serve the slave? For myself, no words can adequately tell the measureless debt I owe him, the moral and intellectual life he opened to me. I feel like the old Greek, who, taught himself by Socrates, called his own scholars "the disciples of Socrates."

This is only another instance added to the roll of the Washingtons and the Hampdens, whose root is not ability, but *character;* that influence which, like the great Master's of Judea (humanly speaking), spreading through the centuries, testifies that the world suffers its grandest changes not by genius, but by the more potent control of *character*. His was an earnestness that would take no denial, that consumed opposition in the intensity of its convictions, that knew nothing but right. As friend after friend gathered slowly, one by one, to his side, in that very meeting of a dozen heroic men to form the New England Anti-slavery Society, it was his compelling hand, his resolute unwillingness to temper or qualify the utterance, that finally dedicated that first organized movement to the doctrine of immediate emancipation. He seems to have understood,— this boy without experience,— he seems to have understood by instinct that righteousness is the only thing which will finally compel submission; that one, with God, is always a majority. He seems to have known it at the very outset, taught of God, the herald and champion, God-endowed and God-sent to arouse a nation, that only by the most absolute assertion of the uttermost truth, without qualification or compromise, can a nation be waked to conscience or strengthened for duty. No man ever understood so thoroughly — not O'Connell nor Cobden — the nature and needs of that *agitation* which alone, in our day, reforms states. In the darkest hour he never doubted the omnipotence of conscience and the moral sentiment.

And then look at the unquailing courage with which he faced the successive obstacles that confronted him! Modest, believing at the outset that America could not be as corrupt as she seemed, he waits at the door of the churches, importunes leading clergymen, begs for a voice from the sanctuary, a consecrated protest from the pulpit. To his utter amazement, he learns, by thus probing it, that the Church will give him no help, but, on the contrary, surges into the movement in opposition. Serene, though astounded by the unexpected revelation, he simply turns his footsteps, and announces that "a Christianity which keeps peace with the oppressor is no Christianity," and goes on his way to supplant the religious element which the Church had allied with sin by a deeper religious faith. Yes, he sets himself to work — this stripling with his sling confronting the angry giant in complete steel, this solitary evangelist — to make Christians of twenty millions of people! I am not exaggerating. You know, older men, who can go back to that period; I know that when one, kindred to a voice that you have heard to-day, whose pathway Garrison's bloody feet had made easier for the treading, when he uttered in a pulpit in Boston only a few strong words, injected in the course of a sermon, his venerable father, between seventy and eighty years, was met the next morning and his hand shaken by a much moved friend. "Colonel, you have my sympathy. I cannot tell you how much I pity you." "What," said the brusque old man, "what is your pity?" "Well, I hear your son went crazy at 'Church Green' yesterday." Such was the utter indifference. At that time bloody feet had smoothed the pathway for other men to tread. Still, then and for years afterwards, insanity was the only kind-hearted excuse that partial friends could find for sympathy with such a madman!

If anything strikes one more prominently than another in this career,— to your astonishment, young men, you may say, — it is the plain, sober common sense, the robust English element which underlay Cromwell, which explains Hampden, which gives the color that distinguishes 1640 in England from 1790 in France. Plain, robust, well-balanced common sense. Nothing erratic; no enthusiasm which had lost its hold on firm earth; no mistake of method; no unmeasured confidence; no miscalculation of the enemy's strength. Whoever mistook, Garrison seldom mistook. Fewer mistakes in that long agitation of fifty years can be charged to his account than to any other American. Erratic as men supposed him, intemperate in utterance, mad in judgment, an enthusiast gone crazy, the moment you sat down at his side, patient in explanation, clear in statement, sound in judgment, studying carefully every step, calculating every assault, measuring the force to meet it, never in haste, always patient, waiting until the time ripened,— fit for a great leader. Cull, if you please, from the statesmen who obeyed him, whom he either whipped into submission or summoned into existence,— cull from among them the man whose career, fairly examined, exhibits fewer miscalculations and fewer mistakes than this career which is just ended.

I know what I claim. As Mr. Weld has said, I am speaking to-day to men who judge by their ears, by rumors; who see, not with their eyes, but with their prejudices. History, fifty years hence, dispelling your prejudices, will do justice to the grand sweep of the orbit which, as my friend said, to-day we are hardly in a position, or mood, to measure. As Coleridge avers, "The truth-haters of to-morrow will give the right name to the truth-haters of to-day, for even such men the stream of time bears onward." I do not fear that, if my words are remembered by the next generation, they will be thought unsupported or extravagant. When history seeks the sources of New England character, when men begin to open up and examine the hidden springs and note the convulsions and the throes of American life within the last half-century, they will remember Parker, that Jupiter of the pulpit; they will remember the long unheeded but measureless influence that came to us from the seclusion of Concord; they will do justice to the masterly statesmanship which guided, during a part of his life, the efforts of Webster. But they will recognize that there was only one man north of Mason and Dixon's line who met squarely, with an absolute logic, the else impregnable position of John C. Calhoun; only one brave, far-sighted, keen, logical intellect, which discerned that there were only two moral points in the universe, *right* and *wrong;* that, when one was asserted, subterfuge and evasion would be sure to end in defeat.

Here lies the brain and the heart; here lies the statesman-like intellect, logical as Jonathan Edwards, brave as Luther, which confronted the logic of South Carolina with an assertion direct and broad enough to make an issue and necessitate a conflict of two civilizations. Calhoun said, Slavery is *right.* Webster and Clay shrunk from him, and evaded his assertion. Garrison, alone at that time, met him face to face, proclaiming slavery a sin and daring all the inferences. It is true, as New Orleans complains to-day in her journals, that this man brought upon America everything they call the disaster of the last twenty years; and it is equally true that, if you seek through the hidden causes and unheeded events for the hand that wrote "emancipation" on the statute-book and on the flag, it lies still there to-day.

I have no time to number the many kindred reforms to which he lent as profound an earnestness and almost as large aid.

I hardly dare enter that home. There is one other marked and, as it seems to me, unprecedented, element in this career. His was the happiest life I ever saw. No need for pity. Let no tear fall over his life. No man gathered into his bosom a fuller sheaf of blessing, delight, and joy. In his seventy years there were not arrows enough in the whole quiver of the Church or State to wound him. As Guizot once said from the tribune, "Gentlemen, you cannot get high enough to reach the level of my contempt." So Garrison, from the serene level of his daily life, from the faith that never faltered, was able to say to American hate, "You cannot reach up to the level of my home mood, my daily existence." I have seen him intimately for thirty years, while raining on his head was the hate of the community, when by every possible form of expression malignity let him know that it wished him all sorts of harm. I never saw him unhappy. I never saw the moment that serene, abounding faith in the rectitude of his motive, the soundness of his method, and the certainty of his success did not lift him above all posssibility of being reached by any clamor about him. Every one of his near friends will agree with me that this was the happiest life God has granted in our day to any American standing in the foremost rank of influence and effort.

Adjourned from the stormiest meeting, where hot debate had roused all his powers as near to anger as his nature ever let him come, the music of a dozen voices — even of those who had just opposed him — or a piano, if the house held one, changed his mood in an instant, and made the hour laugh with more than content; unless, indeed, a baby and playing with it proved metal even more attractive.

To champion wearisome causes, bear with disordered intellects, to shelter the wrecks of intemperance and fugitives whose pulse trembled at every touch on the door-latch,— this was his home. Keenly alive to human suffering, ever prompt to help relieve it, pouring out his means for that more lavishly than he ought, all this was no burden, never clouded or depressed the inextinguishable buoyancy and gladness of his nature. God ever held over him unclouded the sunlight of his countenance.

And he never grew old. The tabernacle of flesh grew feebler, and the step was less elastic. But the ability to work, the serene faith and unflagging hope, suffered no change. To the day of his death he was as ready as in his boyhood to confront and defy a mad majority. The keen insight and clear judgment never failed him. His tenacity of purpose never weakened. He showed nothing either of the intellectual sluggishness or the timidity of age. The bugle-call which last year woke the nation to its peril and duty on the Southern question showed all the old fitness to lead and mould a people's course. Younger men might be confused or dazed by plausible pretensions, and half the North was befooled; but the old pioneer detected the false ring as quickly as in his youth. The words his dying hand traced, welcoming the Southern exodus and foretelling its result, had all the defiant courage and prophetic solemnity of his youngest and boldest days.

Serene, fearless, marvellous man! Mortal, with so few shortcomings!

Farewell, for a very little while, noblest of Christian men! Leader, brave, tireless, unselfish! When the ear heard thee, then it blessed thee; the eye that saw thee gave witness to thee. More truly than it could ever heretofore be said since the great patriarch wrote it, "the blessing of him that was ready to perish" was thine eternal great reward.

Though the clouds rest for a moment to-day on the great work that you set your heart to accomplish, you knew, God in his love let you see, that your work was done; that one thing, by his blessing on your efforts, is fixed beyond the possibility of change. While that ear could listen, God gave what he has so rarely given to man, the plaudits and prayers of four millions of victims, thanking you for emancipation; and through the clouds of to-day your heart, as it ceased to beat, felt certain, *certain*, that, whether one flag or two shall rule this continent in time to come, one thing is settled,— it never henceforth can be trodden by a slave!

THE MURDER OF LOVEJOY.

WENDELL PHILLIPS'S FIRST SPEECH IN FANEUIL HALL, DECEMBER 8, 1837.

At the great meeting held in Faneuil Hall, Dec. 8, 1837, to denounce the murder of Lovejoy by the mob at Alton, Ill., while defending his printing-press, after addresses by Dr. Channing and George S. Hillard, Hon. James T. Austin, attorney-general of the Commonwealth, rose, and in a speech of great bitterness compared the slaves to a menagerie of wild beasts and the rioters at Alton to the "orderly mob" which threw the tea overboard in 1773, and declared that Lovejoy was presumptuous, and "died as the fool dieth." The speech produced great excitement. Wendell Phillips, then a young man of twenty-six, who had not expected to take part in the meeting, was unable to keep silent, and rose to reply, while that portion of the assembly which sympathized with the attorney-general became so boisterous that he had difficulty in gaining the audience. Mr. Phillips had spoken before this at a meeting of the Massachusetts Anti-slavery Society in Lynn, March 28, 1837; but this speech in Faneuil Hall was the real beginning of his great public career.

Mr. Chairman,—We have met for the freest discussion of these resolutions, and the events which gave rise to them. [Cries of "Question," "Hear him," "Go on," "No gagging," etc.] I hope I shall be permitted to express my surprise at the sentiments of the last speaker,— surprise not only at such sentiments from such a man, but at the applause they have received within these walls. A comparison has been drawn between the events of the Revolution and the tragedy at Alton. We have heard it asserted here, in Faneuil Hall, that Great Britain had a right to tax the colonies; and we have heard the mob at Alton, the drunken murderers of Lovejoy, compared to those patriot fathers who threw the tea overboard! [Great applause.] Fellow-citizens, is this Faneuil Hall doctrine? ["No, no."] The mob at Alton were met to wrest from a citizen his just rights,— met to resist the laws. We have been told that our fathers did the same; and the glorious mantle of Revolutionary precedent has been thrown over the mobs of our day. To make out their title to such defence, the gentleman says that the British Parliament had a *right* to tax these colonies. It is manifest that, without this, his parallel falls to the ground; for Lovejoy had stationed himself within constitutional bulwarks. He was not only defending the freedom of the press, but he was under his own roof, in arms with the sanction of the civil authority. The men who assailed him went against and over the laws. The *mob*, as the gentleman terms it,— mob, forsooth! certainly we sons of the tea-spillers are a marvellously patient generation!— the "orderly mob" which assembled in the Old South to destroy the tea were met to resist, not the laws, but illegal exactions. Shame on the American who calls the tea tax and stamp act *laws!* Our fathers resisted, not the king's prerogative, but the king's usurpation. To find any other account, you must read our Revolutionary history upside down. Our State archives are loaded with arguments of John Adams to prove the taxes laid by the British Parliament unconstitutional,— beyond its power. It was not till this was made out that the men of New England rushed to arms. The arguments of the Council Chamber and the House of Representatives preceded and sanctioned the contest. To draw the conduct of our ancestors into a precedent for mobs, for a right to resist laws we ourselves have enacted, is an insult to their memory. The difference between the excitements of those days and our own, which the gentleman in kindness to the latter has overlooked, is simply this: the men of that day went for the right, as secured by the laws. They were the people rising to sustain the laws and constitution of the province. The rioters of our day go for their own wills, right or wrong. Sir, when I heard the gentleman lay down principles which place the murderers of Alton side by side with Otis and Hancock, with Quincy and Adams, I thought those pictured lips [pointing to the portraits in the Hall] would have broken into voice to rebuke the recreant American,— the slanderer of the dead. [Great applause and counter-applause.] The gentleman said that he should sink into insignificance if he dared not gainsay the principles of these resolutions. Sir, for the sentiments he has uttered, on soil consecrated by the prayers of Puritans and the blood of patriots, the earth should have yawned and swallowed him up.

[Applause and hisses, with cries of "Take that back." The uproar became so great that for a long time no one could be heard. At length the Hon. William Sturgis came to Mr. Phillips's side at the front of the platform. He was met with cries of "Phillips or nobody," "Make him take back 'recreant,'" "He sha'n't go on till he takes it back." When it was understood that Mr. Sturgis meant to sustain, not to interrupt, Mr. Phillips, he was listened to, and said, "I did not come here to take any part in this discussion, nor do I intend to; but I do entreat you, fellow-citizens, by everything you hold sacred,— I conjure you by every association connected with this Hall, consecrated by our fathers to freedom of discussion,— that you listen to every man who addresses you in a decorous manner." Mr. Phillips resumed.]

Fellow-citizens, I cannot take back my words. Surely, the Attorney-general, so long and well known here, needs not the aid of your hisses against one so young as I am,— my voice never before heard within these walls!

Another ground has been taken to excuse the mob, and throw doubt and discredit on the conduct of Lovejoy and his associates. Allusion has been made to what lawyers understand very well,— the "conflict of laws." We are told that nothing but the Mississippi River rolls between St. Louis and Alton; and the conflict of laws somehow or other gives the citizens of the former a right to find fault with the defender of the press for publishing his opinions so near their limits. Will the gentleman venture that argument before lawyers? How the laws of the two States could be said to come into conflict in such circumstances I question whether any lawyer in this audience can explain or understand. No matter whether the line that divides one sovereign State from another be an imaginary one or ocean-wide, the moment you cross it, the State you leave is blotted out of existence, so far as you are concerned. The czar might as well claim to control the deliberations of Faneuil Hall, as the laws of Missouri demand reverence, or the shadow of obedience, from an inhabitant of Illinois.

I must find some fault with the statement which has been made of the events at Alton. It has been asked why Lovejoy and his friends did not appeal to the executive,— trust their defence to the police of the city. It has been hinted that, from hasty and ill-judged excitement, the men within the building provoked a quarrel, and that he fell in the course of it, one mob resisting another. Recollect, sir, that they did act with the approbation and sanction of the mayor. In strict truth there was no executive to appeal to for protection. The mayor acknowledged that he could not protect them. They asked him if it was lawful for them to defend themselves. He told them it was, and sanctioned their assembling in arms to do so. They were not, then, a mob; they were not merely citizens defending their own property: they were in some sense the *posse comitatus*, adopted for the occasion into the police of the city, acting under the order of a magistrate. It was civil authority resisting lawless violence. Where, then, was the imprudence? Is the doctrine to be sustained here that it is *imprudent* for men to aid magistrates in executing the laws?

Men are continually asking each other, Had Lovejoy a right to resist? Sir, I protest against the question instead of answering it. Lovejoy did not resist, in the sense they mean. He did not throw himself back on the natural right of self-defence. He did not cry anarchy, and let slip the dogs of civil war, careless of the horrors which would follow.

Sir, as I understand this affair, it was not an individual protecting his property; it was not one body of armed men resisting another, and making the streets of a peaceful city run blood with their contentions. It did not bring back the scenes in some old Italian cities, where family met family, and faction met faction, and mutually trampled the laws under foot. No: the men in that house were regularly *enrolled*, under the sanction of the mayor. There being no militia in Alton, about seventy men were enrolled with the approbation of the mayor. These relieved each other every other night. About thirty men were in arms on the night of the 6th, when the press was landed. The next evening it was not thought necessary to summon more than half that number: among these was Lovejoy. It was, therefore, you perceive, sir, the police of the city resisting rioters,— civil government breasting itself to the shock of lawless men.

Here is no question about the right of self-defence. It is in fact simply this: Has the civil magistrate a right to put down a riot?

Some persons seem to imagine that anarchy existed at Alton from the commencement of these disputes. Not at all. "No one of us," says an eye-witness and a comrade of Lovejoy, "has taken up arms during these disturbances but at the command of the mayor." Anarchy did not settle down on that devoted city till Lovejoy breathed his last. Till then the law, represented in his person, sustained itself against its foes. When he fell, civil authority was trampled under foot. He had "planted himself on his constitutional rights,"—appealed to the laws,—claimed the protection of the civil authority,—taken refuge under "the broad shield of the Constitution. When through that he was pierced and fell, he fell but one sufferer in a common catastrophe." He took refuge under the banner of liberty,—amid its folds; and, when he fell, its glorious stars and stripes, the emblem of free institutions, around which cluster so many heart-stirring memories, were blotted out in the martyr's blood.

It has been stated, perhaps inadvertently, that Lovejoy or his comrades fired first. This is denied by those who have the best means of knowing. Guns were first fired by the mob. After being twice fired on, those within the building consulted together, and deliberately returned the fire. But suppose they did fire first. They had a right so to do,—not only the right which every citizen has to defend himself, but the further right which every civil officer has to resist violence. Even if Lovejoy fired the first gun, it would not lessen his claim to our sympathy or destroy his title to be considered a martyr in defence of a free press. The question now is, Did he act within the Constitution and the laws? The men who fell in State Street on the 5th of March, 1770, did more than Lovejoy is charged with. They were the *first* assailants. Upon some slight quarrel they pelted the troops with every missile within reach. Did this bate one jot of the eulogy with which Hancock and Warren hallowed their memory, hailing them as the first martyrs in the cause of American liberty?

If, sir, I had adopted what are called Peace principles, I might lament the circumstances of this case. But all you who believe, as I do, in the right and duty of magistrates to execute the laws, join with me, and brand as base hypocrisy the conduct of those who assemble year after year on the 4th of July to fight over the battles of the Revolution, and yet "damn with faint praise" or load with obloquy the memory of this man, who shed his blood in defence of life, liberty, property, and the freedom of the press!

Throughout that terrible night I find nothing to regret but this, that within the limits of our country civil authority should have been so prostrated as to oblige a citizen to arm in his own defence, and to arm in vain. The gentleman says Lovejoy was presumptuous and imprudent,—he "died as the fool dieth." And a reverend clergyman of the city * tells us that no citizen has a right to publish opinions disagreeable to the community! If any mob follows such publication, on *him* rests its guilt! He must wait, forsooth, till the people come up to it and agree with him! This libel on liberty goes on to say that the want of right to speak as we think is an evil inseparable from republican institutions! If this be so, what are they

---

* See Rev. Hubbard Winslow's discourse on *Liberty!* in which he defines "republican liberty" to be "liberty to say and do what the *prevailing* voice and will of the brotherhood will allow and protect."

worth? Welcome the depotism of the sultan, where one knows what he may publish and what he may not, rather than the tyranny of this many-headed monster, the mob, where we know not what we may do or say till some fellow-citizen has tried it, and paid for the lesson with his life. This clerical absurdity chooses as a check for the abuses of the press, not the *law*, but the dread of a mob. By so doing, it deprives not only the individual and the minority of their rights, but the majority also, since the expression of *their* opinion may sometimes provoke disturbance from the minority. A few men may make a mob as well as many. The majority, then, have no right, as Christian men, to utter their sentiments, if by any possibility it may lead to a mob! Shades of Hugh Peters and John Cotton, save us from such pulpits!

Imprudent to defend the liberty of the press! Why? Because the defence was unsuccessful? Does success gild crime into patriotism, and the want of it change heroic self-devotion to imprudence? Was Hampden imprudent when he drew the sword and threw away the scabbard? Yet he, judged by that single hour, was unsuccessful. After a short exile the race he hated sat again upon the throne.

Imagine yourself present when the first news of Bunker Hill battle reached a New England town. The tale would have run thus: "The patriots are routed,— the redcoats victorious,— Warren lies dead upon the field." With what scorn would that *Tory* have been received who should have charged Warren with *imprudence!* who should have said that, bred a physician, he was "out of place" in that battle, and "died as the *fool dieth*"! [Great applause.] How would the intimation have been received that Warren and his associates should have waited a better time? But, if success be indeed the only criterion of prudence, *Respice finem*,— Wait till the end.

Presumptuous to assert the freedom of the press on American ground! Is the assertion of such freedom before the age? So much before the age as to leave one no right to make it because it displeases the community? Who invents this libel on his country? It is this very thing which entitles Lovejoy to greater praise. The disputed right which provoked the Revolution — taxation without representation — is far beneath that for which he died. [Here there was a strong and general expression of disapprobation.] One word, gentlemen. As much as *thought* is better than money, so much is the cause in which Lovejoy died nobler than a mere question of taxes. James Otis thundered in this hall when the king did but touch his *pocket*. Imagine, if you can, his indignant eloquence, had England offered to put a gag upon his lips. [Great applause.]

The question that stirred the Revolution touched our civil interests. *This* concerns us not only as citizens, but as immortal beings. Wrapped up in its fate, saved or lost with it, are not only the voice of the statesman, but the instructions of the pulpit, and the progress of our faith.

The clergy "marvellously out of place" where free speech is battled for, —liberty of speech on national sins? Does the gentleman remember that freedom to preach was first gained, dragging in its train freedom to print? I thank the clergy here present, as I reverence their predecessors, who did not so far forget their country in their immediate profession as to deem it duty to separate themselves from the struggle of '76,— the Mayhews and Coopers, who remembered they were citizens before they were clergymen.

Mr. Chairman, from the bottom of my heart I thank that brave little band at Alton for resisting. We must remember that Lovejoy had fled from city to city, suffered the destruction of three presses patiently. At length he took counsel with friends, men of character, of tried integrity, of wide views, of Christian principle. They thought the crisis had come. It was full time to assert the laws. They saw around them, not a community like our own, of fixed habits, of character moulded and settled, but one "in the gristle, not yet hardened into the bone of manhood." The people there, children of our older States, seem to have forgotten the blood-tried principles of their fathers the moment they lost sight of our New England hills. Something was to be done to show them the priceless value of the freedom of the press, to bring back and set right their wandering and confused ideas. He and his advisers looked out on a community staggering like a drunken man, indifferent to their rights and confused in their feelings. Deaf to argument, haply they might be stunned into sobriety. They saw that of which we cannot judge, the *necessity* of resistance. Insulted law called for it. Public opinion, fast hastening on the downward course, must be arrested.

Does not the event show they judged rightly? Absorbed in a thousand trifles, how has the nation all at once come to a stand! Men begin, as in 1776 and 1640, to discuss principles, to weigh characters, to find out where they are. Haply we may awake before we are borne over the precipice.

I am glad, sir, to see this crowded house. It is good for us to be here. When Liberty is in danger, Faneuil Hall has the right, it is her duty, to strike the key-note for these United States. I am glad, for one reason, that remarks such as those to which I have alluded have been uttered here. The passage of these resolutions, in spite of this opposition, led by the Attorney-general of the Commonwealth, will show more clearly, more decisively, the deep indignation with which Boston regards this outrage.

Phillips's eulogy of Garrison may almost be regarded as his verdict upon himself, being a survey at its triumphant close of the great conflict in which through life he stood shoulder to shoulder with Garrison. His speech at Faneuil Hall in 1837 takes us back to the dark and stormy beginnings of the conflict. The two volumes of "Phillips's Speeches, Lectures, and Letters" contain his fiery utterances at every stage of the anti-slavery struggle, as well as his addresses upon other great reforms. A third volume is yet to come. There are biographies of Phillips by George Lowell Austin and Carlos Martyn, a brief sketch by Mrs. Stowe, and noble eulogies by George William Curtis, A. H. Grimké, and Colonel Higginson. The fine sonnet by Lowell is memorable. See also the beautiful poem by Wendell Phillips Stafford, in the *Atlantic Monthly*, July, 1896.

PUBLISHED BY

THE DIRECTORS OF THE OLD SOUTH WORK,
Old South Meeting-house, Boston, Mass.

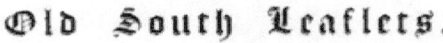

Old South Leaflets.

No. 86.

The Dangers from Slavery.

By THEODORE PARKER.

FROM A SERMON ON "THE DANGERS WHICH THREATEN THE RIGHTS OF MAN IN AMERICA," PREACHED IN MUSIC HALL, BOSTON, SUNDAY, JULY 2, 1854.

There can be no national welfare without national Unity of Action. That cannot take place unless there is national Unity of Idea in fundamentals. Without this a nation is a "house divided against itself": of course it cannot stand. It is what mechanics call a figure without equilibrium: the different parts thereof do not balance.

Now in the American State there are two distinct ideas,— Freedom and Slavery.

The Idea of Freedom first got a national expression seventy-eight years ago next Tuesday. Here it is. I put it in a philosophic form. There are five points to it.

First. All men are endowed by their Creator with certain natural rights, amongst which is the right to life, liberty, and the pursuit of happiness.

Second. These rights are unalienable; they can be alienated and forfeited only by the possessor thereof; the father cannot alienate them for the son, nor the son for the father; nor the husband for the wife, nor the wife for the husband; nor the strong for the weak, nor the weak for the strong; nor the few for the many, nor the many for the few; and so on.

Third. In respect to these all men are equal; the rich man has not more, and the poor less; the strong man has not more, and the weak man less: all are exactly equal in these rights, however unequal in their powers.

Fourth. It is the function of government to secure these natural, unalienable, and equal rights to every man.

Fifth. Government derives all its divine right from its conformity with these ideas, all its human sanction from the consent of the governed.

That is the Idea of Freedom. I used to call it "the American Idea"; it was when I was younger than I am to-day. It is derived from human nature; it rests on the immutable Laws of God; it is part of the natural religion of mankind. It demands a government after natural Justice, which is the point common between the conscience of God and the conscience of mankind, the point common also between the interests of one man and of all men.

Now this government, just in its substance, in its form must be democratic; that is to say, the government of all, by all, and for all. You see what consequences must follow from such an idea, and the attempt to re-enact the Law of God into political institutions. There will follow the freedom of the people, respect for every natural right of all men, the rights of their body, and of their spirit,— the rights of mind and conscience, heart and soul. There must be some restraint,— as of children by their parents, as of bad men by good men; but it will be restraint for the joint good of all parties concerned, not restraint for the exclusive benefit of the restrainer. The ultimate consequence of this will be the material and spiritual welfare of all,— riches, comfort, noble manhood, all desirable things.

That is the Idea of Freedom. It appears in the Declaration of Independence; it reappears in the Preamble to the American Constitution, which aims "to establish Justice, insure domestic tranquillity, provide for the common defence, promote the general welfare, and secure the blessings of Liberty." That is a religious idea; and, when men pray for the "Reign of Justice" and the "Kingdom of Heaven" to come on earth politically, I suppose they mean that there may be a Commonwealth where every man has his natural rights of mind, body, and estate.

Next is the Idea of Slavery. Here it is. I put it also in a philosophic form. There are three points which I make.

First. There are no natural, unalienable, and equal rights, wherewith men are endowed by their Creator; no natural, unalienable, and equal right to life, liberty, and the pursuit of happiness.

Second. There is a great diversity of powers, and in virtue thereof the strong man may rule and oppress, enslave and ruin the weak, for his interest and against theirs.

Third. There is no natural law of God to forbid the strong to oppress the weak, and enslave and ruin the weak.

That is the Idea of Slavery. It has never got a national expression in America; it has never been laid down as a Principle in any act of the American people, nor in any single State, so far as I know. All profess the opposite; but it is involved in the measures of both State and Nation. This Idea is founded in the selfishness of man; it is atheistic.

The idea must lead to a corresponding government; that will be unjust in its substance,— for it will depend not on natural right, but on personal force; not on the Constitution of the Universe, but on the compact of men. It is the abnegation of God in the universe and of conscience in man. Its form will be despotism,— the government of all, by a part, for the sake of a part. It may be a single-headed despotism, or a despotism of many heads; but, whether a Cyclops or a Hydra, it is alike "the abomination which maketh desolate." Its ultimate consequence is plain to foresee,— poverty to a nation, misery, ruin.

At first, Slavery came as a Measure; nothing was said about it as a Principle. But in a country full of schoolmasters, legislatures, newspapers, talking men,— a measure without a principle to bear it up is like a single twig of willow cast out on a wooden floor; there is nothing for it to grow by; it will die. So of late the principle has been boldly avowed. Mr. Calhoun denied the self-evident truths of the Declaration of Independence; denied the natural, unalienable, and equal rights of man. Many since have done the same,— political, literary, and mercantile men, and, of course, ecclesiastical men; there are enough of them always in the market. All parts of the Idea of Slavery have been affirmed by prominent men at the North and the South. It has been acted on in the formation of the Constitution of every Slave State, and in the passage of many of its laws. It lies at the basis of a great deal of national legislation. . . .

These two Ideas are now fairly on foot. They are hostile; they are both mutually invasive and destructive. They are in exact opposition to each other, and the nation which embodies these two is not a figure of equilibrium. As both are active forces in the minds of men, and as each idea tends to become a fact,— a universal and exclusive fact, — as men with these ideas organize into parties as a means to make their idea into a fact, — it follows that there must not only be strife amongst philosophical men about these antagonistic Principles and Ideas, but a strife of practical men about corresponding Facts and Measures. So the quarrel, if not otherwise ended, will pass from words to what seems more serious; and one will overcome the other.

So long as these two Ideas exist in the nation as two political forces, there is no national Unity of Idea, of course no Unity of Action. For there is no centre of gravity common to Freedom and Slavery. They will not compose an equilibrious figure. You may cry, "Peace! peace!" but so long as these two antagonistic Ideas remain, each seeking to organize itself and get exclusive power, there is no peace; there can be none.

The question before the nation to-day is, Which shall prevail, — the Idea and Fact of Freedom or the Idea and the Fact of Slavery; Freedom, exclusive and universal, or Slavery, exclusive and universal? The question is not merely, Shall the African be bond or free? but, Shall America be a Democracy or a Despotism? For nothing is so remorseless as an idea, and no logic is so strong as the historical development of a national idea by millions of men. A measure is nothing without its Principle. The idea which allows Slavery in South Carolina will establish it also in New England. The bondage of a black man in Alexandria imperils every white woman's daughter in Boston. You cannot escape the consequences of a first Principle more than you can "take the leap of Niagara and stop when half-way down." The Principle which recognizes Slavery in the Constitution of the United States would make all America a Despotism; while the principle which made John Quincy Adams a free man would extirpate Slavery from Louisiana and Texas. It is plain America cannot long hold these two contradictions in the national consciousness. Equilibrium must come.

Now there are three possible ways of settling the quarrel between these two Ideas; only three. The categories are exhaustive.

This is the first: The discord may rend the nation asunder, and the two elements separate and become distinct nations,— a Despotism with the Idea of Slavery, a Democracy with the

Idea of Freedom. Then each will be an equilibrious figure. The Anglo-Saxon Despotism may go to ruin on its own account, while the Anglo-Saxon Democracy marches on to national welfare. That is the first hypothesis.

Or, second: The Idea of Freedom may destroy Slavery, with all its accidents,— attendant and consequent. Then the nation may have unity of idea, and so a unity of action, and become a harmonious whole, a Unit of Freedom, a great industrial Democracy, re-enacting the laws of God, and pursuing its way, continually attaining greater degrees of freedom and prosperity. That is the second hypothesis.

Here is the third: The Idea of Slavery may destroy Freedom, with all its accidents,— attendant and consequent. Then the nation will become an integer; only it will be a Unit of Despotism. This involves, of course, the destructive revolution of all our liberal institutions, State as well as national. Democracy must go down; the free press go down; the free church go down; the free school go down. There must be an industrial despotism, which will soon become a military despotism. Popular legislation must end; the Federal Congress will be a club of officials, like Nero's senate, which voted his horse first consul. The State legislature will be a knot of commissioners, tide-waiters, postmasters, district attorneys, deputy marshals. The town-meeting will be a gang of government officers, like the "Marshal's Guard," revolvers in their pockets, soldiers at their back. The *Habeas Corpus* will be at an end; trial by jury never heard of, and open courts as common in America as in Spain or Rome. Commissioners Curtis, Loring, and Kane, will not be exceptional men; there will be no other "judges"; all courts, courts of the kidnapper; all process summary; all cases decided by the will of the government; arbitrary force the only rule. The constable will disappear, the soldier come forth. All newspapers will be like the "Satanic press" of Boston and New York, like the Journal of St. Petersburg or the Diario Romano, which tell lies when the ruler commands, or tell truth when he insists upon it. Then the wicked will walk on every side, for the vilest of men will be exalted, and America, become the mock and scorn and hissing of the nations, will go down to worse shame than was ever heaped upon Sodom; for with her lust for wealth, land, and power, she also will have committed the crime against nature. Then America will be another Italy, Greece, Asia Minor, yea, like Gomorrah; for the Dead Sea will have settled down upon us with nothing living in its breast, and the rulers will proclaim Peace where they have made solitude.

Which of these three hypotheses shall we take?

I. Will there be a Separation of the two elements, and a formation of two distinct States,— Freedom with Democracy, and Slavery with a tendency to despotism? That may save one-half the nation, and leave the other to voluntary ruin. Certainly, it is better to enter into life halt or maimed rather than having two hands and two feet to be cast into everlasting fire. . . .

But I do not think this "dissolution of the Union" will take place immediately or very soon. For America is not now ruled — as it is commonly thought — either by the mass of men who follow their national, ethnological, and human instincts, or by a few far-sighted men of genius for politics, who consciously obey the Law of God made clear in their own masterly mind and conscience, and make statutes in advance of the calculation or even the instincts of the people, and so manage the Ship of State that every occasional tack is on a great circle of the Universe, a right line of Justice, and therefore the shortest way to welfare, but by two very different classes of men,— by Mercantile men, who covet money, actual or expectant Capitalists; and by Political men, who want power, actual or expectant office-holders. These appear diverse; but there is a strong unanimity between the two,— for the mercantile men want money as a means of power and the political men power as a means of money. There are noble men in both classes, exceptional, not instantial, men with great riches even, and great office. But, as a class, these men are not above the average morality of the people, often below it; they have no deep religious faith, which leads them to trust the Higher Law of God. They do not look for Principles that are right, conformable to the Constitution of the Universe, and so creative of the nation's permanent welfare, but only for expedient Measures, productive to themselves of selfish money or selfish power. In general, they have the character of adventurers, the aims of adventurers, the morals of adventurers; they begin poor, and of course obscure, and are then "democratic," and hurrah for the people: "Down with the powerful and the rich," is the private maxim of their heart. If they are successful and become rich, famous, attaining high office, they commonly despise the people: "Down with the people!" is the axiom of their heart,— only they dare not say it; for there are so many others with the same selfishness, who have not yet achieved their end, and raise the opposite cry. The line of the nation's course is a resultant of the compound selfishness of these two classes.

From these two, with their mercantile and political selfishness, we are to expect no comprehensive Morality, which will secure the Rights of mankind; no comprehensive policy which will secure expedient measures for a long time. Both will unite in what serves their apparent interest, brings money to the trader, power to the politician,— whatever be the consequence to the country.

As things now are, the Union favors the schemes of both of these classes of men; thereby the politician gets power, the trader makes money.

If the Union were to be dissolved and a great Northern Commonwealth were to be organized, with the Idea of Freedom, three-quarters of the Politicians, Federal and State, would pass into contempt and oblivion; all that class of Northern demagogues who scoff at God's Law, such as filled the offices of the late Whig administration in its day of power or as fill the offices of the Democratic administration to-day,— they would drop down so deep that no plummet would ever reach them; you would never hear of them again.

Gratitude is not a very common virtue; but gratitude to the hand of Slavery, which feeds these creatures, is their sole and single moral excellence; they have that form of gratitude. When the hand of Slavery is cut off, that class of men will perish just as caterpillars die when, some day in May, the farmer cuts off from the old tree a great branch to graft in a better fruit. The caterpillars will not vote for the grafting. That class of men will go for the Union while it serves them.

Look at the other class. Property is safe in America; and why? Because we have aimed to establish a government on natural rights, and property is a natural right; say oligarchic Blackstone and socialistic Proudhon what they may, property is not the mere creature of compact or the child of robbery; it is founded in the Nature of Man. It has a very great and important function to perform. Nowhere in the world is it so much respected as here.

But there is one kind of property which is not safe just now,

— Property in Men. It is the only kind of property which is purely the creature of violence and law; it has no root in itself.

Now the Union protects that " property." There are three hundred thousand Slave-holders, owning thirteen hundred millions of dollars invested in men. Their wealth depends on the Union; destroy that, and their unnatural property will take to itself legs and run off, seeking liberty by flight, or else stay at home and, like an Anglo-Saxon, take to itself firebrands and swords, and burn down the master's house and cut the master's throat. So the Slave-holder wants the Union; he makes money by it. Slavery is unprofitable to the nation. No three millions earn so little as the three million Slaves. It is costly to every State. But it enriches the owner of the Slaves. The South is agricultural; that is all. She raises cotton, sugar, and corn; she has no commerce, no manufactures, no mining. The North has mills, ships, mines, manufactures; buys and sells for the South, and makes money by what impoverishes the South. So all the great commercial centres of the North are in favor of Union, in favor of Slavery. The instinct of American trade just now is hostile to American Freedom. The Money Power and the Slave Power go hand in hand. Of course such editors and ministers as are only the tools of the Money Power or the Slave Power will be fond of " Union at all hazards." They will sell their mothers to keep it. Now these are the controlling classes of men; these ministers and editors are the mouth-pieces of these controlling classes of men; and, as these classes make money and power out of the Union, for the present I think the Union will hold together. Yet I know very well that there are causes now at work which embitter the minds of men, and which, if much enforced, will so exasperate the North that we shall rend the Union asunder at a blow. That I think not likely to take place, for the South sees the peril and its own ruin.

II. The next hypothesis is, Freedom may triumph over Slavery. That was the expectation once, at the time of the Declaration of Independence; nay, at the formation of the Constitution. But only two national steps have been taken against Slavery since then,— one the Ordinance of 1787, the other the abolition of the African Slave-trade; really that was done in 1788, formally twenty years after. In the individual States the white man's freedom enlarges every year; but the Federal Government becomes more and more addicted to

Slavery. This hypothesis does not seem very likely to be adopted.

III. Shall Slavery destroy Freedom? It looks very much like it. Here are nine great steps, openly taken since '87, in favor of Slavery. First, America put Slavery into the Constitution. Second, out of old soil she made four new Slave States. Third, America, in 1793, adopted Slavery as a Federal institution, and guaranteed her protection for that kind of property as for no other. Fourth, America bought the Louisiana territory in 1803, and put Slavery into it. Fifth, she thence made Louisiana, Missouri, and then Arkansas Slave States. Sixth, she made Slavery perpetual in Florida. Seventh, she annexed Texas. Eighth, she fought the Mexican War, and plundered a feeble sister republic of California, Utah, and New Mexico, to get more Slave Soil. Ninth, America gave ten millions of money to Texas to support Slavery, passed the Fugitive Slave Bill, and has since kidnapped men in New England, New York, New Jersey, Pennsylvania, Ohio, Michigan, Wisconsin, Illinois, Indiana, in all the East, in all the West, in all the Middle States. All the great cities have kidnapped their own citizens. Professional Slave-hunters are members of New England Churches; kidnappers sit down at the Lord's table in the city of Cotton, Chauncey, and Mayhew. In this very year, before it is half through, America has taken two more steps for the destruction of freedom. The repeal of the Missouri Compromise and the enslavement of Nebraska: that is the tenth step. Here is the eleventh: The Mexican Treaty, giving away ten millions of dollars and buying a little strip of worthless land, solely that it may serve the cause of Slavery.

Here are eleven great steps openly taken towards the ruin of Liberty in America. Are these the worst? Very far from it! Yet more dangerous things have been done in secret.

I. Slavery has corrupted the Mercantile Class. Almost all the leading merchants of the North are Pro-slavery men. They hate freedom, hate your freedom and mine! This is the only Christian country in which commerce is hostile to freedom.

II. See the corruption of the Political Class. There are forty thousand officers of the Federal Government. Look at them in Boston,—their character is as well known as this Hall. Read their journals in this city,—do you catch a whisper of freedom in them? Slavery has sought its menial servants,—men basely born and basely bred: it has corrupted them still further, and put them in office. America, like Russia, is the country for mean men to thrive in. Give him time and mire enough, a worm can crawl as high as an eagle flies. State rights are sacrificed at the North; centralization goes on with rapid strides: State laws are trodden under foot. The Northern President is all for Slavery. The Northern Members of the Cabinet are for Slavery; in the Senate, fourteen Northern Democrats were for the enslavement of Nebraska; in the House of Representatives, forty-four Northern Democrats voted for the bill, — fourteen in the Senate, forty-four in the House; fifty-eight Northern men voted against the conscience of the North and the Law of God. Only eight men out of all the South could be found friendly to justice and false to their own local idea of injustice. The present administration, with its supple tools of tyranny, came into office while the cry of "No Higher Law" was echoing through the land!

III. Slavery has debauched the Press. How many leading journals of commerce and politics in the great cities do you know that are friendly to Freedom and opposed to Slavery? Out of the five large daily commercial papers in Boston, Whig or Democratic, I know of only one that has spoken a word for freedom this great while. The American newspapers are poor defenders of American liberty. Listen to one of them, speaking of the last kidnapping in Boston: "We shall need to employ the same measures of coercion as are necessary in monarchical countries." There is always some one ready to do the basest deeds. Yet there are some noble journals,— political and commercial,— such as the New York *Tribune* and *Evening Post*.

IV. Then our Colleges and Schools are corrupted by Slavery. I do not know of five colleges in all the North which publicly appear on the side of freedom. What the hearts of the presidents and professors are, God knows, not I. The great crime against humanity, practical atheism, found ready support in Northern colleges, in 1850 and 1851. Once the common reading books of our schools were full of noble words. Read the school-books now made by Yankee pedlers of literature, and what liberal ideas do you find there? They are meant for the Southern market. Slavery must not be offended!

V. Slavery has corrupted the Churches! There are twenty-eight thousand Protestant clergymen in the United States. There are noble hearts, true and just men among them, who have fearlessly borne witness to the truth. I need not mention their names. Alas! they are not very numerous; I should not have to go over my fingers many times to count them all. I honor these exceptional men. Some of them are old, far older than I am; older than my father need have been; some of them are far younger than I; nay, some of them younger than my children might be: and I honor these men for the fearless testimony which they have borne,— the old, the middle-aged, and the young. But they are very exceptional men. Is there a minister in the South who preaches against Slavery? How few in all the North!

Look and see the condition of the Sunday-schools. In 1853 the Episcopal Methodists had 9,438 Sunday-schools; 102,732 Sunday-school teachers; 525,008 scholars. There is not an Anti-slavery Sunday-school in the compass of the Methodist Episcopal Church. Last year, in New York, they issued, on an average, two thousand bound volumes every day in the year, not a line against Slavery in them. They printed also two thousand pamphlets every day; there is not a line in them all against Slavery; they printed more than two hundred and forty million pages of Sunday-school books, not a line against Slavery in them all; not a line showing that it is wicked to buy and sell a man, for whom, according to the Methodist Episcopal Church, Christ died!

The Orthodox Sunday School Union spent last year $248,-201: not a cent against Slavery, our great National Sin. They print books by the million. Only one of them contains a word against Slavery; that is Cowper's "Task," which contains these words,— my mother taught them to me when I was a little boy, and sat in her lap:—

> "I would not have a slave to till my ground,
> To carry me, to fan me when I sleep,
> And tremble when I wake, for all the wealth
> That sinews, bought and sold, have ever earned!"

You all know it: if you do not, you had better learn and teach it to your children. That is the only Anti-slavery work they print. Once they published a book written by Mr. Gallaudet, which related the story, I think, of the selling of Joseph: at any rate, it showed that Egyptian Slavery was wrong. A little girl in a Sunday-school in one of the Southern States one day said to her teacher, "If it was wrong to make Joseph a Slave, why is it not wrong to make Dinah and Sambo and Chloe

Slaves?" The Sunday-school teacher and the Church took the alarm, and complained of the Sunday School Union: "You are poisoning the South with your religion, telling the children that Slavery is wicked." It was a serious thing, "dissolution of the Union," "levying war," or, at least, "misdemeanor," for aught I know, "obstructing an officer of the United States." What do you think the Sunday School Union did? It suppressed the book! It printed one Sunday-school book which had a line against Egyptian Slavery and then suppressed it; and it cannot be had to-day! Amid all their million books there is not a line against Slavery, save what Cowper sung. There are five million Sunday-school scholars in the United States, and there is not a Sunday-school manual which has got a word against Slavery in it.

You all know the American Tract Society. Last year the American Tract Society in Boston spent $79,983.46; it visited more than fourteen thousand families; it distributed 3,334,920 tracts,— not a word against Slavery in them all. The American Tract Society in New York last year visited 568,000 families, containing three million persons; it spent for home purposes $406,707, for foreign purposes $422,294; it distributed tracts in English, French, German, Dutch, Danish, Swedish, Norwegian, Italian, Hungarian, and Welsh — and it did not print one single line nor whisper a single word against this great national sin of Slavery! Nay, worse: if it finds English books which suit its general purpose, but containing matter adverse to Slavery, it strikes out all the Anti-slavery matter, then prints and circulates the book. Is the Tract Society also managed by Jesuits from the Roman Church?

At this day 600,000 Slaves are directly and personally owned by men who are called "professing Christians," "members in good fellowship" of the churches of this land; 80,000 owned by Presbyterians, 225,000 by Baptists, 250,000 owned by Methodists,— 600,000 Slaves in this land owned by men who profess themselves Christians, and in churches sit down to take the Lord's Supper, in the name of Christ and God! There are ministers who own their fellow-men,— "bought with a price."

Does this not look as if Slavery were to triumph over Freedom?

VI. Slavery corrupts the Judicial Class. In America, especially in New England, no class of men has been so much respected as the judges; and for this reason: we have had wise, learned, excellent men for our judges; men who reverenced the Higher Law of God, and sought by human statutes to execute Justice. You all know their venerable names, and how reverentially we have looked up to them. Many of them are dead; some are still living, and their hoary hairs are a crown of glory on a judicial life, without judicial blot. But of late Slavery has put a different class of men on the benches of the Federal Courts,— mere tools of the government; creatures which get their appointment as pay for past political service, and as pay in advance for iniquity not yet accomplished. You see the consequences. Note the zeal of the Federal Judges to execute iniquity by statute and destroy Liberty. See how ready they are to support the Fugitive Slave Bill, which tramples on the spirit of the Constitution, and its letter, too; which outrages Justice and violates the most sacred principles and precepts of Christianity. Not a United States Judge, Circuit or District, has uttered one word against that "bill of abominations." Nay, how greedy they are to get victims under it! No wolf loves better to rend a lamb into fragments than these judges to kidnap a Fugitive Slave, and punish any man who dares to speak against it. You know what has happened in Fugitive Slave Bill Courts. You remember the "miraculous" rescue of Shadrach: the peaceable snatching of a man from the hands of a cowardly kidnapper was "high treason"; it was "levying war." You remember the "trial" of the rescuers! Judge Sprague's charge to the Grand Jury that, if they thought the question was which they ought to obey, the law of man or the Law of God, then they must "Obey both!" serve God and Mammon, Christ and the Devil, in the same act! You remember the "trial," the "ruling" of the Bench, the swearing on the stand, the witness coming back to alter and "enlarge his testimony" and have another gird at the prisoner! You have not forgotten the trials before Judge Kane at Philadelphia, and Judge Grier at Christiana and Wilkesbarre.

These are natural results of causes well known. You cannot escape a Principle. Enslave a negro, will you? — you doom to bondage your own sons and daughters, by your own act. . . .

All this looks as if the third hypothesis would be fulfilled, and Slavery triumph over Freedom; as if the nation would expunge the Declaration of Independence from the scroll of time, and, instead of honoring Hancock and the Adamses and Washington, do homage to Kane and Grier and Curtis and Hallett and Loring. Then the preamble to our Constitution might read "to establish injustice, insure domestic strife, hinder the common defence, disturb the general welfare, and inflict the curse of bondage on ourselves and our posterity." Then we shall honor the Puritans no more, but their Prelatical tormentors; nor reverence the Great Reformers, only the Inquisitors of Rome. Yea, we may tear the name of Jesus out of the American Bible; yes, God's name. . . .

See the steady triumph of Despotism! Ten years more like the ten years past, and it will be all over with the liberties of America. Everything must go down, and the heel of the tyrant will be on our neck. It will be all over with the Rights of Man in America, and you and I must go to Austria, to Italy, or to Siberia for our freedom; or perish with the liberty which our fathers fought for and secured to themselves, — not to their faithless sons! Shall America thus miserably perish? Such is the aspect of things to-day!

But are the people alarmed? No, they fear nothing; only the tightness in the money market! Next Tuesday at sunrise every bell in Boston will ring joyously; every cannon will belch sulphurous Welcome from its brazen throat. There will be processions, — the Mayor and the Aldermen and the Marshal and the Naval Officer, and, I suppose, the "Marshal's Guard," very appropriately taking their places. There is a chain on the Common to-day: it is the same chain that was around the Court House in 1851; it is the chain that bound Sims: now it is a festal chain. There are mottoes about the Common, — "They mutually pledged to each other their lives, their fortunes, and their sacred honor." I suppose it means that the mayor and the kidnappers did this. "The spirit of '76 still lives." Lives, I suppose, in the Supreme Court of Fugitive Slave Bill judges. "Washington, Jefferson, and their compatriots! — their names are sacred in the heart of every American." That, I suppose, is the opinion of Thomas Sims and of Anthony Burns. And opposite the great Park Street Church, — where a noble man is this day, I trust, discoursing noble words, for he has never yet been found false to freedom, — "Liberty and Independence, our Fathers' Legacy! — God forbid that we their sons should prove recreant to the trust!"

It ought to read, "God forgive us that we their sons have proved so recreant to the trust!" So they will celebrate the Fourth of July, and call it "Independence Day"! The foolish press of France, bought and beaten and trodden on by Napoleon the Crafty, is full of talk about the welfare of the "Great Nation"! Philip of Macedon was conquering the Athenian allies town by town; he destroyed and swept off two-and-thirty cities, selling their children as Slaves. All the Cassandrian eloquence of Demosthenes could not rouse degenerate Athens from her idle sleep. She also fell,—the fairest of all free States; corrupted first,—forgetful of God's Higher Law. Shall America thus perish, all immature!

So was it in the days of old: they ate, they drank, they planted, they built, they married, they were given in marriage, until the day that Noah entered into the ark, and the Flood came and devoured them all!

Well, is this to be the end? Was it for this the Pilgrims came over the sea? Does Forefathers' Rock assent to it? Was it for this that the New England clergy prayed, and their prayers became the law of the land for a hundred years? Was it for this that Cotton planted in Boston a little branch of the Lord's vine, and Roger Williams and Higginson — he still lives in an undegenerate son — did the same in the city which they called of Peace, Salem? Was it for this that Eliot carried the Gospel to the Indians? that Chauncey, and Edwards, and Hopkins, and Mayhew, and Channing, and Ware labored and prayed? for this that our fathers fought,— the Adamses, Washington, Hancock? for this that there was an eight years' war, and a thousand battlefields? for this the little monuments at Acton, Concord, Lexington, West Cambridge, Danvers, and the great one over there on the spot which our fathers' blood made so red? Shall America become Asia Minor? New England, Italy? Boston such as Athens,— dead and rotten? Yes! if we do not mend, and speedily mend. Ten years more, and the liberty of America is all gone. We shall fall,— the laugh, the byword, the proverb, the scorn, the mock of the nations, who shall cry against us. Hell from beneath shall be moved to meet us at our coming, and in derision shall it welcome us,—

"The Heir of all the ages, and the youngest born of time!"

We shall lie down with the unrepentant prodigals of old time, damned to everlasting infamy and shame.

Would you have it so? Shall it be?

To-day America is a debauched young man, of good blood, fortune, and family, but the companion of gamesters and brawlers; reeking with wine; wasting his substance in riotous living; in the lap of harlots squandering the life which his mother gave him. Shall he return? Shall he perish? One day may determine.

Shall America thus die? I look to the past,— Asia, Africa, Europe, and they answer, "Yes!" Where is the Hebrew Commonwealth; the Roman Republic; where is liberal Greece, — Athens and many a far-famed Ionian town; where are the Commonwealths of Mediæval Italy; the Teutonic free cities,— German, Dutch, or Swiss? They have all perished. Not one of them is left. Parian Statues of Liberty, sorely mutilated, still remain; but the Parian rock whence Liberty once hewed her sculptures out,— it is all gone. Shall America thus perish? Greece and Italy both answer, "Yes!" I question the last fifty years of American history, and it says, "Yes." I look to the American pulpit, I ask the five million Sunday-school scholars, and they say, "Yes." I ask the Federal Court, the Democratic Party, and the Whig, and the answer is still the same.

But I close my eyes on the eleven past missteps we have taken for Slavery; on that sevenfold clandestine corruption; I forget the Whig party; I forget the present Administration; I forget the Judges of the Courts; I remember the few noblest men that there are in society, Church and State; I remember the grave of my father, the lessons of my mother's life; I look to the Spirit of this Age,— it is the nineteenth century, not the ninth; I look to the history of the Anglo-Saxons in America, and the history of Mankind; I remember the story and the song of Italian and German Patriots; I recall the dear words of those great-minded Greeks,— Ionian, Dorian, Ætolian; I remember the Romans who spoke and sang and fought for truth and right; I recollect those old Hebrew Prophets, earth's nobler sons, Poets and Saints; I call to mind the greatest, noblest, purest soul that ever blossomed in this dusty world; — and I say, "No!" Truth shall triumph, Justice shall be law! And if America fail, though she is one-fortieth of God's family, and it is a great loss, there are other nations behind us; our Truth shall not perish, even if we go down.

But we shall not fail! I look into your eyes,— young men

and women, thousands of you, and men and women far enough from young! I look into the eyes of fifty thousand other men and women whom in the last eight months I have spoken to face to face, and they say, "No! America shall not fail!" I remember the women, who were never found faithless when a sacrifice was to be offered to great principles; I look up to my God, and I look into my own heart, and I say, We shall not fail! We shall not fail!

THEODORE PARKER.

FROM THE ADDRESS BY RALPH WALDO EMERSON AT THE MEMORIAL MEETING AT MUSIC HALL, BOSTON, JUNE 15, 1860.

It is plain to me that Theodore Parker has achieved a historic immortality here, that he has so woven himself in these few years into the history of Boston that he can never be left out of your annals. It will not be in the acts of city councils, nor of obsequious mayors; nor, in the State House, the proclamations of governors, with their failing virtue,— failing them at critical moments,— that coming generations will study what really befell, but in the plain lessons of Theodore Parker in this Music Hall, in Faneuil Hall, or in legislative committee rooms, that the true temper and authentic record of these days will be read. The next generation will care little for the chances of elections that govern governors now, it will care little for fine gentlemen who behaved shabbily; but it will read very intelligently in his rough story, fortified with exact anecdotes, precise with names and dates, what part was taken by each actor,— who threw himself into the cause of humanity and came to the rescue of civilization at a hard pinch and who blocked its course.

The vice charged against America is the want of sincerity in leading men. It does not lie at his door. He never kept back the truth for fear to make an enemy. But, on the other hand, it was complained that he was bitter and harsh, that his zeal burned with too hot a flame. It is so difficult, in evil times, to escape this charge! for the faithful preacher, most of all. It was his merit, like Luther, Knox, and Latimer, and John Baptist, to speak tart truth, when that was peremptory and when there were few to say it. His commanding merit as a reformer is this: that he insisted beyond all men in pulpits — I cannot think of one rival — that the essence of Christianity is its practical morals; it is there for use, or it is nothing; and if you combine it with sharp trading, or with ordinary city ambitions to gloze over municipal corruptions, or private intemperance, or successful fraud, or immoral politics, or unjust wars, or the cheating of Indians, or the robbery of frontier nations, or leaving your principles at home to follow on the high seas or in Europe a supple complaisance to tyrants, it is a hypocrisy, and the truth is not in you; and no love of religious music or of dreams of Swedenborg, or praise of John Wesley or of Jeremy Taylor, can save you from the Satan which you are.

His ministry fell on a political crisis also, — on the years when Southern slavery broke over its old banks, made new and vast pretensions, and wrung from the weakness or treachery of Northern people fatal concessions in the Fugitive Slave Bill and the repeal of the Missouri Compromise. Two days, bitter in the memory of Boston, the days of the rendition of Sims and of Burns, made the occasion of his most remarkable discourses. He kept nothing back. In terrible earnest he denounced the public crime, and meted out to every official, high and low, his due portion. By the incessant power of his statement he made and held a party. It was his great service to freedom. He took away the reproach of silent consent that would otherwise have lain against the indignant minority by uttering in the hour and place wherein these outrages were done the stern protest. . . .

Theodore Parker was a son of the soil, charged with the energy of New England, strong, eager, inquisitive of knowledge, of a diligence that never tired, upright, of a haughty independence, yet the gentlest of companions; a man of study, fit for a man of the world; with decided opinions and plenty of power to state them; rapidly pushing his studies so far as to leave few men qualified to sit as his critics. He elected his part of duty, or accepted nobly that assigned him in his rare constitution. Wonderful acquisition of knowledge, a rapid wit that heard all, and welcomed all that came, by seeing its bearing. Such was the largeness of his reception of facts and his skill to employ them that it looked as if he were some president of council to whom a score of telegraphs were ever bringing in reports; and his information would have been excessive but for the noble use he made of it ever in the interest of humanity. . . .

There were, of course, multitudes to censure and defame this truth-speaker. But the brave know the brave. Fops, whether in hotels or churches, will utter the fop's opinion, and faintly hope for the salvation of his soul; but his manly enemies, who despised the fops, honored him; and it is well known that his great hospitable heart was the sanctuary to which every soul conscious of an earnest opinion came for sympathy,— alike the brave slaveholder and the brave slave-rescuer. These met in the house of this honest man,— for every sound heart loves a responsible person, one who does not in generous company say generous things, and in mean company base things, but says one thing,— now cheerfully, now indignantly,— but always because he must, and because he sees that, whether he speak or refrain from speech, this is said over him; and history, nature, and all souls testify to the same.

Ah, my brave brother! it seems as if, in a frivolous age, our loss were immense, and your place cannot be supplied. But you will already be consoled in the transfer of your genius, knowing well that the nature of the world will affirm to all men, in all times, that which for twenty-five years you valiantly spoke; that the winds of Italy murmur the same truth over your grave; the winds of America over these bereaved streets; that the sea which bore your mourners home affirms it, the stars in their courses, and the inspirations of youth; whilst the polished and pleasant traitors to human rights, with perverted learning and disgraced graces, rot and are forgotten with their double tongue saying all that is sordid for the corruption of man.

A complete uniform American edition of the works of Theodore Parker is a desideratum. There is an English edition, carefully edited many years ago by Frances Power Cobbe; but this is now rare. Two volumes of this English edition are devoted to Parker's anti-slavery discourses. Most of these are also contained in four volumes of addresses prepared for the press by Parker himself in his lifetime, but now out of print. The famous address on Webster, the discourses following the rendition of Sims and Burns, addresses before the Anti-slavery Society, and various sermons on slavery are included in these volumes. There are many volumes of

Parker's religious works. His lectures on Franklin, Washington, John Adams, and Jefferson were published in a volume entitled "Historic Americans."

There are two valuable biographies of Parker, that by Weiss in two volumes, and the later, briefer, and more interesting work by Frothingham. Albert Réville's little book on Parker has been translated; and there are important sketches and eulogies by Wendell Phillips, James Freeman Clarke, Higginson, Johnson, Emerson, and others. Extracts from Emerson's eulogy are given in the present leaflet.

PUBLISHED BY

THE DIRECTORS OF THE OLD SOUTH WORK,
Old South Meeting-house, Boston, Mass.

Old South Leaflets.
No. 81.

The Anti-slavery Convention of 1833.

By John G. Whittier.

Written in 1874.*

In the gray twilight of a chill day of late November, forty years ago, a dear friend of mine, residing in Boston, made his appearance at the old farm-house in East Haverhill. He had been deputed by the abolitionists of the city, William L. Garrison, Samuel E. Sewall, and others, to inform me of my appointment as a delegate to the convention about to be held in Philadelphia for the formation of an American Anti-slavery Society, and to urge upon me the necessity of my attendance.

Few words of persuasion, however, were needed. I was unused to travelling, my life had been spent on a secluded farm; and the journey, mostly by stage-coach, at that time was really a formidable one. Moreover, the few abolitionists were everywhere spoken against, their persons threatened, and in some instances a price set on their heads by Southern legislators. Pennsylvania was on the borders of slavery, and it needed small effort of imagination to picture to one's self the breaking up of the convention and mltreatment of its members. This latter consideration I do not think weighed much with me, although I was better prepared for serious danger than for anything like personal indignity. I had read Governor Trumbull's description of the tarring and feathering of his hero MacFingal, when, after the application of the melted tar, the feather bed was ripped open and shaken over him, until

"Not Maia's son, with wings for ears,
Such plumes about his visage wears,
Nor Milton's six-winged angel gathers
Such superfluity of feathers";

* *Reprinted by permission from Whittier's Prose Works, published by Houghton, Mifflin & Co.*

and, I confess, I was quite unwilling to undergo a martyrdom which my best friends could scarcely refrain from laughing at. But a summons like that of Garrison's bugle-blast could scarcely be unheeded by one who, from birth and education, held fast the traditions of that earlier abolitionism which, under the lead of Benezet and Woolman, had effaced from the Society of Friends every vestige of slave-holding. I had thrown myself, with a young man's fervid enthusiasm, into a movement which commended itself to my reason and conscience, to my love of country and my sense of duty to God and my fellow-men. My first venture in authorship was the publication at my own expense, in the spring of 1833, of a pamphlet entitled "Justice and Expediency," on the moral and political evils of slavery, and the duty of emancipation. Under such circumstances I could not hesitate, but prepared at once for my journey. It was necessary that I should start on the morrow; and the intervening time, with a small allowance of sleep, was spent in providing for the care of the farm and homestead during my absence.

So the next morning I took the stage for Boston, stopping at the ancient hostelry known as the Eastern Stage Tavern; and on the day following, in company with William Lloyd Garrison, I left for New York. At that city we were joined by other delegates, among them David Thurston, a Congregational minister from Maine. On our way to Philadelphia we took, as a matter of necessary economy, a second-class conveyance, and found ourselves, in consequence, among rough and hilarious companions, whose language was more noteworthy for strength than refinement. Our worthy friend the clergyman bore it awhile in painful silence, but at last felt it his duty to utter words of remonstrance and admonition. The leader of the young roisterers listened with ludicrous mock gravity, thanked him for his exhortation, and, expressing fears that the extraordinary effort had exhausted his strength, invited him to take a drink with him. Father Thurston buried his grieved face in his coat-collar, and wisely left the young reprobates to their own devices.

On reaching Philadelphia, we at once betook ourselves to the humble dwelling on Fifth Street occupied by Evan Lewis, a plain, earnest man and lifelong abolitionist, who had been largely interested in preparing the way for the convention. In one respect the time of our assembling seemed unfavorable.

The Society of Friends, upon whose co-operation we had counted, had but recently been rent asunder by one of those unhappy controversies which so often mark the decline of practical righteousness. The martyr-age of the society had passed, wealth and luxury had taken the place of the old simplicity, there was a growing conformity to the maxims of the world in trade and fashion, and with it a corresponding unwillingness to hazard respectability by the advocacy of unpopular reforms. Unprofitable speculation and disputation on one hand, and a vain attempt on the other to enforce uniformity of opinion, had measurably lost sight of the fact that the end of the gospel is love, and that charity is its crowning virtue. After a long and painful struggle the disruption had taken place. The shattered fragments, under the name of Orthodox and Hicksite, so like and yet so separate in feeling, confronted each other as hostile sects; and

> "Never either found another
> To free the hollow heart from paining:
> They stood aloof, the scars remaining,
> Like cliffs that have been torn asunder
> A dreary sea now flows between;
> But neither rain nor frost nor thunder
> Can wholly do away, I ween,
> The marks of that which once has been."

We found about forty members assembled in the parlors of our friend Lewis, and after some general conversation Lewis Tappan was asked to preside over an informal meeting preparatory to the opening of the convention. A handsome, intellectual-looking man, in the prime of life, responded to the invitation, and in a clear, well-modulated voice, the firm tones of which inspired hope and confidence, stated the objects of our preliminary council, and the purpose which had called us together, in earnest and well-chosen words. In making arrangements for the convention, it was thought expedient to secure, if possible, the services of some citizen of Philadelphia, of distinction and high social standing, to preside over its deliberations. Looking round among ourselves in vain for some titled civilian or doctor of divinity, we were fain to confess that to outward seeming we were but "a feeble folk," sorely needing the shield of a popular name. A committee, of which I was a member, was appointed to go in search of a president of this description. We visited two prominent gentlemen, known as friendly to emancipation and of high social standing. They received us with the dignified courtesy of the old school, declined our proposition in civil terms, and bowed us out with a cool politeness equalled only by that of the senior Winkle towards the unlucky deputation of Pickwick and his unprepossessing companions. As we left their doors, we could not refrain from smiling in each other's faces at the thought of the small inducement our proffer of the presidency held out to men of their class. Evidently, our company was not one for respectability to march through Coventry with.

On the following morning we repaired to the Adelphi Building, on Fifth Street, below Walnut, which had been secured for our use. Sixty-two delegates were found to be in attendance. Beriah Green, of the Oneida (New York) Institute, was chosen president, a fresh-faced, sandy-haired, rather common-looking man, but who had the reputation of an able and eloquent speaker. He had already made himself known to us as a resolute and self-sacrificing abolitionist. Lewis Tappan and myself took our places at his side as secretaries, on the elevation at the west end of the hall.

Looking over the assembly, I noticed that it was mainly composed of comparatively young men, some in middle age, and a few beyond that period. They were nearly all plainly dressed, with a view to comfort rather than elegance. Many of the faces turned towards me wore a look of expectancy and suppressed enthusiasm. All had the earnestness which might be expected of men engaged in an enterprise beset with difficulty and perhaps with peril. The fine, intellectual head of Garrison, prematurely bald, was conspicuous. The sunny-faced young man at his side, in whom all the beatitudes seemed to find expression, was Samuel J. May, mingling in his veins the best blood of the Sewalls and Quincys,— a man so exceptionally pure and large-hearted, so genial, tender, and loving, that he could be faithful to truth and duty without making an enemy.

> "The de'il wad look into his face,
> And swear he couldna wrang him."

That tall, gaunt, swarthy man, erect, eagle-faced, upon whose somewhat martial figure the Quaker coat seemed a little out of place, was Lindley Coates, known in all Eastern Pennsylvania as a stern enemy of slavery. That slight, eager man, intensely alive in every feature and gesture, was Thomas Shipley, who for thirty years had been the protector of the free colored people of Philadelphia, and whose name was whispered reverently in the slave cabins of Maryland as the friend of the black man, one of a class peculiar to old Quakerism, who in doing what they felt to be duty and walking as the Light within guided them knew no fear and shrank from no sacrifice. Braver men the world has not known. Beside him, differing in creed, but united with him in works of love and charity, sat Thomas Whitson, of the Hicksite school of Friends, fresh from his farm in Lancaster County, dressed in plainest homespun, his tall form surmounted by a shock of unkempt hair, the odd obliquity of his vision contrasting strongly with the clearness and directness of his spiritual insight. Elizur Wright, the young professor of a Western college, who had lost his place by his bold advocacy of freedom, with a look of sharp concentration in keeping with an intellect keen as a Damascus blade, closely watched the proceedings through his spectacles, opening his mouth only to speak directly to the purpose. The portly form of Dr. Bartholomew Fussell, the beloved physician, from that beautiful land of plenty and peace which Bayard Taylor has described in his "Story of Kennett," was not to be overlooked. Abolitionist in heart and soul, his house was known as the shelter of runaway slaves; and no sportsman ever entered into the chase with such zest as he did into the arduous and sometimes dangerous work of aiding their escape and baffling their pursuers. The youngest man present was, I believe, James Miller McKim, a Presbyterian minister from Columbia, afterwards one of our most efficient workers. James Mott, E. L. Capron, Arnold Buffum, and Nathan Winslow, men well known in the anti-slavery agitation, were conspicuous members. Vermont sent down from her mountains Orson S. Murray, a man terribly in earnest, with a zeal that bordered on fanaticism, and who was none the more genial for the mob-violence to which he had been subjected. In front of me, awakening pleasant associations of the old homestead in Merrimack valley, sat my first school-teacher, Joshua Coffin, the learned and worthy antiquarian and historian of Newbury. A few spectators, mostly of the Hicksite division of Friends, were present, in broad brims and plain bonnets, among them Esther Moore and Lucretia Mott.

Committees were chosen to draft a constitution for a national Anti-slavery Society, nominate a list of officers, and prepare a declaration of principles to be signed by the members. Dr. A. L. Cox of New York, while these committees were absent, read something from my pen eulogistic of William Lloyd Garrison; and Lewis Tappan and Amos A. Phelps, a Congregational clergyman of Boston, afterwards one of the most devoted laborers in the cause, followed in generous commendation of the zeal, courage, and devotion of the young pioneer. The president, after calling James McCrummell, one of the two or three colored members of the convention, to the chair, made some eloquent remarks upon those editors who had ventured to advocate emancipation. At the close of his speech a young man rose to speak, whose appearance at once arrested my attention. I think I have never seen a finer face and figure; and his manner, words, and bearing were in keeping. "Who is he?" I asked of one of the Pennsylvania delegates. "Robert Purvis, of this city, a colored man," was the answer. He began by uttering his heart-felt thanks to the delegates who had convened for the deliverance of his people. He spoke of Garrison in terms of warmest eulogy, as one who had stirred the heart of the nation, broken the tomb-like slumber of the Church, and compelled it to listen to the story of the slave's wrongs. He closed by declaring that the friends of colored Americans would not be forgotten. "Their memories," he said, "will be cherished when pyramids and monuments shall have crumbled in dust. The flood of time, which is sweeping away the refuge of lies, is bearing on the advocates of our cause to a glorious immortality."

The committee on the constitution made their report, which after discussion was adopted. It disclaimed any right or intention of interfering, otherwise than by persuasion and Christian expostulation, with slavery as it existed in the States, but affirming the duty of Congress to abolish it in the District of Columbia and Territories, and to put an end to the domestic slave-trade. A list of officers of the new society was then chosen: Arthur Tappan, of New York, president, and Elizur Wright, Jr., William Lloyd Garrison, and A. L. Cox, secretaries. Among the vice-presidents was Dr. Lord, of Dartmouth College, then professedly in favor of emancipation, but who afterwards turned a moral somersault, a self-inversion which left him ever after on his head instead of his feet. He became a querulous advocate of slavery as a divine institution, and denounced woe upon the abolitionists for interfering with the will and purpose of the Creator. As the cause of freedom gained ground, the poor man's heart failed him, and his hope for Church and State grew fainter and fainter. A sad prophet of the evangel of slavery, he testified in the unwilling ears of an unbelieving generation, and died at last, despairing of a world which seemed determined that Canaan should no longer be cursed, nor Onesimus sent back to Philemon.

The committee on the declaration of principles, of which I was a member, held a long session discussing the proper scope and tenor of the document. But little progress being made, it was finally decided to intrust the matter to a sub-committee, consisting of William L. Garrison, S. J. May, and myself; and, after a brief consultation and comparison of each other's views, the drafting of the important paper was assigned to the former gentleman. We agreed to meet him at his lodgings in the house of a colored friend early the next morning. It was still dark when we climbed up to his room, and the lamp was still burning by the light of which he was writing the last sentence of the declaration. We read it carefully, made a few verbal changes, and submitted it to the large committee, who unanimously agreed to report it to the convention.

The paper was read to the convention by Dr. Atlee, chairman of the committee, and listened to with the profoundest interest.

Commencing with a reference to the time, fifty-seven years before, when, in the same city of Philadelphia, our fathers announced to the world their Declaration of Independence,— based on the self-evident truths of human equality and rights,— and appealed to arms for its defence, it spoke of the new enterprise as one "without which that of our fathers is incomplete," and as transcending theirs in magnitude, solemnity, and probable results as much "as moral truth does physical force." It spoke of the difference of the two in the means and ends proposed, and of the trifling grievances of our fathers compared with the wrongs and sufferings of the slaves, which it forcibly characterized as unequalled by any others on the face of the earth. It claimed that the nation was bound to repent at once, to let the oppressed go free, and to admit them to all the rights and privileges of others; because, it asserted, no man has a right to enslave or imbrute his brother; because liberty is inalienable; because there is no difference in principle between slave-holding and man-stealing, which the law brands as piracy; and because no length of bondage can invalidate man's claim to himself, or render slave laws anything but "an audacious usurpation."

It maintained that no compensation should be given to planters emancipating slaves, because that would be a surrender of fundamental principles. "Slavery is a crime, and is, therefore, not an article to be sold"; because slave-holders are not just proprietors of what they claim; because emancipation would destroy only nominal, not real, property; and because compensation, if given at all, should be given to the slaves.

It declared any "scheme of expatriation" to be "delusive, cruel, and dangerous." It fully recognized the right of each state to legislate exclusively on the subject of slavery within its limits, and conceded that Congress, under the present national compact, had no right to interfere, though still contending that it had the power, and should exercise it, "to suppress the domestic slave-trade between the several states," and "to abolish slavery in the District of Columbia, and in those portions of our territory which the Constitution has placed under its exclusive jurisdiction."

After clearly and emphatically avowing the principles underlying the enterprise, and guarding with scrupulous care the rights of persons and states under the Constitution, in prosecuting it, the declaration closed with these eloquent words: —

"We also maintain that there are at the present time the highest obligations resting upon the people of the free states to remove slavery by moral and political action, as prescribed in the Constitution of the United States. They are now living under a pledge of their tremendous physical force to fasten the galling fetters of tyranny upon the limbs of millions in the Southern states; they are liable to be called at any moment to suppress a general insurrection of the slaves; they authorize the slave-holder to vote on three-fifths of his slaves as property, and thus enable him to perpetuate his oppression: they support a standing army at the South for its protection; and they seize the slave who has escaped into their territories, and send him back to be tortured by an enraged master or a brutal driver. This relation to slavery is criminal and full of danger. It must be broken up.

"These are our views and principles,— these our designs and measures. With entire confidence in the overruling justice of God, we plant ourselves upon the Declaration of Independence and the truths of divine revelation as upon the everlasting rock.

"We shall organize anti-slavery societies, if possible, in every city, town, and village in our land.

"We shall send forth agents to lift up the voice of remonstrance, of warning, of entreaty and rebuke.

"We shall circulate unsparingly and extensively anti-slavery tracts and periodicals.

"We shall enlist the pulpit and the press in the cause of the suffering and the dumb.

"We shall aim at a purification of the churches from all participation in the guilt of slavery.

"We shall encourage the labor of freemen over that of the slaves, by giving a preference to their productions; and

"We shall spare no exertions nor means to bring the whole nation to speedy repentance.

"Our trust for victory is solely in God. We may be personally defeated, but our principles never. Truth, justice, reason, humanity, must and will gloriously triumph. Already a host is coming up to the help of the Lord against the mighty, and the prospect before us is full of encouragement.

"Submitting this declaration to the candid examination of the people of this country and of the friends of liberty all over the world, we hereby affix our signatures to it, pledging ourselves that, under the guidance and by the help of Almighty God, we will do all that in us lies, consistently with this declaration of our principles, to overthrow the most execrable system of slavery that has ever been witnessed upon earth, to deliver our land from its deadliest curse, to wipe out the foulest stain which rests upon our national escutcheon, and to secure to the colored population of the United States all the rights and privileges which belong to them as men and as Americans, come what may to our persons, our interests, or our reputations, whether we live to witness the triumph of justice, liberty, and humanity, or perish untimely as martyrs in this great, benevolent, and holy cause."

The reading of the paper was followed by a discussion which lasted several hours. A member of the Society of Friends moved its immediate adoption. "We have," he said, "all given it our assent: every heart here responds to it. It is a doctrine of Friends that these strong and deep impressions should be heeded." The convention, nevertheless, deemed it important to go over the declaration carefully, paragraph by paragraph. During the discussion one of the spectators asked leave to say a few words. A beautiful and graceful woman, in the prime of life, with a face beneath her plain cap as finely intellectual as that of Madame Roland, offered some wise and valuable suggestions, in a clear, sweet voice, the charm of which I have never forgotten. It was Lucretia Mott, of Philadelphia. The president courteously thanked her, and encouraged her to take a part in the discussion. On the morning of the last day of our session the declaration, with its few verbal amendments, carefully engrossed on parchment, was brought before the convention. Samuel J. May rose to read it for the last time. His sweet, persuasive voice faltered with the intensity of his emotions as he repeated the solemn pledges of the concluding paragraphs. After a season of silence, David Thurston, of Maine, rose as his name was called by one of the secretaries, and affixed his name to the document. One after another passed up to the platform, signed, and retired in silence. All felt the deep responsibility of the occasion: the shadow and forecast of a lifelong struggle rested upon every countenance.

Our work as a convention was now done. President Green arose to make the concluding address. The circumstances under which it was uttered may have lent it an impressiveness not its own; but, as I now recall it, it seems to me the most powerful and eloquent speech to which I have ever listened. He passed in review the work that had been done, the constitution of the new society, the declaration of sentiments, and the union and earnestness which had marked the proceedings. His closing words will never be forgotten by those who heard them: —

"Brethren, it has been good to be here. In this hallowed atmosphere I have been revived and refreshed. This brief interview has more than repaid me for all that I have ever suffered. I have here met congenial minds. I have rejoiced in sympathies delightful to the soul. Heart has beat responsive to heart, and the holy work of seeking to benefit the outraged and despised has proved the most blessed employment.

"But now we must retire from these balmy influences, and breathe another atmosphere. The chill hoar frost will be upon us. The storm and tempest will rise, and the waves of persecution will dash against our souls. Let us be prepared for the worst. Let us fasten ourselves to the throne of God as with hooks of steel. If we cling not to him, our names to that document will be but as dust.

"Let us court no applause, indulge in no spirit of vain boasting. Let us be assured that our only hope in grappling with the bony monster is in an Arm that is stronger than ours. Let us fix our gaze on God, and walk in the light of his countenance. If our cause be just,— and we know it is,— his omnipotence is pledged to its triumph. Let this cause be entwined around the very fibres of our hearts. Let our hearts grow to it, so that nothing but death can sunder the bond."

He ceased, and then, amidst a silence broken only by the deep-drawn breath of emotion in the assembly, lifted up his voice in a prayer to Almighty God, full of fervor and feeling, imploring his blessing and sanctification upon the convention and its labors. And with the solemnity of this supplication in our hearts we clasped hands in farewell, and went forth each man to his place of duty, not knowing the things that should befall us as individuals, but with a confidence never shaken by abuse and persecution in the certain triumph of our cause.

FORMATION OF THE AMERICAN ANTI-SLAVERY SOCIETY.

A LETTER TO WILLIAM LLOYD GARRISON, PRESIDENT OF THE SOCIETY.

AMESBURY, 24th 11th mo., 1863.

My dear Friend,— I have received thy kind letter with the accompanying circular, inviting me to attend the commemoration of the thirtieth anniversary of the formation of the American Anti-slavery Society at Philadelphia. It is with the deepest regret that I am compelled by the feeble state of my health to give up all hope of meeting thee and my other old and dear friends on an occasion of so much interest. How much it costs me to acquiesce in the hard necessity thy own feelings will tell thee better than any words of mine.

I look back over thirty years, and call to mind all the circumstances of my journey to Philadelphia, in company with thyself and the excellent Dr. Thurston, of Maine, even then as we thought an old man, but still living, and true as ever to the good cause. I recall the early gray morning when, with

Samuel J. May, our colleague on the committee to prepare a Declaration of Sentiments for the convention, I climbed to the small "upper chamber" of a colored friend to hear thee read the first draft of a paper which will live as long as our national history. I see the members of the convention, solemnized by the responsibility, rise one by one, and solemnly affix their names to that stern pledge of fidelity to freedom. Of the signers, many have passed away from earth, a few have faltered and turned back; but I believe the majority still live to rejoice over the great triumph of truth and justice, and to devote what remains of time and strength to the cause to which they consecrated their youth and manhood thirty years ago.

For, while we may well thank God and congratulate one another on the prospect of the speedy emancipation of the slaves of the United States, we must not for a moment forget that from this hour new and mighty responsibilities devolve upon us to aid, direct, and educate these millions left free, indeed, but bewildered, ignorant, naked, and foodless in the wild chaos of civil war. We have to undo the accumulated wrongs of two centuries, to remake the manhood which slavery has well-nigh unmade, to see to it that the long-oppressed colored man has a fair field for development and improvement, and to tread under our feet the last vestige of that hateful prejudice which has been the strongest external support of Southern slavery. We must lift ourselves at once to the true Christian altitude where all distinctions of black and white are overlooked in the heartfelt recognition of the brotherhood of man.

I must not close this letter without confessing that I cannot be sufficiently thankful to the Divine Providence which, in a great measure through thy instrumentality, turned me away so early from what Roger Williams calls "the world's great trinity, pleasure, profit, and honor," to take side with the poor and oppressed. I am not insensible to literary reputation. I love, perhaps too well, the praise and good-will of my fellow-men; but I set a higher value on my name as appended to the Antislavery Declaration of 1833 than on the title-page of any book. Looking over a life marked by many errors and shortcomings, I rejoice that I have been able to maintain the pledge of that signature, and that, in the long intervening years,

> "My voice, though not the loudest, has been heard
> Wherever Freedom raised her cry of pain."

Let me, through thee, extend a warm greeting to the friends, whether of our own or the new generation, who may assemble on the occasion of commemoration. There is work yet to be done which will task the best efforts of us all. For thyself, I need not say that the love and esteem of early boyhood have lost nothing by the test of time; and

I am, very cordially, thy friend,
JOHN G. WHITTIER.

ANTI-SLAVERY ANNIVERSARY.

READ AT THE SEMI-CENTENNIAL CELEBRATION OF THE AMERICAN ANTI-SLAVERY SOCIETY AT PHILADELPHIA ON THE 3d DECEMBER, 1883.

OAK KNOLL, DANVERS, MASS.,
11th mo., 30, 1883.

I need not say how gladly I would be with you at the semi-centennial of the American Anti-slavery Society. I am, I regret to say, quite unable to gratify this wish, and can only represent myself by a letter.

Looking back over the long years of half a century, I can scarcely realize the conditions under which the convention of 1833 assembled. Slavery was predominant. Like Apollyon in *Pilgrim's Progress*, it "straddled over the whole breadth of the way." Church and state, press and pulpit, business interests, literature, and fashion were prostrate at its feet. Our convention, with few exceptions, was composed of men without influence or position, poor and little known, strong only in their convictions and faith in the justice of their cause. To onlookers our endeavor to undo the evil work of two centuries and convert a nation to the "great renunciation" involved in emancipation must have seemed absurd in the last degree. Our voices in such an atmosphere found no echo. We could look for no response but laughs of derision or the missiles of a mob.

But we felt that we had the strength of truth on our side; we were right, and all the world about us was wrong. We had faith, hope, and enthusiasm, and did our work, nothing doubting, amidst a generation who first despised and then feared and hated us. For myself I have never ceased to be grateful to the Divine Providence for the privilege of taking a part in that work.

And now for more than twenty years we have had a free country. No slave treads its soil. The anticipated dangerous consequences of complete emancipation have not been felt. The emancipated class, as a whole, have done wisely and well under circumstances of peculiar difficulty. The masters have learned that cotton can be raised better by free than by slave labor, and nobody now wishes a return to slave-holding. Sectional prejudices are subsiding, the bitterness of the civil war is slowly passing away. We are beginning to feel that we are one people, with no really clashing interests, and none more truly rejoice in the growing prosperity of the South than the old abolitionists, who hated slavery as a curse to the master as well as to the slave.

In view of this commemorative semi-centennial occasion, many thoughts crowd upon me; memory recalls vanished faces and voices long hushed. Of those who acted with me in the convention fifty years ago nearly all have passed into another state of being. We who remain must soon follow; we have seen the fulfilment of our desire; we have outlived scorn and persecution; the lengthening shadows invite us to rest. If, in looking back, we feel that we sometimes erred through impatient zeal in our contest with a great wrong, we have the satisfaction of knowing that we were influenced by no merely selfish considerations. The low light of our setting sun shines over a free, united people, and our last prayer shall be for their peace, prosperity, and happiness.

With a feeling of gratitude to God, I recall the great happiness of laboring with the noble company of whom Garrison was the central figure. I love to think of him as he seemed to me, when in the fresh dawn of manhood he sat with me in the old Haverhill farmhouse, revolving even then schemes of benevolence; or, with cheery smile, welcoming me to his frugal meal of bread and milk in the dingy Boston printing-room; or, as I found him in the gray December morning in the small attic of a colored man, in Philadelphia, finishing his night-long task of drafting his immortal *Declaration of Sentiments* of the American Anti-slavery Society; or, as I saw him in the jail of Leverett Street, after his almost miraculous escape from the mob, playfully inviting me to share the safe lodgings which the state had provided for him; and in all the varied scenes and situations where we acted together our parts in the great endeavor and success of Freedom. — From Whittier's Introduction to Oliver Johnson's *William Lloyd Garrison and His Times.*

HYMN

FOR THE CELEBRATION OF EMANCIPATION AT NEWBURYPORT.

Not unto us who did but seek
The word that burned within to speak,
Not unto us this day belong
The triumph and exultant song.

Upon us fell in early youth
The burden of unwelcome truth,
And left us, weak and frail and few,
The censor's painful work to do.

Thenceforth our life a fight became,
The air we breathed was hot with blame;
For not with gauged and softened tone
We made the bondman's cause our own.

We bore, as Freedom's hope forlorn,
The private hate, the public scorn,
Yet held through all the paths we trod
Our faith in man and trust in God.

We prayed and hoped; but still, with awe,
The coming of the sword we saw;
We heard the nearing steps of doom,
We saw the shade of things to come.

In grief which they alone can feel
Who from a mother's wrong appeal,
With blended lines of fear and hope
We cast our country's horoscope.

For still within her house of life
We marked the lurid sign of strife,
And, poisoning and imbittering all,
We saw the star of Wormwood fall.

Deep as our love for her became
Our hate of all that wrought her shame;
And if, thereby, with tongue and pen
We erred, we were but mortal men.

We hoped for peace: our eyes survey
The blood-red dawn of Freedom's day;
We prayed for love to loose the chain:
'Tis shorn by battle's axe in twain!

Nor skill nor strength nor zeal of ours
Has mined and heaved the hostile towers;
Not by our hands is turned the key
That sets the sighing captives free.

A redder sea than Egypt's wave
Is piled and parted for the slave;
A darker cloud moves on in light;
A fiercer fire is guide by night!

The praise, O Lord, is Thine alone,
In Thy own way Thy work is done!
Our poor gifts at Thy feet we cast,
To whom be glory, first and last!

February, 1865.

Whittier was pre-eminently the poet of the anti-slavery conflict. There is almost no phase of the great wrong and almost no episode in the struggle for its abolition which is not the subject of some burning poem from his pen. There are almost a hundred of the anti-slavery poems now printed together in the editions of his works (vol. iii. in the Riverside edition), beginning with the poem "To William Lloyd Garrison" (1832) and ending with the "Hymn for the Celebration of Emancipation" (1865), reprinted in the present leaflet. Whittier's prose writings against slavery were also numerous,—he was a vigorous polemic,—and these papers, twenty in number, may be found together in vol. vii. of the Riverside edition. Among them are the pamphlet "Justice and Expediency," which he refers to in his account of the convention of 1833, as his first venture in authorship, and his two letters to the *Jeffersonian and Times*, Richmond, Va. (1833), on "The Abolitionists: their Sentiments and Objects," which suggests comparison with Phillips's great address later on "The Philosophy of the Abolition Movement." In vol. vi. of the Riverside edition is Whittier's sketch of Lydia Maria Child, originally written in 1882 as an introduction to an edition of Mrs. Child's Letters.

The Life of Whittier, by Samuel T. Pickard, is especially full, touching his work against slavery and his general political life, which was much more active than is commonly supposed. There are briefer biographies by Underwood, Kennedy, and Linton, and interesting volumes of personal reminiscences by Mrs. Mary B. Claflin and Mrs. James T. Fields. Stedman, in his "American Poets," pays high tribute to Whittier as the great poet of the anti-slavery conflict.

PUBLISHED BY

THE DIRECTORS OF THE OLD SOUTH WORK,
Old South Meeting-house, Boston, Mass.

Old South Leaflets.

No. 82.

The Story of "Uncle Tom's Cabin."

By HARRIET BEECHER STOWE.

WRITTEN IN 1878, AS AN INTRODUCTION TO A NEW EDITION OF "UNCLE TOM'S CABIN." *

The introduction of a new American edition of "Uncle Tom's Cabin" gives an occasion for a brief account of that book,— how it came to be, how it was received in the world, and what has been its history throughout all the nations and tribes of the earth, civilized and uncivilized, into whose languages it has been translated.

Its author had for many years lived in Ohio on the confines of a slave state, and had thus been made familiar with facts and occurrences in relation to the institution of American slavery. Some of the most harrowing incidents related in the story had from time to time come to her knowledge in conversation with former slaves now free in Ohio. The cruel sale and separation of a married woman from her husband, narrated in Chapter XII., "Select Incident of Lawful Trade," had passed under her own eye while passenger on a steamboat on the Ohio River. Her husband and brother had once been obliged to flee with a fugitive slave woman by night, as described in Chapter IX.; and she herself had been called to write the letters for a former slave woman, servant in her own family, to a slave husband in Kentucky, who, trusted with unlimited liberty, free to come and go on business between Kentucky and Ohio, still refused to break his pledge of honor to his master, though that master from year to year deferred the keeping of his promise

* *Copyright, 1878, by Harriet Beecher Stowe. Reprinted by special arrangement with Messrs. Houghton, Mifflin & Co., publishers of Mrs. Stowe's works.*

of freedom to the slave. It was the simple honor and loyalty of this Christian black man, who remained in slavery rather than violate a trust, that first impressed her with the possibility of such a character as, years after, was delineated in Uncle Tom.

From time to time incidents were brought to her knowledge which deepened her horror of slavery. In her own family she had a private school for her children; and, as there was no provision for the education of colored children in her vicinity, she allowed them the privilege of attending. One day she was suddenly surprised by a visit from the mother of one of the brightest and most amusing of these children. It appeared that the child had never been emancipated, and was one of the assets of an estate in Kentucky, and had been seized and carried off by one of the executors, and was to be sold by the sheriff at auction to settle the estate. The sum for the little one's ransom was made up by subscription in the neighborhood, but the incident left a deep mark in Mrs. Stowe's mind as to the practical workings of the institution of slavery.

But it was not for many years that she felt any call to make use of the materials thus accumulating. In fact, it was a sort of general impression upon her mind, as upon that of many humane people in those days, that the subject was so dark and painful a one, so involved in difficulty and obscurity, so utterly beyond human hope or help, that it was of no use to read or think or distress one's self about it. There was a class of professed abolitionists in Cincinnati and the neighboring regions, but they were unfashionable persons and few in number. Like all asserters of pure abstract right as applied to human affairs, they were regarded as a species of moral monomaniacs, who, in the consideration of one class of interests and wrongs, had lost sight of all proportion and all good judgment. Both in Church and in State they were looked upon as "those that troubled Israel."

It was a general saying among conservative and sagacious people that this subject was a dangerous one to investigate, and that nobody could begin to read and think upon it without becoming practically insane; moreover, that it was a subject of such delicacy that no discussion of it could be held in the free states without impinging upon the sensibilities of the slave states, to whom alone the management of the matter belonged.

So when Dr. Bailey — a wise, temperate, and just man, a

model of courtesy in speech and writing — came to Cincinnati and set up an anti-slavery paper, proposing a fair discussion of the subject, there was an immediate excitement. On two occasions a mob led by slave-holders from Kentucky attacked his office, destroyed his printing-press, and threw his types into the Ohio River. The most of the Cincinnati respectability, in Church and State, contented themselves on this occasion with reprobating the imprudence of Dr. Bailey in thus "arousing the passions of our fellow-citizens of Kentucky." In these mobs and riots the free colored people were threatened, maltreated, abused, and often had to flee for their lives. Even the servants of good families were often chased to the very houses of their employers, who rescued them with difficulty; and the story was current in those days of a brave little woman who defended her black waiter, standing, pistol in hand, on her own doorstep, and telling the mob face to face that they should not enter except over her dead body.

Professor Stowe's house was more than once a refuge for frightened fugitives on whom the very terrors of death had fallen; and the inmates slept with arms in the house and a large bell ready to call the young men of the adjoining Institution, in case the mob should come up to search the house. Nor was this a vain or improbable suggestion; for the mob, in their fury, had more than once threatened to go up and set fire to Lane Seminary, where a large body of students were known to be abolitionists. Only the fact that the Institution was two miles from the city, with a rough and muddy road up a long high hill, proved its salvation. Cincinnati mud, far known for its depth and tenacity, had sometimes its advantages.

The general policy of the leaders of society, in cases of such disturbances, was after the good old pattern in Judea, where a higher One had appeared, who disturbed the traders in swine: "they besought him that he would depart out of their coasts." Dr. Bailey at last was induced to remove his paper to Washington, and to conduct his investigation under the protection of the national Capitol; and there for years he demonstrated the fact that the truth may be spoken plainly, yet courteously and with all honorable and Christian fairness, on the most exciting of subjects. In justice to the South, it must be said that his honesty, courage, and dignity of character won for him friends even among the most determined slave-holders. Manly men have a sort of friendship for an open, honest opponent, like that of Richard Cœur de Lion for Saladin.

Far otherwise was the fate of Lovejoy, who essayed an anti-slavery paper at Alton, Ill. A mob from Missouri besieged the office, set the house on fire, and shot him at the door. It was for some days reported that Dr. Beecher's son, Rev. Edward Beecher, known to have been associated with Lovejoy at this period, had been killed at the same time. Such remembrances show how well grounded were the fears which attended every effort to agitate this subject. People who took the side of justice and humanity in those days had to count the cost and pay the price of their devotion. In those times, when John G. Fee, a young Kentucky student in Lane Seminary, liberated his slaves, and undertook to preach the gospel of emancipation in Kentucky, he was chased from the state, and disinherited by his own father. Berea College, for the education of colored and white, stands to-day a triumphant monument of his persistence in well-doing. Mr. Van Zandt, a Kentucky farmer, set free his slaves, and came over and bought a farm in Ohio. Subsequently, from an impulse of humanity, he received and protected fugitive slaves in the manner narrated in Chapter IX. of "Uncle Tom's Cabin." For this he was seized, imprisoned, his property attached, and he was threatened with utter ruin. Salmon P. Chase, then a rising young lawyer in Cincinnati, had the bravery to appear as his lawyer. As he was leaving the court-room, after making his plea, one of the judges remarked, "There goes a young man who has *ruined* himself to-day"; and the sentiment was echoed by the general voice of society. The case went against Van Zandt; and Mr. Chase carried it up to the Supreme Court of the United States, which, utterly ignoring argument and justice, decided it against him. But a few years more, and Salmon P. Chase was himself Chief Justice of the United States. It was one of those rare dramatic instances in which courage and justice sometimes bring a reward even in this life.

After many years' residence in Ohio, Mrs. Stowe returned to make her abode in New England, just in the height of the excitement produced by the Fugitive Slave Law. Settled in Brunswick, Me., she was in constant communication with friends in Boston, who wrote to her from day to day of the terror and despair which that law had occasioned to industrious, worthy colored people who had from time to time escaped to Boston, and were living in peace and security. She heard of families broken up and fleeing in the dead of winter to the frozen shores of Canada. But what seemed to her more inexplicable, more dreadful, was the apparent apathy of the Christian world of the free North to these proceedings. The pulpits that denounced them were exceptions, the voices raised to remonstrate few and far between.

In New England, as at the West, professed abolitionists were a small, despised, unfashionable band, whose constant remonstrances from year to year had been disregarded as the voices from impracticable fanatics. It seemed now as if the system once confined to the Southern States was rousing itself to new efforts to extend itself all over the North, and to overgrow the institutions of free society.

With astonishment and distress Mrs. Stowe heard on all sides, from humane and Christian people, that the slavery of the blacks was a guaranteed constitutional right, and that all opposition to it endangered the national Union. With this conviction she saw that even earnest and tender-hearted Christian people seemed to feel it a duty to close their eyes, ears, and hearts to the harrowing details of slavery, to put down all discussion of the subject, and even to assist slave-owners to recover fugitives in Northern States. She said to herself, These people cannot know what slavery is: they do not see what they are defending; and hence arose a purpose to write some sketches which should show to the world slavery as she had herself seen it. Pondering this subject, she was one day turning over a little bound volume of an anti-slavery magazine, edited by Mrs. Dr. Bailey, of Washington, and there she read the account of the escape of a woman with her child on the ice of the Ohio River from Kentucky. The incident was given by an eye-witness, one who had helped the woman to the Ohio shore. This formed the first salient point of the story. She began to meditate. The faithful slave husband in Kentucky occurred to her as a pattern of Uncle Tom, and the scenes of the story began gradually to form themselves in her mind.

The first part of the book ever committed to writing was the death of Uncle Tom. This scene presented itself almost as a tangible vision to her mind while sitting at the communion table in the little church in Brunswick. She was perfectly overcome by it, and could scarcely restrain the convulsion of tears and sobbings that shook her frame. She hastened home, and wrote it; and, her husband being away, she read it to her two sons of ten and twelve years of age. The little fellows broke out into convulsions of weeping, one of them saying, through his sobs, "O mamma, slavery is the most cursed thing in the world!" From that time the story can less be said to have been composed by her than imposed upon her. Scenes, incidents, conversations, rushed upon her with a vividness and importunity that would not be denied. The book insisted upon getting itself into being, and would take no denial. After the first two or three chapters were written, she wrote to Dr. Bailey of the *National Era* that she was planning a story that might probably run through several numbers of the *Era*. In reply she received an instant application for it, and began immediately to send off weekly instalments. She was then in the midst of heavy domestic cares, with a young infant, with a party of pupils in her family, to whom she was imparting daily lessons with her own children, and with untrained servants requiring constant supervision; but the story was so much more intense a reality to her than any other earthly thing that the weekly instalment never failed. It was there in her mind day and night waiting to be written, and requiring but a few moments to bring it into visible characters.

The weekly number was always read to the family circle before it was sent away, and all the household kept up an intense interest in the progress of the story.

As the narrative appeared in the *Era*, sympathetic words began to come to her from old workers who had long been struggling in the anti-slavery cause. She visited Boston, went to the Anti-slavery Rooms, and re-enforced her *répertoire* of facts by such documents as Theodore D. Weld's "Slavery As It Is," the Lives of Josiah Henson and Lewis Clarke, particulars from both whose lives were inwoven with the story in the characters of Uncle Tom and George Harris.

In shaping her material, the author had but one purpose, to show the institution of slavery truly, just as it existed. She had visited in Kentucky, had formed the acquaintance of people who were just, upright, and generous, and yet slaveholders. She had heard their views, and appreciated their situation. She felt that justice required that their difficulties should be recognized and their virtues acknowledged. It was her object to show that the evils of slavery were the inherent evils of a bad *system*, and not always the fault of those who had become involved in it and were its actual administrators.

Then she was convinced that the presentation of slavery alone, in its most dreadful forms, would be a picture of such unrelieved horror and darkness as noboby could be induced to look at. Of set purpose, she sought to light up the darkness by humorous and grotesque episodes and the presentation of the milder and more amusing phases of slavery, for which her recollection of the never-failing wit and drollery of her former colored friends in Ohio gave her abundant material. As the story progressed, a young publisher, J. P. Jewett, of Boston, set his eye upon it, and made overtures for the publication of it in book form, to which she consented. After a while she had a letter from him expressing his fears that she was making the story too long for a one-volume publication. He reminded her that it was an unpopular subject, and that people would not willingly hear much about it; that one short volume might possibly sell, but, if it grew to two, it might prove a fatal obstacle to its success. Mrs. Stowe replied that she did not make the story, that the story made itself, and that she could not stop it till it was done. The feeling that pursued her increased in intensity to the last, till, with the death of Uncle Tom, it seemed as if the whole vital force had left her. A feeling of profound discouragement came over her. Would anybody read it? Would anybody listen? Would this appeal, into which she had put heart, soul, mind, and strength, which she had written with her heart's blood,— would it, too, go for nothing, as so many prayers and groans and entreaties of these poor suffering souls had already gone? There had just been a party of slaves who had been seized and thrown into prison in Washington for a vain effort to escape. They were, many of them, partially educated, cultivated young men and women, to whom slavery was intolerable. When they were retaken and marched through the streets of Washington, followed by a jeering crowd, one of them, named Emily Edmundson, answered one man, who cried shame upon her, that she was not ashamed, that she was proud that she and all the rest of them had made an effort for liberty! It was the sentiment of a heroine, but she and her sisters were condemned no less to the auction-block.

It was when the last proof-sheet had been sent to the office that Mrs. Stowe, alone and thoughtful, sat reading Horace Mann's eloquent plea for those young men and women, then about to be consigned to the slave warehouse of Bruin & Hill in Alexandria,— a plea eloquent, impassioned, but vain, as all other pleas on that side had ever proved in all courts hitherto. It seemed to her that there was no hope, that nobody would hear, nobody would read, nobody would pity; that this frightful system, which had already pursued its victims into the free states, might at last even threaten them in Canada.

So, determined to leave nothing undone which remotely could help the cause she pleaded, she wrote one letter to Prince Albert, to accompany a copy of her work; another to T. B. Macaulay, of whose father she had heard in her youth as an anti-slavery laborer; one to Charles Dickens, whose sympathy for the slave had been expressed more than once; one to Charles Kingsley; and one to Lord Carlisle. These letters were despatched to their destination with early copies of the book, and all in due time acknowledged to the author.

"Uncle Tom's Cabin" was published March 20, 1852. The despondency of the author as to the question whether anybody would read or attend to her appeal was soon dispelled. Ten thousand copies were sold in a few days, and over three hundred thousand within a year; and eight power-presses, running day and night, were barely able to keep pace with the demand for it. It was read everywhere, apparently, and by everybody; and she soon began to hear echoes of sympathy all over the land. The indignation, the pity, the distress, that had long weighed upon her soul, seemed to pass off from her and into the readers of the book. The following note from a lady, an intimate friend, was a specimen of many which the post daily brought her. [*Omitted.*]

Mrs. Stowe at this period visited New York. It was just at the time of Jenny Lind's first visit to this country, when the young Swedish vocalist was the idol of the hour, and tickets to her concerts were selling at fabulous prices. Mrs. Stowe's friends, applying for tickets, found all sold; but, on hearing of the application, the cantatrice immediately sent Mrs. Stowe two tickets to two of the best seats in the house. In reply to Mrs. Stowe's note of thanks came this answer:—

May 23, 1852.

My dear Madam,— Allow me to express my most sincere thanks for your very kind letter, which I was very happy to receive.

You must feel and know what deep impression "Uncle Tom's Cabin" has made upon every heart that can feel for the dignity of human existence; so I, with my miserable English, would not even try to say a word about the great excellency of that most beautiful book, but *I must* thank you for the great joy I have felt over that book.

Forgive me, my dear madam; it is a great liberty I take, in thus addressing you, I know, but I have *so* wished to find an opportunity to pour out my thankfulness in a few words to you that I cannot help this intruding. I have the feeling about "Uncle Tom's Cabin" that great changes will take place by and by from the impression people receive out of it, and that the writer of that book can "fall asleep" to-day or to-morrow with the bright sweet conscience of having been a strong, powerful means, in the Creator's hand, of operating essential good in one of the most important questions for the welfare of our black *brethren*. God bless and protect you and yours, dear madam, and certainly God's hand will remain with a blessing over your head.

Once more, forgive my bad English and the liberty I have taken, and believe me to be, dear madam,
      Yours most truly,
        JENNY GOLDSCHMIDT, *née* LIND.

A more cheering result was in the testimony of many colored persons and fugitive slaves who said to her: "Since that book has come out, everybody is good to us: we find friends everywhere. It's wonderful how kind everybody is."

In one respect, Mrs. Stowe's expectations were strikingly different from fact. She had painted slave-holders as amiable, generous, and just. She had shown examples among them of the noblest and most beautiful traits of character, had admitted fully their temptations, their perplexities, and their difficulties, so that a friend of hers who had many relatives in the South wrote to her in exultation, "Your book is going to be the great pacificator: it will unite both North and South." Her expectation was that the professed abolitionists would denounce it as altogether too mild in its dealings with slaveholders. To her astonishment, it was the extreme abolitionists who received, and the entire South who rose up against it.

Whittier wrote to Garrison in May, 1852: —

It did me good to see thy handwriting, friend William, reminding me of the old days when we fought the beasts at Ephesus together in Philadelphia. Ah me! I am no longer able to take active part in the conflicts and skirmishes which are preparing the way for the great battle of Armageddon, — the world-wide, final struggle between freedom and slavery, — but, sick or well, in the body or out, I shall be no unconcerned spectator. I bless God that, through the leadings of his Providence, I have a right to rejoice in the certain victory of the right.

What a glorious work Harriet Beecher Stowe has wrought! *Thanks for the Fugitive Slave Law!* Better for slavery that law had never been enacted, for it gave occasion for "Uncle Tom's Cabin"!

In a letter from Garrison to Mrs. Stowe, he said that he estimated the value of anti-slavery writing by the abuse it brought. "Since 'Uncle Tom's Cabin' has been published," he adds, "all the defenders of slavery have let me alone, and are spending their strength in abusing you." In fact, the post-office began about this time to bring her threatening and insulting letters from the Legrees and Haleys of the slave-markets,— letters so curiously compounded of blasphemy, cruelty, and obscenity that their like could only be expressed by John Bunyan's account of the speech of Apollyon,— "He spake as a dragon."

After a little, however, responses began to come from across the water. The author had sent copies to Prince Albert, to Charles Dickens, to T. B. Macaulay, to Kingsley, and to Lord Carlisle. The receipt of the copy sent to Prince Albert was politely acknowledged, with thanks, by his private secretary. Her letter is here given:—

To his Royal Highness Prince Albert:

The author of this work feels that she has an apology for presenting it to Prince Albert, because it concerns the great interests of humanity; and, from those noble and enlarged views of human progress which she has at different times seen in his public speeches, she has inferred that he has an eye and a heart for all that concerns the development and welfare of the human family.

Ignorant of the forms of diplomatic address and the etiquette of rank, may she be pardoned for speaking with the republican simplicity of her own country, as to one who possesses a nobility higher than that of rank or station.

This simple narrative is an honest attempt to enlist the sympathies both of England and America in the sufferings of an oppressed race, to whom in less enlightened days both England and America were unjust.

The wrong on England's part has been atoned in a manner worthy of herself, nor in all her strength and glory is there anything that adds such lustre to her name as the position she holds in relation to human freedom. (May America yet emulate her example!)

The appeal is in greater part, as it should be, to the writer's own country; but, when fugitives by thousands are crowding British shores, she would enlist for them the sympathy of British hearts.

We, in America, have been told that the throne of earth's mightiest nation is now filled by one less adorned by all this world can give of power and splendor than by a good and noble heart,— a heart ever ready to feel for the suffering, the oppressed, and the lowly.

The author is encouraged by the thought that beneath the royal insignia of England throbs that woman's and mother's heart. May she ask that he who is nearest to her would present to her notice this simple story? Should it win from her compassionate nature pitying thoughts for those multitudes of poor outcasts who have fled for shelter to the shadow of her throne, it were enough.

May the blessing of God rest on the noble country from which America draws her lineage, and on *her*, the Queen of it. Though all the thrones be shaken, may *hers*, founded deep in the hearts of her subjects, be established to her and *to her children*, through all generations!

With deep respect,

HARRIET BEECHER STOWE.

BRUNSWICK, ME., March 20, 1852.

Her letter to Charles Dickens and his reply are as follows:—

TO THE AUTHOR OF "DAVID COPPERFIELD":

The Author of the following sketches offers them to your notice as the first writer in our day who turned the attention of the high to the joys and sorrows of the lowly. In searching out and embellishing the forlorn, the despised, the lonely, the neglected, and forgotten, lies the true mission which you have performed for the world. There is a moral bearing in it that far outweighs the amusement of a passing hour. If I may hope to do only something like the same, for a class equally ignored and despised by the fastidious and refined of my country, I shall be happy.

Yours very truly,

HARRIET BEECHER STOWE.

TAVISTOCK HOUSE, LONDON, July 17, 1852.

Dear Madam,— I have read your book with the deepest interest and sympathy, and admire, more than I can express to you, both the generous feeling which inspired it and the admirable power with which it is executed.

If I might suggest a fault in what has so charmed me, it would be that you go too far and seek to prove too much. The wrongs and atrocities of slavery are, God knows, case enough. I doubt there being any warrant for making out the African race to be a great race or for supposing the future destinies of the world to lie in that direction; and I think this extreme championship likely to repel some useful sympathy and support.

Your book is worthy of any head and any heart that ever inspired a book. I am much your debtor, and I thank you most fervently and sincerely.

CHARLES DICKENS.

MRS. HARRIET B. STOWE.

The following is the letter addressed to Macaulay and his reply:—

HON. T. B. MACAULAY:

One of the most vivid recollections of my early life is the enthusiasm excited by reading your review of Milton,— an enthusiasm deepened as I followed successively your writings as they appeared. A desire to hold some communion with minds that have strongly swayed and controlled our own is, I believe, natural to every one, and suggested to my mind the idea of presenting to you this work. When a child between eight and ten years of age, I was a diligent reader of the *Christian Observer*, and in particular of the articles in which the great battle was fought against the slave-trade. An impression was then made on my mind which will never be obliterated. A similar conflict is now convulsing this nation,—an agitation which every successive year serves to deepen and widen. In this conflict the wise and good of *other lands* can materially aid us.

The *public sentiment of Christianized humanity* is the last court of appeal in which the cause of a helpless race is to be tried, and nothing operates more sensibly on this country than the temperate and just expression of the sentiments of distinguished men in your own. Every such expression is a shot which strikes the citadel. There is a public sentiment on this subject in England which often expresses itself in a way which does far less good than it might if those who expressed it had a more accurate knowledge and a more skilful touch; and yet even that has done good, though it has done harm also. The public sentiment of nations is rising to be a power stronger than that of fleets and armies, and it needs to be skilfully and wisely guided. He who should direct the feelings of England on this subject wisely and effectively, might do a work worthy of your father, of Clarkson and Wilberforce and all those brave men who began the great conflict for God and humanity.

I much misjudge your mind and heart if the subject is one on which you can be indifferent, or can speak otherwise than justly, humanely, and effectively. Yours with deep respect,

HARRIET BEECHER STOWE.

BRUNSWICK, ME., March 20, 1852.

THE ALBANY, LONDON, May 20, 1852.

Madam,— I sincerely thank you for the volumes which you have done me the honor to send me. I have read them,— I cannot say with pleasure, for no work on such a subject can give pleasure,— but with high respect for the talents and for the benevolence of the writer. I have the honor to be, madam, Your most faithful servant,

T. B. MACAULAY.

In October of 1856 Macaulay wrote to Mrs. Stowe: —

I have just returned from Italy, where your fame seems to throw that of all other writers into the shade. There is no place where "Uncle Tom" (transformed into "Il Zio Tom") is not to be found. By this time I have no doubt he has "Dred" for a companion.

Soon after Macaulay's letter came to her, Mrs. Stowe began to receive letters from other distinguished persons, expressing a far warmer sympathy with the spirit and motive of her work.

FROM LORD CARLISLE.

LONDON, July 8, 1852.

Madam,— I have allowed some time to elapse before I thanked you for the great honor and kindness you did me in sending to me from yourself a copy of "Uncle Tom's Cabin." I thought it due to the subject of which I perceived that it treated not to send a mere acknowledgment, as I confess from a motive of policy I am apt to do upon the first arrival of a book. I therefore determined to read before I wrote.

Having thus read, it is not in the stiff and conventional form of compliment, still less in the technical language of criticism, that I am about to speak of your work. I return my deep and solemn thanks to Almighty God, who has led and enabled you to write such a book. I do feel, indeed, the most thorough assurance that, in his good Providence, such a book cannot have been written in vain. I have long felt that Slavery is by far the *topping* question of the world and age we live in, including all that is most thrilling in heroism and most touching in distress,—in short, the real Epic of the Universe. The self-interest of the parties most nearly concerned on the one hand, the apathy and ignorance of unconcerned observers on the other, have left these august pretensions to drop very much out of sight, and hence my rejoicing that a writer has appeared who will be read and must be felt, and that, happen what may to the transactions of slavery, they will no longer be suppressed.

I trust that what I have just said was not required to show the entire sympathy I entertain with respect to the main truth and leading scope of your high argument, but we live in a world only too apt to regard the accessories and accidents of a subject above its real and vital essence. No one can know so well as you how much the external appearance of the negro detracts from the romance and sentiment which undoubtedly might attach to his position and to his wrongs; and on this account it does seem to me proportionately important that you should have brought to your portraiture great grace of style, great power of language, a play of humor which relieves and lightens even the dark depth of the background which you were called upon to reveal, a force of pathos which, to give it the highest praise, does not lag behind all the dread reality, and, above all, a variety, a discrimination, and a truth in the delineation of character which, even to my own scanty and limited experience of the society you describe, accredits itself instantaneously and irresistibly. There is one point which, in face of all that your book has aimed at and achieved, I think of extremely slight importance, but which I will nevertheless just mention, if only to show that I have not been bribed into this fervor of admiration. I think, then, that whenever you speak of England and her institutions it is in a tone which fails to do them justice. I do not know what distinct charges you think could be established against our aristocracy and capitalists; but you generally convey the impression that the same oppressions in degree, though not in kind, might be brought home to them which are now laid to the charge of Southern slave-holders. Exposed to the same ordeal, I grant they might very probably not stand the test better. All I contend for is that the circumstances in which they are placed, and the institutions by which they are surrounded, make the parallel wholly inapplicable. I cannot but suspect that your view has been in many respects derived from composers of fiction and others among ourselves, who, writing with distinguished ability, have been more successful in delineating and dissecting the morbid features of our modern society than in detecting the principle which is at fault or suggesting the appropriate remedy. My own belief is — liable, if you please, to national bias — that our capitalists are very much the same sort of persons as your own in the Northern States, with the same mixtures and inequalities of motive and action. With respect to our aristocracy, I should really be tempted to say that, tried by their conduct on the question of Free Trade, they do not sustain an unfavorable comparison with your uppermost classes. I need not repeat how irrelevant, after all, I feel what I have said upon this head to be to the main issues included in your work. There is little doubt, too, that as a nation we have our special failings; and one of them probably is that we care too little about what other nations think of us. Nor can I wish my countrymen ever to forget that their own past history should prevent them from being forward in casting accusations at their transatlantic brethren on the subject of slavery. With great ignorance of its actual miseries and horrors, there is also among us great ignorance of the fearful perplexities and difficulties with which its solution could not fail to be attended. I feel, however, that there is a considerable difference between reluctant acquiescence in what you inherit from the past and voluntary fresh enlargements and reinforcements of the system. For instance, I should not say that the mode in which such an enactment as the Fugitive Slave Law has been considered in this country has at all erred upon the side of overmuch indignation.

I need not detain you longer. I began my letter with returning thanks to Almighty God for the appearance of your work; and I offer my humble and ardent prayer to the same Supreme Source that it may have a marked agency in hastening the great consummation, which I should feel it a practical atheism not to believe must be among the unfulfilled purposes of the Divine Power and Love.

I have the honor to be, madam,
Your sincere admirer and well-wisher,
CARLISLE.

MRS. BEECHER STOWE.

FROM REV. CHARLES KINGSLEY.

EVERSLEY, Aug. 12, 1852.

My dear Madam,— Illness and anxiety have prevented my acknowledging long ere this your kind letter and your book, which, if success be a pleasure to you, has a success in England which few novels, and certainly no American book whatsoever, ever had. I cannot tell you how pleased I am to see coming from across the Atlantic a really healthy indigenous growth, "autochthones," free from all second and third hand Germanisms and Italianisms and all other unrealisms.

Your book will do more to take away the reproach from your great and growing nation than many platform agitations and speechifyings.

Here there is but one opinion about it. Lord Carlisle (late Morpeth) assured me that he believed the book, independent of its artistic merit (of which hereafter), calculated to produce immense good; and he can speak better concerning it than I can, for I pay you a compliment in saying that I have actually not read it through. It is too painful,— I cannot bear the sight of misery and wrong that I can do nothing to alleviate. But I will read it through and reread it in due time, though, when I have done so, I shall have nothing more to say than what every one says now, that it is perfect.

I cannot resist transcribing a few lines which I received this morning from an excellent critic: "To my mind it is the greatest novel ever written, and, though it will seem strange, it reminded me in a lower sphere more of Shakespeare than anything modern I have ever read; not in the style nor in the humor nor in the pathos,—though Eva set me a-crying worse than Cordelia did at sixteen,—but in the many-sidedness, and, above all, in that marvellous clearness of insight and outsight, which makes it seemingly impossible for her to see any one of her characters without showing him or her at once as a distinct man or woman different from all others."

I have a debt of personal thanks to you for the book, also, from a most noble and great woman, my own mother, a West-Indian, who in great sickness and sadness read your book with delighted tears. What struck her was the way in which you, first of all writers, she said, had dived down into the depths of the negro heart, and brought out his common humanity without losing hold for a moment of his race peculiarities. But I must really praise you no more to your face, lest I become rude and fulsome. May God bless and prosper you, and all you write, is the earnest prayer, and, if you go on as you have begun, the assured hope, of your faithful and obliged servant,

CHARLES KINGSLEY.

FROM THE EARL OF SHAFTESBURY.*

LONDON, Dec. 14, 1852.

Madam,— It is very possible that the writer of this letter may be wholly unknown to you. But whether my name be familiar to your ears, or whether you now read it for the first time, I cannot refrain from expressing to you the deep gratitude that I feel to Almighty God, who has inspired both your heart and your head in the composition of "Uncle Tom's Cabin."

It would be out of place here to enumerate the various beauties, singular, original, and lasting, which shine throughout the work. One conviction, however, is constantly present to my mind,— the conviction that the gospel alone can elevate the intellect, even to the highest point. None but a Christian believer could have composed "Paradise Lost." None but a Christian believer could have produced such a book as yours, which has absolutely startled the whole world, and impressed many thousands by revelations of cruelty and sin which give us an idea of what would be the uncontrolled dominion of Satan on this fallen earth.

Your character of Eva is true. I have, allowing for the difference in sex, and the influences of a southern as compared with a northern climate, seen such myself in zeal, simplicity, and overflowing affection to God and man. It pleases God to show, every now and then, such specimens of his grace, and then remove them before they are tarnished by the world.

You are right, too, about Topsy. Our Ragged Schools will afford you many instances of poor children, hardened by kicks, insults, and neglect, moved to tears and to docility by the first word of kindness. It opens new feelings, develops, as it were, a new nature, and brings the wretched outcast into the family of man. I live in hope — God grant that it may rise to faith! — that this system is drawing to a close. It seems as though our Lord had sent out this book as the messenger before his face to prepare his way before him. It may be that these unspeakable horrors are now disclosed to drive us to the only "hope of all the ends of the earth," the second advent of our blessed Saviour. Let us continue, as Saint Paul says, "fervent and instant in prayer"; and may we at the great day of

---

* Formerly Lord Ashley.

account be found, with millions of this oppressed race, among the sheep at the right hand of our common Lord and Master!

Believe me, madam, with deep respect,

Your sincere admirer and servant,

SHAFTESBURY.

Mrs. Harriet Beecher Stowe.

About the same time with this Mrs. Stowe received a letter from Hon. Arthur Helps, accompanying a review of her work, written by himself, in a leading periodical. The main subject of Mr. Helps's letter was the one already alluded to in Lord Carlisle's letter, on the relation of the capitalists and higher classes of England to the working-classes as compared with the relations of slave-holders and slaves in America. Her reply to this letter being shown to Archbishop Whately, she was surprised by a letter from him to the following purport:—

Madam.—The writer of the article in *Fraser's Magazine* has favored me with a copy of your most interesting letter to him; and from it I collect that you will be glad to learn that I have been negotiating for the insertion of articles by very able hands on your truly valuable work in the *Edinburgh Review* and the *North British*, both which are of wider circulation and more influence than that magazine.

The subject was discussed at the Statistical Section, of which I was president, of the British Association meeting in Belfast; and I then took occasion to call attention to your work.

It became evident, then, that the book had found powerful support and sympathy on English shores.

Sampson Low, who afterwards became Mrs. Stowe's English publisher, thus records its success in England:—

From April to December, 1852, twelve different editions (not reissues), at one shilling, were published; and within the twelve months of its first appearance no less than eighteen different houses in London were engaged in supplying the demand that had set in. The total number of editions was forty, varying from the fine illustrated edition of 15s. to the cheap popular one at 6d.

After carefully analyzing these editions and weighing probabilities with ascertained facts, I am able pretty confidently to say that the aggregate number circulated in Great Britain and her colonies exceeded one million and a half.

Meanwhile Mrs. Stowe received intelligence of its appearance in Sweden from the pen of the accomplished Frederika Bremer.

FROM FREDERIKA BREMER.

STOCKHOLM, Jan. 4, 1853.

My dearest Lady,— How shall I thank you for your most precious, most delightful gift? Could I have taken your hand many a time, while I was reading your work, and laid it on my beating heart, you would have known the joy, the happiness, the exultation it made me experience. It was the work I had long wished for, that I had anticipated, that I wished while in America to have been able to write, that I thought must come in America, as the uprising of the woman's and mother's heart on the question of slavery. I wondered that it had not come earlier. I wondered that the woman, the *mother*, could look at these things, and be silent,— that no cry of noble indignation and anger would escape her breast, and rend the air and pierce to the ear of humanity. I wondered; and, God be praised, it has come! The woman, the mother, has raised her voice out of the very soil of the New World in behalf of the wronged ones; and her voice vibrates still through two great continents, opening all hearts and minds to the light of truth.

How happy you are to have been able to do it so well, to have been able to win all hearts while you so daringly proclaimed strong and bitter truths, to charm while you instructed, to amuse while you defended the cause of the little ones, to touch the heart with the softest sorrow while you aroused all our boldest energies against the powers of despotism.

In Sweden your work has been translated and published as feuilleton in our largest daily paper, and has been read, enjoyed, and praised by men and women of all parties as I think no book here has been enjoyed and praised before.... I look upon you as a heroine who has won the battle. I think it is won! I have a deep, unwavering faith in the strong humanity of the American mind. It will ever work to throw out whatever is at war with that humanity; and, to make it fully alive, nothing is needed but a truly strong appeal of heart to heart, and that has been done in "Uncle Tom."

You have done it, dear, blessed, happy lady. Receive in these poor words my congratulations, my expressions of love and joy, my womanly pride in you as my sister in faith and love. God bless you forever!

FREDERIKA BREMER.

The author also received letters from France, announcing the enthusiastic reception of her work there. Madame George Sand, then one of the greatest powers of the literary world of France, thus introduced it to the public:—

To review a book the very morrow after its appearance, in the very journal where it has just been published, is doubtless contrary to usage: but in this case it is the most disinterested homage that can be rendered, since the immense success attained by this work at its publication does not need to be set forth.

This book is in all hands and in all journals. It has, and will have, editions in every form: people devour it, they cover it with tears. It is no longer permissible to those who can read not to have read it; and one mourns that there are so many souls condemned never to read it,—helots of poverty, slaves through ignorance, for whom society has been unable as yet to solve the double problem of uniting the food of the body with the food of the soul.

It is not, then, it cannot be, an officious and needless task to review this book of Mrs. Stowe. We repeat, it is a homage; and never did a generous and pure work merit one more tender and spontaneous. She is far from us: we do not know her who has penetrated our hearts with emotions so sad and yet so sweet. Let us thank her the more. Let the gentle voice of woman, the generous voice of man, with the voices of little children, so adorably glorified in this book, and those of the oppressed of this old world,—let them cross the seas, and hasten to say to her that she is esteemed and beloved. . . .

Mrs. Stowe is all instinct: it is the very reason that she appears to some not to have talent. Has she not talent? What is talent? Nothing, doubtless, compared to genius; but has she genius? I cannot say that she has talent, as one understands it in the world of letters; but she has genius, as humanity feels the need of genius,—the genius of goodness, not that of the man of letters, but of the saint. Yes, a saint! Thrice holy the soul which thus loves, blesses, and consoles the martyrs. Pure, penetrating, and profound the spirit which thus fathoms the recesses of the human soul. Noble, generous, and great the heart which embraces in her pity, in her love, an entire race, trodden down in blood and mire under the whip of ruffians and the maledictions of the impious.

Thus should it be, thus should we value things ourselves. We should feel that genius is *heart*, that power is *faith*, that talent is *sincerity*, and, finally, success is *sympathy*, since this book overcomes us, since it penetrates the breast, pervades the spirit, and fills us with a strange sentiment of mingled tenderness and admiration for a poor negro lacerated by blows, prostrate in the dust, there gasping on a miserable pallet, his last sigh exhaled towards God.

In matters of art there is but one rule, to paint and to move. And where shall we find creations more complete, types more vivid, situations more touching, more original than in "Uncle Tom,"—those beautiful relations of the slave with the child of his master, indicating a state of things unknown among us; the protest of the master himself against slavery during that innocent part of life when his soul belongs to God alone? Afterwards, when society takes him, the law chases away God, and interest deposes conscience. In coming to mature years, the infant ceases to be *man* and becomes master. God dies in his soul.

What hand has ever drawn a type more fascinating and admirable than St. Clare,—this exceptional nature, noble, generous, and loving, but too soft and too nonchalant to be really great? Is it not man himself, human nature itself, with its innate virtues, its good aspirations, and its deplorable failures?—this charming master who loves and is beloved, who thinks and reasons, but concludes nothing and does nothing! He spends in his day treasures of indulgence, of consideration, of goodness. He dies without having accomplished anything. The story of his precious life is all told in a word,—"to aspire and to regret." He has never learned to *will*. Alas! is there not something of this even among the bravest and best of men?

The life and death of a little child and a negro slave!—that is the whole book! This negro and this child are two saints of heaven! The affection that unites them, the respect of these two perfect ones for each other, is the only love story, the only passion of the drama. I know not what other genius but that of sanctity itself could shed over this affection and this situation a charm so powerful and so sustained. The child reading the Bible on the knees of the slave, dreaming over its mysteries and enjoying them in her exceptional maturity; now covering him with flowers like a doll, and now looking to him as something sacred, passing from tender playfulness to tender veneration, and then fading away through a mysterious malady which seems to be nothing but the wearing of pity in a nature too pure, too divine, to accept earthly law; dying finally in the arms of the slave, and calling him after her to the bosom of God,— all this is so new, so beautiful, that one asks one's self in thinking of it whether the success which has attended the work is after all equal to the height of the conception.

Children are the true heroes of Mrs. Stowe's works. Her soul, the most motherly that could be, has conceived of these little creatures in a halo of grace. George Shelby, the little Harry, the cousin of Eva, the regretted babe of the little wife of the Senator, and Topsy, the poor diabolic, excellent Topsy,— all the children that one sees, and even those that one does not see in this romance, but of whom one has only a few words from their desolate mothers, seem to us a world of little angels, white and black, where any mother may recognize some darling of her own, source of her joys and tears. In taking form in the spirit of Mrs. Stowe, these children, without ceasing to be children, assume ideal graces, and come at last to interest us more than the personages of an ordinary love story.

Women, too, are here judged and painted with a master hand,— not merely mothers who are sublime, but women who are not mothers either in heart or in fact, and whose infirmities are treated with indulgence or with rigor. By the side of the methodical Miss Ophelia, who ends by learning that duty is good for nothing without love, Marie St. Clare is a frightfully truthful portrait. One shudders in thinking that she exists, that she is everywhere, that each of us has met her and seen her, perhaps not far from us; for it is only necessary that this charming creature should have slaves of torture, and we should see her revealed complete through her vapors and her nervous complaints.

The saints also have their claw! it is that of the lion. She buries it deep in the conscience; and a little of burning indignation and of terrible sarcasm does not, after all, misbecome this Harriet Stowe, this woman so gentle, so humane, so religious, and full of evangelical unction. Ah! yes, she is a very good woman, but not what we derisively call "goody-good." Hers is a heart strong and courageous, which, in blessing the unhappy and applauding the faithful, tending the feeble and succoring the irresolute, does not hesitate to bind to the pillory the hardened tyrant, to show to the world his deformity.

She is, in the true spirit of the word, consecrated. Her fervent Christianity sings the praise of the martyr, but permits no man the right to perpetuate the wrong. She denounces that strange perversion of Scripture which tolerates the iniquity of the oppressor because it gives opportunity for the virtues of the victims. She calls on God himself, and threatens in his name: she shows us human law on one side and God on the other!

Let no one say that, because she exhorts to patient endurance of wrong, she justifies those who do the wrong. Read the beautiful page where George Harris, the white slave, embraces for the first time the shores of a free territory, and presses to his heart wife and child, who at last are *his own*. What a beautiful picture, that! What a large heart-throb! what a triumphant protest of the eternal and inalienable right of man to liberty!

Honor and respect to you, Mrs. Stowe! Some day your recompense, which is already recorded in heaven, will come also in this world.

GEORGE SAND.

NOHANT, Dec. 17, 1852.

Madame L. S. Belloc, also a well-known and distinguished writer, the translator of Miss Edgeworth's and of other English works into French, says: —

When the first translation of "Uncle Tom" was published in Paris, there was a general hallelujah for the author and for the cause. A few weeks after, M. Charpentier, one of our best publishers, called on me to ask a new translation. I objected that there were already so many it might prove a failure. He insisted, saying, "Il n'y aura jamais assez de lecteurs pour un tel livre"; and he particularly desired a special translation for his own collection, "Bibliothèque Charpentier," where it is catalogued, and where it continues now to sell daily. "La Case de l'Oncle Tom" was the fifth, if I recollect rightly; and a sixth illustrated edition appeared some months after. It was read by high and low, by grown persons and children. A great enthusiasm for the anti-slavery cause was the result. The popularity of the work in France was immense, and no doubt influenced the public mind in favor of the North during the War of Secession.

The next step in the history of "Uncle Tom" was a meeting at Stafford House, when Lord Shaftesbury recommended to the women of England the sending of an "affectionate and Christian address to the women of America."

This address, composed by Lord Shaftesbury, was taken in hand for signatures by energetic canvassers in all parts of England, and also among resident English on the Continent. The demand for signatures went as far forth as the city of Jerusalem. When all the signatures were collected, the document was forwarded to the care of Mrs. Stowe in America, with a letter from Lord Carlisle, recommending it to her, to be presented to the ladies of America in such way as she should see fit.

It was exhibited first at the Boston Anti-slavery Fair, and now remains in its solid oak case, a lasting monument of the feeling called forth by "Uncle Tom's Cabin."

It is in twenty-six thick folio volumes, solidly bound in morocco, with the American eagle on the back of each. On the first page of the first volume is the address, beautifully illuminated on vellum; and following are the subscribers' names, filling the volumes. There are 562,448 names of women of every rank of life, from the nearest in rank to the throne of England to the wives and daughters of the humblest artisan and laborer. Among all who signed, it is fair to presume there was not one who had not read the book, and did not, at the time of signing, feel a sympathy for the cause of the oppressed people whose wrongs formed its subject. The address, with its many signatures, was simply a relief to that impulsive desire to *do* something for the cause of the slave which the reading of "Uncle Tom's Cabin" appeared to inspire.

Of the wisdom of this step there have been many opinions. Nobody, however, can doubt that Lord Shaftesbury, who had spent a long life in labors to lift burdens from the working-classes of England, and who had redeemed from slavery and degradation English women and children in its mines and collieries, had thereby acquired a certain right to plead for the cause of the oppressed working-classes in all countries.

The address was received as a welcome word of cheer and encouragement by that small band of faithful workers who for years had stood in an unfashionable minority; but, so far as the feeling expressed in it was one of real Christian kindliness and humility, it was like a flower thrown into the white heat of a furnace. It added intensity, if that were possible, to that terrible conflict of forces which was destined never to cease till slavery was finally abolished.

It was a year after the publication of "Uncle Tom" that Mrs. Stowe visited England, and was received at Stafford House, there meeting all the best known and best worth knowing of the higher circles of England.

The Duchess of Sutherland, then in the height of that majestic beauty and that noble grace of manner which made her a fit representative of English womanhood, took pleasure in showing by this demonstration the sympathy of the better class of England with that small unpopular party in the United States who stood for the rights of the slave.

On this occasion she presented Mrs. Stowe with a solid gold bracelet made in the form of a slave's shackle, with the words, "We trust it is a memorial of a chain that is soon to be broken." On two of the links were inscribed the date of the abolition of the slave-trade, March 25, 1807, and of slavery in English territory, Aug. 1, 1834. On another link was recorded the number of signatures to the address of the women of England.

At the time such a speech and the hope it expressed seemed like a Utopian dream. Yet that bracelet has now inscribed upon its other links the steps of American emancipation: "Emancipation in District of Columbia, April 16, 1862"; "President's proclamation abolishing slavery in rebel States, Jan. 1. 1863"; "Maryland free, Oct. 13, 1864"; "Missouri free, Jan. 11, 1865." "Constitutional amendment" (forever abolishing slavery in the United States) is inscribed on the clasp of the bracelet. Thus what seemed the vaguest and most sentimental possibility has become a fact of history.

A series of addresses presented to Mrs. Stowe at this time by public meetings in different towns of England, Scotland, and Ireland, still remain among the literary curiosities relating to this book. The titles of these are somewhat curious: "Address from the Inhabitants of Berwick-upon-Tweed"; "Address from the Inhabitants of Dalkeith"; "Address from the Committee of the Glasgow Female Anti-slavery Society"; "Address from the Glasgow University Abstainers' Society"; "Address from a Public Meeting in Belfast, Ireland"; "Address from the Committee of the Ladies' Anti-slavery Society, Edinburgh"; "Address from the City of Leeds."

All these public meetings, addresses, and demonstrations of sympathy were, in their time and way, doubtless of perfect sincerity. But, when the United States went into a state of civil war, these demonstrations ceased.

But it is due to the brave true working-classes of England to say that in this conflict, whenever they thought the war was one of justice to the slave, they gave it their sympathy, and, even when it brought hardship and want to their very doors, refused to lend themselves to any popular movement which would go to crush the oppressed in America.

It is but justice also to the Duchess of Sutherland to say that, although by the time our war was initiated she had retired from her place as leader of society to the chamber of the invalid, yet her sympathies expressed in private letters ever remained true to the cause of freedom.

Her son-in-law, the Duke of Argyll, stood almost alone in the

House of Lords in defending the cause of the Northern States. It is, moreover, a significant fact that the Queen of England, in concurrence with Prince Albert, steadily resisted every attempt to enlist the warlike power of England against the Northern States.

But Almighty God had decreed the liberation of the African race; and, though presidents, senators, and representatives united in declaring that such were not *their* intentions, yet by great signs and mighty wonders was this nation compelled to listen to the voice that spoke from heaven,—"Let my people go."

In the darkest hour of the war, when defeat and discouragement had followed the Union armies, and all hearts were trembling with fear, Mrs. Stowe was in the Senate Chamber at Washington, and heard these words in the Message of President Lincoln:—

If this struggle is to be prolonged till there be not a house in the land where there is not one dead, till all the treasure amassed by the unpaid labor of the slave shall be wasted, till every drop of blood drawn by the lash shall be atoned by blood drawn by the sword, we can only bow and say, "Just and true are thy ways, thou King of Saints!"

Such words were a fit exponent of the Emancipation Proclamation, which, though sown in weakness, was soon raised in power, and received the evident benediction of God's providence.

"Uncle Tom's Cabin," in the fervor which conceived it, in the feeling which it inspired through the world, was only one of a line of ripples marking the commencement of mighty rapids, moving by forces which no human power could stay to an irresistible termination,—towards human freedom.

Now the war is over, slavery is a thing of the past: slave-pens, blood-hounds, slave-whips, and slave-coffles are only bad dreams of the night; and now the humane reader can afford to read "Uncle Tom's Cabin" without an expenditure of torture and tears.

For many years Mrs. Stowe has had a home in the Southern States, and she has yet to meet an intelligent Southern man or woman who does not acquiesce in the extinction of slavery, and feel that the life of free society is as great an advantage to the whites as to the blacks. Slavery has no mourners: there is nobody who wishes it back.

As to the influence of "Uncle Tom's Cabin" in various other lands of the earth whither it has been carried, intelligence has sometimes come to the author through the American missionaries and other sources. The three following letters are specimens.

In a letter from Miss Florence Nightingale, Oct. 26, 1856, she says: —

> I hope it may be some pleasure to you, dear madam, to hear that "Uncle Tom" was read by the sick and suffering in our Eastern military hospitals with intense interest. The interest in that book raised many a sufferer who, while he had not a grumble to bestow upon his own misfortunes, had many a thought of sorrow and just indignation for those which you brought before him. It is from the knowledge of such evils so brought home to so many honest hearts that they feel as well as know them that we confidently look to their removal in God's good time.

From the Armenian Convent in the Lagoon of Venice came a most beautiful Armenian translation of "Uncle Tom," with a letter from the principal translator.

Rev. Mr. Dwight thus wrote to Professor Stowe from Constantinople. Sept. 8, 1855: —

> "Uncle Tom's Cabin" in the Armenian language! Who would have thought it? I do not suppose your good wife, when she wrote that book, thought that she was going to missionate it among the sons of Haig in all their dispersions, following them along the banks of the Euphrates, sitting down with them in their towns and villages under the shade of hoary Ararat, travelling with them in their wanderings even to India and China. But I have it in my hands! in the Armenian of the present day, the same language in which I speak and think and dream. Now do not suppose this is any of *my* work or that of any missionary in the field. The translation has been made and book printed at Venice by a fraternity of Catholic Armenian Monks perched there on the island of St. Lazarus. It is in two volumes, neatly printed and with plates, I think translated from the French. It has not been in any respect materially altered, and, when it is so, not on account of religious sentiment. The account of the negro prayer and exhortation meetings is given in full, though the translator, not knowing what we mean by people's becoming Christians, took pains to insert at the bottom of the page that at these meetings of the negroes great effects were sometimes produced by the warm-hearted exhortations and prayers, and it often happened that heathen negroes embraced Christianity on the spot.
>
> One of your former scholars is now in my house studying Armenian, and the book which I advised him to take as the best for the language is this "Uncle Tom's Cabin."

Two or three other letters will conclude this *répertoire*.

86 Sauchiehall Street, Glasgow, April 16, 1853.

Mrs. H. B. Stowe:

Madam,— When persons of every rank in this country are almost vying with each other who is to show you most respect, you might perhaps think but little at being addressed by an exile, who offers you his heartfelt thanks, not for the mere gratification which the reading of "Uncle Tom's Cabin" afforded, but for the services you have rendered to the cause of humanity and of my country. You may be surprised at hearing of services rendered to my country (Poland); yet so it is. The unvarnished tale you published cannot fail to awaken the nobler feelings of man in every reader: it instils into their minds that fundamental Christian precept to love our fellow-beings; and it is by the spread of universal benevolence, and not by revolutions, that the cause of humanity is best promoted.

But you have done more than that, although you may be unconscious of it. A mother yourself, you have given comfort to other mothers. That foreign land where such pure benevolence as is taught in "Uncle Tom's Cabin" is honored cannot be a bad land; and, though letters from their children do not always reach Polish mothers, your book is accessible to them, and gives them the conviction that their offspring, far as they are from them, are still within reach of maternal feelings.

A still higher good you have done to many a man by the picture of the patient faith of Uncle Tom. It was the custom of some persons to sneer at faith, on the supposition that it implied a blind belief in all that the clergyman utters. Your book has helped to dispel that delusion, and faith begins to be seen by some as something nobler, as the firm conviction of the mind that higher aims are placed before man than the gratification of his appetites and desires; that it is, in short, that strength of mind which restrains him from doing evil when his bad passions lead him into temptation.

I cannot address you in the name of a body; but as an exile, as a man belonging to the family of mankind, I beg to offer you my thanks and my wishes. May God bless you, may your days be many and prosperous, and may the noble aim you proposed yourself in writing "Uncle Tom's Cabin" be speedily accomplished! If I may add a request, I would beg of you to pray now and then for the poor Polish mothers,— a good person's prayer may be acceptable.

I am, madam, your most obedient servant,

Charles F. Müller.

Waverley in Belmont, Oct. 26, 1860.

Mrs. H. B. Stowe:

Dear Madam,— I will not make any apology for the liberty which I take of writing to you, although I cannot claim any personal acquaintance. At any rate, I think you will excuse me. The facts which I wish to communicate will, I doubt not, be of sufficient interest to justify me.

It was my privilege, for such I shall esteem it on many accounts, to receive into my family and have under my especial care the young Brahmin whose recent visit to this country you must be acquainted with. I mean Joguth Chunder Gangooly, the first and only individual of his caste who has visited this country. Being highly intelligent and familiar with the social and intellectual character of the Hindoos of his native land, he gave me much information for which, in my scanty knowledge of that country, I was unprepared. Among other things he assured me that "Uncle Tom's Cabin" was a book as well known and as much read in Bengal among his own people as here in America, that it had been translated into their language, and been made a household book. He himself showed a familiar acquaintance with its contents, and assured me that it had done not a little to deepen the loathing of slavery in the minds of the Hindoos, and also to qualify their opinion of our country.

The facts which he gave me I believe to be substantially true, and deemed them such as would have an interest for the author of the book in question. Though I grieve for the wrong and shame which disgraces my country, I take a laudable pride in those productions of the true-hearted that appeal to the sympathies of all nations, and find a ready response in the heart of humanity. With high respect,

Yours truly,

JAMES THURSTON.

FROM MRS. LEONOWENS, FORMERLY ENGLISH GOVERNESS IN THE FAMILY OF THE KING OF SIAM.

48 INGLIS STREET, HALIFAX, N.S., Oct. 15, 1878.

MRS. H. B. STOWE:

Dear Madam,—The following is the fact, the result of the translation of "Uncle Tom's Cabin" into the Siamese language, by my friend, Sonn Klean, a lady of high rank at the court of Siam. I enclose it to you here, as related in one of my books.

"Among the ladies of the harem I knew one woman who more than all the rest helped to enrich my life, and to render fairer and more beautiful every lovely woman I have since chanced to meet. Her name translated itself, and no other name could have been more appropriate, into 'Hidden Perfume.' Her dark eyes were clearer and calmer, her full lips had a stronger expression of tenderness about them, and her brow, which was at times smooth and open, and at others contracted with pain, grew nobler and more beautiful as through her studies in English the purposes of her life strengthened and grew deeper and broader each day. Our daily lessons and translations from English into Siamese had become a part of her happiest hours. The first book we translated was 'Uncle Tom's Cabin,' and it soon became her favorite book. She would read it over and over again, though she knew all the characters by heart, and spoke of them as if she had known them all her life. On the 3d of January, 1867, she voluntarily liberated all her slaves,— men, women, and children,— one hundred and thirty in all, saying, 'I am wishful to be good like Harriet Beecher Stowe, and never again to buy human bodies, but only to let them go free once more.' Thenceforth, to express her entire sympathy and affection for the author of 'Uncle Tom's Cabin,' she always signed herself Harriet Beecher Stowe; and her sweet voice trembled with love and music whenever she spoke of the lovely American lady who had taught her as even Buddha had taught kings to respect the rights of her fellow-creatures."

I remain,

Yours very truly,

A. H. LEONOWENS.

The distinctively religious influence of "Uncle Tom's Cabin" has been not the least remarkable of the features of its history.

Among other testimonials in the possession of the writer is a Bible presented by an association of workingmen in England on the occasion of a lecture delivered to them on "Uncle Tom as an Illustration of Christianity."

The Christianity represented in the book was so far essential and unsectarian that alike in the Protestant, Catholic, and Greek Church it has found sympathetic readers.

It has, indeed, been reported that "Uncle Tom's Cabin" has been placed in the Index of the Roman Catholic Church; but of this there may be a doubt, as when the author was in Rome she saw it in the hands of the common people, and no less in those of some of the highest officials in the Vatican, and heard from them in conversation expressions of warm sympathy with the purport of the work.

In France it was the testimony of colporteurs that the enthusiasm for the work awakened a demand for the Bible of Uncle Tom, and led to a sale of the Scriptures.

The accomplished translator of M. Charpentier's edition said to the author that, by the researches necessary to translate correctly the numerous citations of Scripture in the work, she had been led to a most intimate knowledge of the sacred writings in French.

The witty scholar and *littérateur*, Heinrich Heine, speaking of his return to the Bible and its sources of consolation in the last years of his life, uses this language :—

The reawakening of my religious feelings I owe to that holy book the Bible. Astonishing! that after I have whirled about all my life over all the dance-floors of philosophy, and yielded myself to all the orgies of the intellect, and paid my addresses to all possible systems, without satisfaction, like Messalina after a licentious night, I now find myself on the same stand-point where poor Uncle Tom stands,— on that of the Bible. I kneel down by my black brother in the same prayer. What a humiliation! With all my science I have come no farther than the poor ignorant negro, who has scarce learned to spell. Poor Tom, indeed, seems to have seen deeper things in the holy book than I. . . . Tom, perhaps, understands them better than I, because more flogging occurs in them,— that is to say, those ceaseless blows of the whip which have æsthetically disgusted me in reading the Gospels and Acts. But a poor negro slave reads with his back, and understands better than we do. But I, who used to make citations from Homer, now begin to quote the Bible as Uncle Tom does.—*Vermischte Schriften*, p. 77.

The acute German in these words has touched the vital point in the catholic religious spirit of the book. "Uncle Tom's Cabin" shows that, under circumstances of utter desolation and despair, the religion of Christ can enable the poorest and most ignorant human being, not merely to submit, but to triumph,— that the soul of the lowest and weakest, by its aid, can become strong in superhuman virtue, and rise above every threat and terror and danger in a sublime assurance of an ever-present love and an immortal life.

It is in this point of view that its wide circulation through all the languages of the earth may justly be a source of devout satisfaction.

Life has sorrows so hopeless, so dreadful,— so many drag through weary, joyless lives,— that a story which carries such a message as this can never cease to be a comforter.

The message is from Christ the Consoler, and too blessed is any one allowed by him to carry it to the sorrowful children of men.

The story of "Uncle Tom's Cabin" given in the present leaflet was written by Mrs. Stowe in 1878 as an introduction for a new edition of the work. With this story of the work in the Riverside edition is included another story of it by Charles Dudley Warner, together with a biographical sketch of Mrs. Stowe; and in the appendix to the second volume is reprinted the "Key to Uncle Tom's Cabin," prepared by Mrs. Stowe in 1853, "presenting the original facts and documents upon which the story is founded, together with corroborative statements verifying the truth of the work." There is also given in this appendix a bibliographical account of "Uncle Tom's Cabin," including lists of the various English editions, translations, and works relating to the story, critical notices, etc.

"Dred," Mrs. Stowe's second anti-slavery novel, was published in 1856, and had a great success, a hundred thousand copies being sold in England in a month. Harriet Martineau thought it "far superior to 'Uncle Tom'"; but that has not been the general verdict. In the appendix to the second volume of "Dred," in the Riverside edition, are reprinted various anti-slavery tales and papers by Mrs. Stowe, including her account of Sojourner Truth. Among the men treated by her in her "Men of our Times" are several of the anti-slavery leaders,— Garrison, Sumner, Wilson, Greeley, Beecher, Phillips, Frederick Douglass, Chase, Andrew, and Lincoln.

There is a good biography of Mrs. Stowe by her son, Rev. Charles Edward Stowe, in which her letters are largely drawn upon.

PUBLISHED BY

THE DIRECTORS OF THE OLD SOUTH WORK,
Old South Meeting-house, Boston, Mass.

Old South Leaflets.

No. 83.

The Crime against Kansas.

By CHARLES SUMNER.

FROM HIS SPEECH IN THE SENATE, MAY 19, 1856.

I UNDERTAKE, in the first place, to expose the CRIME AGAINST KANSAS, in origin and extent. Logically, this is the beginning of the argument. I say Crime, and deliberately adopt this strongest term, as better than any other denoting the consummate transgression. I would go further if language could further go. It is the *Crime of Crimes*,— surpassing far the old *Crimen Majestatis*, pursued with vengeance by the laws of Rome, and containing all other crimes, as the greater contains the less. I do not go too far when I call it the *Crime against Nature*, from which the soul recoils, and which language refuses to describe. To lay bare this enormity I now proceed. The whole subject has become a twice-told tale, and its renewed recital will be a renewal of sorrow and shame; but I shall not hesitate. The occasion requires it from the beginning.

It is well remarked by a distinguished historian of our country that, "at the Ithuriel touch of the Missouri discussion, the Slave Interest, hitherto hardly recognized as a distinct element in our system, started up portentous and dilated,"* with threats and assumptions which are the origin of our existing national politics. This was in 1820. The debate ended with the admission of Missouri as a Slaveholding State, and the prohibition of Slavery in all the remaining territory west of the Mississippi and north of 36° 30′, leaving the condition of other territory south of this line, or subsequently acquired, untouched by the arrangement. Here was a solemn act of

* Hildreth, History of the United States, vol. vi. p. 713.

legislation, called at the time compromise, covenant, compact, first brought forward in this body by a slaveholder, vindicated in debate by slaveholders, finally sanctioned by slaveholding votes,— also upheld at the time by the essential approbation of a slaveholding President, James Monroe, and his Cabinet, of whom a majority were slaveholders, including Mr. Calhoun himself; and this compromise was made the condition of the admission of Missouri, without which that State could not have been received into the Union. The bargain was simple, and was applicable, of course, only to the territory named. Leaving all other territory to await the judgment of another generation, the South said to the North, Conquer your prejudices so far as to admit Missouri as a slave State, and, in consideration of this much coveted boon, slavery shall be prohibited "forever" (mark here the word "*forever*")* in all the remaining Louisiana Territory above 36° 30'; and the North yielded.

In total disregard of history, the President, in his annual message, tells us that this compromise "was *reluctantly* acquiesced in by Southern States." Just the contrary is true. It was the work of slaveholders, and by their concurring votes was crowded upon a reluctant North. It was hailed by slaveholders as a victory. Charles Pinckney, of South Carolina, in an oft-quoted letter, written at eight o'clock on the night of its passage, says, "It is considered here by the slaveholding States as a great triumph." † At the North it was accepted as a defeat, and the friends of freedom everywhere throughout the country bowed their heads with mortification. Little did they know the completeness of their disaster. Little did they dream that the prohibition of slavery in the territory, which was stipulated as the price of their fatal capitulation, would also, at the very moment of its maturity, be wrested from them.

Time passed, and it became necessary to provide for this territory an organized government. Suddenly, without notice in the public press or the prayer of a single petition or one word of open recommendation from the President, after an acquiescence of thirty-four years, and the irreclaimable posses-

---

* Referring to this provision of the Missouri Bill, Mr. Niles italicizes "*forever*," thus showing his construction of the word. Niles's *Weekly Register*, March 11, 1820.

† This letter, which the *Columbian Centinel*, of Boston, April 1, 1820, properly styles "tell-tale," was addressed to the editor of the Charleston *City Gazette*, under date of March 2, 1820.

sion by the South of its special share under this compromise, in breach of every obligation of honor, compact, and good neighborhood, and in contemptuous disregard of the outgushing sentiments of an aroused North, this time-honored prohibition — in itself a landmark of Freedom — was overturned, and the vast region now known as Kansas and Nebraska was open to slavery. It is natural that a measure thus repugnant in character should be pressed by arguments mutually repugnant. It was urged on two principal reasons, so opposite and inconsistent as to fight with each other: one being that, by the repeal of the Prohibition, the Territory would be left open to the entry of slaveholders with their slaves, without hindrance; and the other being that the people would be left absolutely free to determine the question for themselves, and to prohibit the entry of slaveholders with their slaves, if they should think best. With some the apology was the alleged rights of slaveholders; with others it was the alleged rights of the people. With some it was openly the extension of slavery; and with others it was openly the establishment of freedom, under the guise of popular sovereignty. The measure, thus upheld in defiance of reason, was carried through Congress in defiance of all securities of legislation. These things I mention that you may see in what foulness the present crime was engendered.

It was carried, *first*, by *whipping in*, through Executive influence and patronage, men who acted against their own declared judgment and the known will of their constituents; *secondly*, by *thrusting out of place*, both in the Senate and House of Representatives, important business, long pending, and usurping its room; *thirdly*, by *trampling under foot* the rules of the House of Representatives, always before the safeguard of the minority; and, *fourthly*, by *driving it to a close* during the very session in which it originated, so that it might not be arrested by the indignant voice of the People. Such are some of the means by which this snap judgment was obtained. If the clear will of the people had not been disregarded, it could not have passed. If the government had not nefariously interposed, it could not have passed. If it had been left to its natural place in the order of business, it could not have passed. If the rules of the House and the rights of the minority had not been violated, it could not have passed. If it had been allowed to go over to another Congress, when the people might be heard, it would have been ended; and then the Crime we now deplore would have been without its first seminal life.

Mr. President, I mean to keep absolutely within the limits of parliamentary propriety. I make no personal imputations, but only with frankness, such as belongs to the occasion and my own character, describe a great historical act, now enrolled in the Capitol. Sir, the Nebraska Bill was in every respect a swindle. It was a swindle of the North by the South. On the part of those who had already completely enjoyed their share of the Missouri Compromise, it was a swindle of those whose share was yet absolutely untouched; and the plea of unconstitutionality set up — like the plea of usury after the borrowed money has been enjoyed,— did not make it less a swindle. Urged as a bill of peace, it was a swindle of the whole country. Urged as opening the doors to slave-masters with their slaves, it was a swindle of Popular Sovereignty in its asserted doctrine. Urged as sanctioning Popular Sovereignty, it was a swindle of slave-masters in their asserted rights. It was a swindle of a broad territory, thus cheated of protection against slavery. It was a swindle of a great cause, early espoused by Washington, Franklin, and Jefferson, surrounded by the best fathers of the Republic. Sir, it was a swindle of God-given, inalienable rights. Turn it over, look at it on all sides, and it is everywhere a swindle; and, if the word I now employ has not the authority of classical usage, it has, on this occasion, the indubitable authority of fitness. No other word will adequately express the mingled meanness and wickedness of the cheat.

Its character is still further apparent in the general structure of the bill. Amidst overflowing professions of regard for the sovereignty of the people in the Territory, they are despoiled of every essential privilege of sovereignty. They are not allowed to choose governor, secretary, chief justice, associate justices, attorney, or marshal,— all of whom are sent from Washington; nor are they allowed to regulate the salaries of any of these functionaries, or the daily allowance of the legislative body, or even the pay of the clerks and door-keepers: but they are left free to adopt slavery. And this is nicknamed Popular Sovereignty! Time does not allow, nor does the occasion require, that I should stop to dwell on this transparent device to cover a transcendent wrong. Suffice it to say that slavery is in itself an arrogant denial of human rights, and by no human reason can the power to establish such a wrong be placed among the attributes of any just sovereignty. In refusing it such a place, I do not deny popular rights, but uphold them; I do not restrain popular rights, but extend them. And, sir, to this conclusion you must yet come, unless deaf, not only to the admonitions of political justice, but also to the genius of our Constitution, under which, when properly interpreted, no valid claim for slavery can be set up anywhere in the national territory. The Senator from Michigan [Mr. CASS] may say, in response to the Senator from Mississippi [Mr. BROWN], that slavery cannot go into the Territory, under the Constitution, without legislative introduction; and permit me to add, in response to both, that slavery cannot go there at all. *Nothing can come out of nothing;* and there is absolutely nothing in the Constitution out of which slavery can be derived, while there are provisions which, when properly interpreted, make its existence anywhere within the exclusive national jurisdiction impossible.

The offensive provision in the bill is in its form a legislative anomaly, utterly wanting the natural directness and simplicity of an honest transaction. It does not undertake openly to repeal the old prohibition of slavery, but seems to mince the matter, as if conscious of the swindle. It says that this prohibition, "being inconsistent with the principle of non-intervention by Congress with slavery in the States and Territories, as recognized by the legislation of 1850, commonly called the Compromise Measures, is hereby declared inoperative and void." Thus, with insidious ostentation, is it pretended that an act violating the greatest compromise of our legislative history, and loosening the foundations of all compromise, is derived out of a compromise. Then follows in the bill the further declaration, entirely without precedent, which has been aptly called "a stump speech in its belly," namely, "it being the true intent and meaning of this act not to legislate slavery into any Territory or State nor to exclude it therefrom, but to leave the people thereof perfectly free to form and regulate their domestic institutions in their own way, subject only to the Constitution of the United States."* Here are smooth words, such as belong to a cunning tongue enlisted in a bad cause. But, whatever may have been their various hidden

---

* Act to organize the Territories of Nebraska and Kansas, Sect. 14, Statutes at Large, vol. x. p. 283.

meanings, this at least is evident, that, by their effect, the Congressional prohibition of slavery, which had always been regarded as a sevenfold shield, covering the whole Louisiana Territory north of 36° 30', is now removed, while a principle is declared which renders the supplementary prohibition of slavery in Minnesota, Oregon, and Washington "inoperative and void," and thus opens to slavery all these vast regions, now the rude cradles of mighty States. Here you see the magnitude of the mischief contemplated. But my purpose is with the crime against Kansas, and I shall not stop to expose the conspiracy beyond.

Mr. President, men are wisely presumed to intend the natural consequences of their conduct, and to seek what their acts seem to promote. Now the Nebraska Bill, on its very face, openly clears the way for slavery, and it is not wrong to presume that its originators intended the natural consequences of such an act, and sought in this way to extend slavery. Of course they did. And this is the first stage in the Crime against Kansas.

This was speedily followed by other developments. It was soon whispered that Kansas must be a slave State. In conformity with this barefaced scheme was the government of this unhappy Territory organized in all its departments; and thus did the President, by whose complicity the prohibition of slavery was overthrown, lend himself to a new complicity,— giving to the conspirators a lease of connivance, amounting even to copartnership. The governor, secretary, chief justice, associate justices, attorney, and marshal, with a whole caucus of other stipendiaries, nominated by the President and confirmed by the Senate, are all commended as friendly to slavery. No man with the sentiments of Washington or Jefferson or Franklin finds favor; nor is it too much to say that, had these great patriots once more come among us, not one of them, with his recorded, unretracted opinions on slavery, could be nominated by the President or confirmed by the Senate for any post in that Territory. With such auspices the conspiracy proceeded. Even in advance of the Nebraska Bill, secret societies were organized in Missouri, ostensibly to protect her institutions, and afterwards, under the name of "Self-defensive Associations" and "Blue Lodges," these were multiplied throughout the western counties of that State, *before any counter-movement from the North*. It was confidently anticipated, that, by the activity of these societies, and the interest of slaveholders everywhere, with the advantage derived from the neighborhood of Missouri and the influence of the Territorial Government, slavery might be introduced into Kansas, quietly, but surely, without arousing conflict,— that the crocodile egg might be stealthily dropped in the sunburnt soil, there to be hatched, unobserved until it sent forth its reptile monster.

But the conspiracy was unexpectedly balked. The debate, which convulsed Congress, stirred the whole country. From all sides attention was directed upon Kansas, which at once became the favorite goal of emigration. The bill loudly declares that its object is "to leave the people perfectly free to form and regulate their domestic institutions in their own way," and its supporters everywhere challenge the determination of the question between freedom and slavery by a competition of emigration. Thus, while opening the Territory to slavery, the bill also opens it to emigrants from every quarter, who may by votes redress the wrong. The populous North, stung by sense of outrage and inspired by a noble cause, are pouring into the debatable land, and promise soon to establish a supremacy of numbers there, involving, of course, a just supremacy of Freedom.

Then was conceived the consummation of the crime against Kansas. What could not be accomplished peaceably was to be accomplished forcibly. The reptile monster, that could not be quietly and securely hatched there, is to be pushed full-grown into the Territory. All efforts are now applied to the dismal work of forcing slavery upon free soil. In flagrant derogation of the very popular sovereignty whose name helped to impose this bill upon the country, the atrocious object is distinctly avowed. And the avowal is followed by the act. Slavery is forcibly introduced into Kansas, and placed under formal safeguard of pretended law. How this is done belongs to the argument.

In depicting this consummation, the simplest outline, without one word of color, will be best. Whether regarded in mass or detail, in origin or result, it is all blackness, illumined by nothing from itself, but only by the heroism of the undaunted men and women whom it environed. A plain statement of facts is a picture of direst truth, which faithful History will preserve in its darkest gallery. In the foreground all will recognize a familiar character, in himself connecting link between President and border ruffian,— less conspicuous for ability than for the exalted place he has occupied,— who once sat in the seat where you now sit, sir,— where once sat John Adams and Thomas Jefferson,— also, where once sat Aaron Burr. I need not add the name of David R. Atchison.* You do not forget that, at the session of Congress immediately succeeding the Nebraska Bill, he came tardily to his duty here, and then, after a short time, disappeared. The secret was long since disclosed.. Like Catiline, he stalked into this Chamber, reeking with conspiracy,— *immo etiam in Senatum venit,*— and then, like Catiline, he skulked away,— *abiit, excessit, evasit, erupit,*— to join and provoke the conspirators, who at a distance awaited their congenial chief. Under the influence of his malign presence the crime ripened to its fatal fruits, while the similitude with Catiline is again renewed in the sympathy, not even concealed, which he finds in the very Senate itself, where, beyond even the Roman example, a Senator has not hesitated to appear as his open compurgator.

And now, as I proceed to show the way in which this Territory was overrun and finally subjugated to slavery, I desire to remove, in advance, all question with regard to the authority on which I rely. The evidence is secondary, but it is the best which, in the nature of the case, can be had; and it is not less clear, direct, and peremptory than any by which we are assured of the campaigns in the Crimea or the fall of Sebastopol. In its manifold mass, I confidently assert that it is such a body of evidence as the human mind is not able to resist. It is found in the concurring reports of the public press, in the letters of correspondents, in the testimony of travellers, and in the unaffected story to which I have listened from leading citizens, who, during this winter, have "come flocking" here from that distant Territory. It breaks forth in the irrepressible outcry reaching us from Kansas, whose truthful tones leave no ground of mistake. It addresses us in formal complaint, instinct with the indignation of a people determined to be free, and unimpeachable as the declarations of a murdered man on his dying-bed against his murderer. And let me add that all this testimony finds echo in the very statute book of the conspirators, and also in language dropped from the President of the United States.

* Senator from Missouri at Washington from 1843 to 1855, and for several sessions President *pro tempore* of the Senate.

I begin with an admission from the President himself, in whose sight the people of Kansas have little favor. After arraigning the innocent emigrants from the North, he is constrained to declare that their conduct is "far from justifying the *illegal* and *reprehensible* counter-movements which ensued."* By the reluctant admission of the Chief Magistrate, then, there was a counter-movement at once "*illegal* and *reprehensible.*" I thank thee, President, for teaching me these words; and I now put them in the front of this exposition, as in themselves a confession. Sir, this "illegal and reprehensible counter-movement" is none other than the dreadful Crime — under an apologetic *alias* — by which, through successive invasions, slavery is forcibly planted in this Territory.

Next to this Presidential admission must be placed details of invasions, which I now present as not only "illegal and reprehensible," but also unquestionable evidence of the resulting crime.

The violence, for some time threatened, broke forth on the 29th of November, 1854, at the first election of a Delegate to Congress, when companies from Missouri, amounting to upwards of one thousand, crossed into Kansas, and with force and arms proceeded to vote for General Whitfield, the candidate of slavery. An eye-witness, General Pomeroy,† of superior intelligence and perfect integrity, thus describes this scene: —

> The first ballot-box that was opened upon our virgin soil was closed to us by overpowering numbers and impending force. So bold and reckless were our invaders that they cared not to conceal their attack. They came upon us, not in the guise of voters, to steal away our franchise, but boldly and openly, to snatch it with a strong hand. They came directly from their own homes, and in compact and organized bands, with arms in hand and provisions for the expedition, marched to our polls, and, when their work was done, returned whence they came.

Here was an outrage at which the coolest blood of patriotism boils. Though, for various reasons unnecessary to develop, the busy settlers allowed the election to pass uncontested, still the means employed were none the less "illegal and reprehensible."

This infliction was a significant prelude to the grand invasion

---

* Message relative to the Affairs in the Territory of Kansas, Jan. 24, 1856, Executive Documents, 34th Cong., 1st Sess., No. 28, p. 4.

† Hon. S. C. Pomeroy, afterwards for many years Senator of Kansas at Washington.

of the 30th of March, 1855, at the election of the first Territorial legislature under the organic law, when an armed multitude from Missouri entered the Territory in larger numbers than General Taylor commanded at Buena Vista or than General Jackson had within his lines at New Orleans,— much larger than our fathers rallied on Bunker Hill. On they came as "an army with banners," organized in companies, with officers, munitions, tents, and provisions, as though marching upon a foreign foe, and breathing loud-mouthed threats that they would carry their purpose, if need were, by the bowie-knife and revolver. Among them, according to his own confession, was David R. Atchison, belted with the vulgar arms of his vulgar comrades. Arrived at their several destinations on the night before the election, the invaders pitched their tents, placed their sentries, and waited for the coming day. The same trustworthy eye-witness whom I have already quoted says of one locality:—

> Baggage-wagons were there, with arms and ammunition enough for a protracted fight, and among them two brass field-pieces, ready charged. They came with drums beating and flags flying, and their leaders were of the most prominent and conspicuous men of their State.

Of another locality he says:—

> The invaders came together in one armed and organized body, with trains of fifty wagons, besides horsemen, and the night before election pitched their camp in the vicinity of the polls; and having appointed their own judges in place of those who, from intimidation or otherwise, failed to attend, they voted without any proof of residence.

With this force they were able, on the succeeding day, in some places, to intimidate the judges of elections, in others to substitute judges of their own appointment, in others to wrest the ballot-boxes from their rightful possessors, and everywhere to exercise a complete control of the election, and thus, by preternatural audacity of usurpation, impose a legislature upon the free people of Kansas. Thus was conquered the Sebastopol of that Territory!

It was not enough to secure the legislature. The election of a member of Congress recurred on the 1st of October, 1855; and the same foreigners, who had learned their strength, again manifested it. Another invasion, in controlling numbers, came from Missouri, and once more forcibly exercised the electoral franchise in Kansas.

At last, in the latter days of November, 1855, a storm, long gathering, burst upon the heads of the devoted people. The ballot-boxes had been violated and a legislature installed which proceeded to carry out the conspiracy of the invaders; but the good people of the Territory, born to freedom and educated as American citizens, showed no signs of submission. Slavery, though recognized by pretended law, was in many places practically an outlaw. To the lawless borderers this was hard to bear; and, like the heathen of old, they raged particularly against the town of Lawrence, already known by the firmness of its principles and the character of its citizens as citadel of the good cause. On this account they threatened, in their peculiar language, to "wipe it out." Soon the hostile power was gathered for this purpose. The wickedness of this invasion was enhanced by the way in which it began. A citizen of Kansas by the name of Dow was murdered by a partisan of slavery in the name of "law and order." Such an outrage naturally aroused indignation and provoked threats. The professors of "law and order" allowed the murderer to escape, and, still further to illustrate the irony of the name they assumed, seized the friend of the murdered man, whose few neighbors soon rallied for his rescue. This transaction, though totally disregarded in its chief front of wickedness, became the excuse for unprecedented excitement. The weak Governor,* with no faculty higher than servility to slavery,— whom the President, in official delinquency, had appointed to a trust worthy only of a well-balanced character,— was frightened from his propriety. By proclamation he invoked the Territory. By telegraph he invoked the President. The Territory would not respond to his senseless appeal. The President was false. But the proclamation was circulated throughout the border counties of Missouri; and Platte, Clay, Carroll, Saline, Howard, and Jackson, each of them contributed a volunteer company, recruited from the roadsides, and armed with weapons which chance afforded, known as "the shot-gun militia,"— with a Missouri officer as commissary general, dispensing rations, and another Missouri officer as general in chief; with two wagon-loads of rifles belonging to Missouri, drawn by six mules, from its arsenal at Jefferson City; with seven pieces of cannon belonging to the United States from its arsenal at Liberty; and this formidable force amounting to at least

* Hon. Wilson Shannon.

1,800 men, terrible with threats, oaths, and whiskey, crossed the borders, and encamped in larger part on the Wakarusa over against the doomed town of Lawrence, now threatened with destruction. With these invaders was the Governor, who by this act levied war upon the people he was sent to protect. In camp with him was the original Catiline of the conspiracy, while by his side were the docile Chief Justice and the docile judges. But this is not the first instance in which an unjust governor has found tools where he ought to have found justice. In the great impeachment of Warren Hastings the British orator by whom it was conducted exclaims, in words strictly applicable to the misdeed I here denounce: "Had he not the Chief Justice, the tamed and domesticated Chief Justice, who waited on him like a familiar spirit?"* Thus was this invasion countenanced by those who should have stood in the breach against it. For more than a week it continued, while deadly conflict was imminent. I do not dwell on the heroism by which it was encountered or the mean retreat to which it was compelled; for that is not necessary in exhibiting the crime which you are to judge. But I cannot forbear to add other features furnished in a letter written at the time by a clergyman, who saw and was part of what he describes:—

Our citizens have been shot at *and in two instances murdered*, our houses invaded, hay-ricks burnt, corn and other provisions plundered, cattle driven off, all communication cut off between us and the States, wagons on the way to us with provisions stopped and plundered, and the drivers taken prisoners, and we in hourly expectation of an attack. *Nearly every man has been in arms in the village.* Fortifications have been thrown up, by incessant labor night and day. The sound of the drum and the tramp of armed men resounded through our streets, *families fleeing with their household goods for safety.* Day before yesterday the report of cannon was heard at our house, from the direction of Lecompton. Last Thursday one of our neighbors,—one of the most peaceful and excellent of men, from Ohio,—on his way home, was set upon by a gang of twelve men on horseback, and shot down. Over eight hundred men are gathered under arms at Lawrence. As yet no act of violence has been perpetrated by those on our side. *No blood of retaliation stains our hands. We stand, and are ready to act, purely in defence of our homes and lives.*

The catalogue is not yet complete. On the 15th of December, when the people assembled to vote on the Constitution submitted for adoption, only a few days after the Treaty of

---

* Burke, Speech in the Impeachment of Warren Hastings, Feb. 16, 1788, Works (London, 1822), vol. xiii. p. 202.

Peace between the governor on the one side and the town of Lawrence on the other, another and fifth irruption was made. But I leave all this untold. Enough of these details has been given.

Five several times and more have these invaders entered Kansas in armed array, and thus five several times and more have they trampled upon the organic law of the Territory. These extraordinary expeditions are simply the extraordinary witnesses to successive, uninterrupted violence. They stand out conspicuous, but not alone. The spirit of evil, in which they had their origin, is wakeful and incessant. From the beginning it hung upon the skirts of this interesting Territory, harrowing its peace, disturbing its prosperity, and keeping its inhabitants under the painful alarms of war. All security of person, property, and labor, was overthrown; and, when I urge this incontrovertible fact, I set forth a wrong which is small only by the side of the giant wrong for the consummation of which all this is done. Sir, what is man, what is government, without security, in the absence of which nor man nor government can proceed in development or enjoy the fruits of existence? Without security civilization is cramped and dwarfed. Without security there is no true freedom. Nor shall I say too much, when I declare that security, guarded of course by its parent freedom, is the true end and aim of government. Of this indispensable boon the people of Kansas are despoiled, — absolutely, totally. All this is aggravated by the nature of their pursuits, rendering them peculiarly sensitive to interruption, and at the same time attesting their innocence. They are for the most part engaged in the cultivation of the soil, which from time immemorial has been the sweet employment of undisturbed industry. Contented in the returns of bounteous nature and the shade of his own trees, the husbandman is not aggressive. Accustomed to produce, and not to destroy, he is essentially peaceful, unless his home is invaded, when his arm derives vigor from the soil he treads, and his soul inspiration from the heavens beneath whose canopy he daily toils. Such are the people of Kansas, whose security has been overthrown. Scenes from which Civilization averts her countenance are part of their daily life. Border incursions, which in barbarous ages or barbarous lands fretted and harried an exposed people, are here renewed, with this peculiarity, that our border robbers do not simply levy blackmail and drive off a few cattle, like those who acted under the inspiration of the Douglas of other days,— they do not seize a few persons, and sweep them away into captivity, like the African slave-traders, whom we brand as pirates,— but they commit a succession of deeds in which border sorrows and African wrongs are revived together on American soil, while, for the time being, all protection is annulled, and the whole Territory is enslaved.

Private griefs mingle their poignancy with public wrongs. I do not dwell on the anxieties of families exposed to sudden assault, and lying down to rest with the alarms of war ringing in the ears, not knowing that another day may be spared to them. Throughout this bitter winter, with the thermometer at thirty degrees below zero, the citizens of Lawrence were constrained to sleep under arms, with sentinels pacing constant watch against surprise. Our souls are wrung by individual instances. In vain do we condemn the cruelties of another age, the refinements of torture to which men were doomed, the rack and thumb-screw of the Inquisition, the last agonies of the regicide Ravaillac,

"Luke's iron crown and Damien's bed of steel";

for kindred outrages disgrace these borders. Murder stalks, Assassination skulks in the tall grass of the prairie, and the vindictiveness of man assumes unwonted forms. A preacher of the gospel has been ridden on a rail, then thrown into the Missouri, fastened to a log, and left to drift down its muddy, tortuous current. And lately we have the tidings of that enormity without precedent, a deed without a name, where a candidate for the legislature was most brutally gashed with knives and hatchets, and then, after weltering in blood on the snow-clad earth, trundled along with gaping wounds to fall dead before the face of his wife. It is common to drop a tear of sympathy over the sorrows of our early fathers, exposed to the stealthy assault of the savage foe; and an eminent American artist* has pictured this scene in a marble group on the front of the National Capitol, where the uplifted tomahawk is arrested by the strong arm and generous countenance of the pioneer, whose wife and children find shelter at his feet. But now the tear must be dropped over the sorrows of fellow-

---

* Horatio Greenough, the earliest of our sculptors, and also excellent with his pen.

citizens building a new State in Kansas, and exposed to the perpetual assault of murderous robbers from Missouri. Hirelings picked from the drunken spew and vomit of an uneasy civilization, having the form of men,—

> "Ay, in the catalogue ye go for men;
> As hounds and greyhounds, mongrels, spaniels, curs,
> Shoughs, water-rugs, and demi-wolves are clept
> All by the name of dogs,"—

leashed together by secret signs and lodges, renew the incredible atrocities of the Assassins and the Thugs, showing the blind submission of the Assassins to the Old Man of the Mountain in robbing Christians on the road to Jerusalem, and the heartlessness of the Thugs, who, avowing that murder is their religion, waylay travellers on the great road from Agra to Delhi,— with the more deadly bowie-knife for the dagger of the Assassin and the more deadly revolver for the noose of the Thug.

In these invasions, with the entire subversion of all security in this Territory, the plunder of the ballot-box, and the pollution of the electoral franchise, I show simply the process in unprecedented crime. If that be the best government where injury to a single citizen is resented as injury to the whole State, what must be the character of a government which leaves a whole community of citizens thus exposed? In the outrage upon the ballot-box, even without the illicit fruits which I shall soon exhibit, there is a peculiar crime of the deepest dye, though subordinate to the final crime, which should be promptly avenged. In other lands, where royalty is upheld, it is a special offence to rob the crown jewels, which are emblems of that sovereignty before which the loyal subject bows, and it is treason to be found in adultery with the queen, for in this way may a false heir be imposed upon the State; but in our Republic the ballot-box is the single priceless jewel of that sovereignty which we respect, and the electoral franchise, where are born the rulers of a free people, is the royal bed we are to guard against pollution. In this plain presentment, whether as regards security or as regards elections, there is enough, without proceeding further, to justify the intervention of Congress, promptly and completely, to throw over this oppressed people the impenetrable shield of the Constitution and laws. But the half is not yet told.

As every point in a wide-spread horizon radiates from a common centre, so everything said or done in this vast circle of crime radiates from the *One Idea* that Kansas, at all hazards, must be made a slave State. In all the manifold wickednesses that occur and in every successive invasion, this *One Idea* is ever present, as Satanic tempter, motive power, *causing cause*. Talk of "one idea"! Here it is with a vengeance!

To accomplish this result, three things are attempted: *first*, by outrage of all kinds, to drive the friends of freedom out of the Territory; *secondly*, to deter others from coming; and, *thirdly*, to obtain complete control of the government. The process of driving out, and also of deterring, has failed. On the contrary, the friends of freedom there have become more fixed in resolve to stay and fight the battle which they never sought, but from which they disdain to retreat, while the friends of freedom elsewhere are more aroused to the duty of timely succor by men and munitions of just self-defence.

While defeated in the first two processes, the conspirators succeeded in the last. By the violence already portrayed at the election of the 30th of March, when the polls were occupied by armed hordes from Missouri, they imposed a legislature upon the Territory, and thus, under the iron mask of law, established a Usurpation not less complete than any in history. That this was done I proceed to prove. Here is the evidence.

1. Only in this way can this extraordinary expedition be adequately explained. In the words of Molière, once employed by John Quincy Adams in the other House, "*Que diable allaient-ils faire dans cette galère?*" What did they go into the Territory for? If their purposes were peaceful, as has been suggested, why cannons, arms, flags, numbers, and all this violence? As simple citizens, proceeding to the honest exercise of the electoral franchise, they might go with nothing more than a pilgrim's staff. Philosophy always seeks a *sufficient cause*, and only in the *One Idea* already presented can a cause be found in any degree commensurate with the crime; and this becomes so only when we consider the mad fanaticism of slavery.

2. Public notoriety steps forward to confirm the suggestion of reason. In every place where Truth can freely travel it is asserted and understood that the legislature was imposed upon Kansas by foreigners from Missouri; and this universal voice is now received as undeniable verity.

3. It is also attested by harangues of the conspirators. Here is what Stringfellow said *before* the invasion: —

> To those who have qualms of conscience as to violating laws, State or national, the time has come when such impositions must be disregarded, as your rights and property are in danger; *and I advise you, one and all, to enter every election district in Kansas in defiance of Reeder and his vile myrmidons, and vote at the point of the bowie-knife and revolver.* Neither give nor take quarter, as our cause demands it. It is enough that the slaveholding interest wills it, from which there is no appeal. What right has Governor Reeder to rule Missourians in Kansas? His proclamation and prescribed oath must be repudiated. It is your interest to do so. Mind that slavery is established where it is not prohibited.

Here is what Atchison said *after* the invasion: —

> Well, what next? Why, an election for members of the legislature to organize the Territory must be held. What did I advise you to do then? Why, meet them on their own ground, and beat them at their own game again; and, cold and inclement as the weather was, I went over with a company of men. My object in going was not to vote. I had no right to vote, unless I had disfranchised myself in Missouri. I was not within two miles of a voting-place. My object in going was not to vote, but to settle a difficulty between two of our candidates; and the Abolitionists of the North said, *and published it abroad, that Atchison was there with bowie-knife and revolver,—and, by God, 'twas true! I never did go into that Territory, I never intend to go into that Territory, without being prepared for all such kind of cattle.* Well, we beat them, and Governor Reeder gave certificates to a majority of all the members of both Houses; and then, after they were organized, as everybody will admit, they were the only competent persons to say who were and who were not members of the same.

4. It is confirmed by contemporaneous admission of *The Squatter Sovereign*, a paper published at Atchison, and at once the organ of the President and of these Borderers, which, under the date of April 1, thus recounts the victory: —

> INDEPENDENCE [MISSOURI], March 31, 1855.
>
> Several hundred emigrants from Kansas have just entered our city. They were preceded by the Westport and Independence brass bands. They came in at the west side of the public square, and proceeded entirely around it, the bands cheering us with fine music and the emigrants with good news. Immediately following the bands were about two hundred horsemen in regular order; following these were one hundred and fifty wagons, carriages, etc. They gave repeated cheers for Kansas and Missouri. They report that not an anti-slavery man will be in the legislature of Kansas. *We have made a clean sweep.*

5. It is also confirmed by contemporaneous testimony of another paper always faithful to slavery, the New York *Herald*,

in the letter of a correspondent from Brunswick, Mo., under date of April 20, 1855:—

> From five to seven thousand men started from Missouri to attend the election, some to remove, but the most to return to their families, with an intention, if they liked the Territory, to make it their permanent abode at the earliest moment practicable. But they intended to vote. The Missourians were, many of them, Douglas men. There were one hundred and fifty voters from this county, one hundred and seventy-five from Howard, one hundred from Cooper. Indeed, every county furnished its quota; and, when they set out, it looked like an army. . . . They were armed. . . . And, as there were no houses in the Territory, they carried tents. Their mission was a peaceable one,— to vote and to drive down stakes for their future homes. After the election some fifteen hundred of the voters sent a committee to Mr. Reeder to ascertain if it was his purpose to ratify the election. He answered that it was, and said the majority at an election must carry the day. But it is not to be denied that the fifteen hundred, apprehending that the governor might attempt to play the tyrant,— since his conduct had already been insidious and unjust,— wore on their hats bunches of hemp. They were resolved, if a tyrant attempted to trample upon the rights of the sovereign people, to hang him.

6. It is again confirmed by testimony of a lady for five years resident in Western Missouri, who thus writes in a letter published in the New Haven *Register*:—

> MIAMI, SALINE COUNTY, Nov. 26, 1855.
>
> You ask me to tell you something about the Kansas and Missouri troubles. Of course you know in what they have originated. *There is no denying that the Missourians have determined to control the elections, if possible*: and I do not know that their measures would be justifiable, except upon the principle of self-preservation, and that, you know, is the first law of nature.

7. And it is confirmed still further by the Circular of the Emigration Society of Lafayette County, in Missouri, dated as late as 25th of March, 1856, where the efforts of Missourians are openly confessed:—

> The western counties of Missouri have for the last two years been heavily taxed, both in money and time, in fighting the battles of the South. *Lafayette County alone has expended more than one hundred thousand dollars in money, and as much or more in time. Up to this time the border counties of Missouri have upheld and maintained the rights and interests of the South in this struggle, unassisted, and not unsuccessfully.* But the Abolitionists, staking their all upon the Kansas issue, and hesitating at no means, fair or foul, are moving heaven and earth to render that beautiful Territory *a Free State*.

8. Here, also, is amplest testimony to the usurpation, by

the *Intelligencer*, a leading paper of St. Louis, Mo., made in the ensuing summer: —

> Atchison and Stringfellow, with their Missouri followers, overwhelmed the settlers in Kansas, browbeat and bullied them, and took the government from their hands. Missouri votes elected the present body of men, who insult public intelligence and popular rights by styling themselves "the legislature of Kansas." This body of men are helping themselves to fat speculations by locating the "seat of government" and getting town lots for their votes. They are passing laws disfranchising all the citizens of Kansas who do not believe Negro Slavery to be a Christian institution and a national blessing. They are proposing to punish with imprisonment the utterance of views inconsistent with their own. And they are trying to perpetuate their preposterous and infernal tyranny by appointing *for a term of years* creatures of their own, as commissioners in every county, to lay and collect taxes, and see that the laws they are passing are faithfully executed. Has this age anything to compare with these acts in audacity?

9. In harmony with all these is the authoritative declaration of Governor Reeder in a speech to his neighbors at Easton, Penn., at the end of April, 1855, and immediately afterwards published in the Washington *Union*. Here it is: —

> It was, indeed, too true that Kansas had been invaded, conquered, subjugated, by an armed force from beyond her borders, led on by a fanatical spirit, trampling under foot the principles of the Kansas Bill and the right of suffrage.

10. In similar harmony is the complaint of the people of Kansas in public meeting at Big Springs on the 5th of September, 1855, embodied in these words: —

> *Resolved*, That the body of men who for the last two months have been passing laws for the people of our Territory, moved, counselled, and dictated to by the demagogues of Missouri, are to us a foreign body representing only the lawless invaders who elected them, and not the people of the Territory,— that we repudiate their action as the monstrous consummation of an act of violence, usurpation, and fraud, unparalleled in the history of the Union, and worthy only of men unfitted for the duties and regardless of the responsibilities of Republicans.

11. Finally, the invasion which ended in the Usurpation is clearly established from official Minutes laid on our table by the President. But the effect of this testimony has been so amply exposed by the Senator from Vermont [Mr. COLLAMER], in his able and indefatigable argument, that I content myself with simply referring to it.

On this cumulative, irresistible evidence in concurrence with antecedent history I rest. And yet Senators here argue that this cannot be,— precisely as the conspiracy of Catiline was doubted in the Roman Senate. "*Nonnulli sunt in hoc ordine, qui aut ea quæ imminent non videant, aut ea quæ vident dissimulent; qui spem Catilinæ mollibus sententiis aluerunt, conjurationemque nascentem non credendo corroboraverunt.*" * These words of the Roman orator picture the case here. As I listened to the Senator from Illinois while he painfully strove to show that there is no Usurpation, I was reminded of the effort by a distinguished logician to prove that Napoleon Bonaparte never existed. And permit me to say that the fact of his existence is not more entirely above doubt than the fact of this usurpation. This I assert on proofs already presented. But confirmation comes almost while I speak. The columns of the public press are daily filled with testimony solemnly taken before the committee of Congress in Kansas, which attests, in awful light, the violence ending in the Usurpation. Of this I may speak on some other occasion.† Meanwhile I proceed with the development of the crime.

The usurping legislature assembled at the appointed place in the interior, and then at once, in opposition to the veto of the governor, by a majority of two-thirds, removed to the Shawnee Mission, a place in most convenient proximity to the Missouri borderers, by whom it had been constituted, and whose tyrannical agent it was. The statutes of Missouri, in all their text, with their divisions and subdivisions, were adopted bodily, and with such little local adaptation that the word "State" in the original is not even changed to "Territory," but is left to be corrected by an explanatory act. All this general legislation was entirely subordinate to the special chapter entitled "An Act to punish Offences against Slave Property," where the One Idea that provoked this whole conspiracy is at last embodied in legislative form, and Human Slavery openly recognized on Free Soil, under the sanction of pretended law.‡ This chapter, of thirteen sections, is in itself a *Dance of Death*. But its complex completeness of wicked-

---

* Cicero, Oratio in Catilinam, i..12.

† This review Mr. Sumner was disabled from making by the long illness following the assault by Brooks.

‡ Statutes of the Territory of Kansas, passed at the first session of the Legislative Assembly, 1855, and the Act of Congress organizing said Territory, and other Acts of Congress having immediate relation thereto, Shawnee M. L. School, 1855, Chap. 151, pp. 715-717. Mr. Sumner's copy of this curious volume, which once belonged to Mr. Seward, is lettered on the back "Laws of Kansas; Territorial Legislature, *alias* The Ruffian's Legislature."

ness without parallel may be partially conceived, when it is understood that in three sections only is the penalty of death denounced no less than forty-eight different times, by as many changes of language, against the heinous offence, described in forty-eight different ways, of interfering with what does not exist in that Territory, and under the Constitution cannot exist there,— I mean property in human flesh. Thus is Liberty sacrificed to Slavery, and Death summoned to sit at the gates as guardian of the Wrong.

The work of Usurpation was not perfected even yet. It had already cost too much to be left at any hazard.

> "To be thus is nothing,
> But to be safely thus."

Such was the object. And this could not be, except by the entire prostration of all the safeguards of Human Rights. Liberty of speech, which is the very breath of a Republic,— the press, which is the terror of wrong-doers,— the bar, through which the oppressed beards the arrogance of law,— the jury, by which right is vindicated,— all these must be struck down, while officers are provided in all places, ready to be the tools of this Tyranny; and then, to obtain final assurance that their crime is secure, the whole Usurpation, stretching over the Territory, must be fastened and riveted by legislative bolt, spike, and screw, *so as to defy all effort at change through ordinary forms of law.* To this work, in its various parts, were bent the subtlest energies; and never, from Tubal Cain to this hour, was any fabric forged with more desperate skill and completeness.

Mark, sir, three different legislative enactments constituting part of this work. *First,* according to one act, all who deny, by spoken or written word, "the right of persons to hold slaves in this Territory," are denounced as felons, to be punished by imprisonment at hard labor for a term not less than two years, — it may be for life. To show the extravagance of this injustice, it is well put by the Senator from Vermont [Mr. COLLAMER] that, should the Senator from Michigan [Mr. CASS], who believes that Slavery cannot exist in a Territory unless introduced by express legislative act, venture there with his moderate opinions, his doom must be that of a felon! To such extent are the great liberties of speech and of the press subverted! *Secondly,* by another act, entitled "An Act concerning Attorneys-at-law," no person can practise as attorney unless he *shall obtain a license* from the Territorial courts, which, of course, a tyrannical discretion will be free to deny; and, after obtaining such license, he is constrained to take an oath not only "to support" the Constitution of the United States, but also "to support and sustain"—mark here the reduplication—the Territorial Act and the Fugitive Slave Bill, thus erecting a test for admission to the bar calculated to exclude citizens who honestly regard the latter legislative enormity as unfit to be obeyed. And, *thirdly*, by another act, entitled "An Act concerning Jurors," all persons "conscientiously opposed to the holding slaves" or "who do not admit the right to hold slaves in this Territory" are excluded from the jury on every question, civil or criminal, arising out of asserted slave property, while, in all cases, the summoning of the jury is left without one word of restraint to "the marshal, sheriff, or other officer," who is thus free to pack it according to his tyrannical discretion.

For the ready enforcement of all statutes against Human Freedom the President furnished a powerful quota of officers, in the governor, chief justice, judges, secretary, attorney, and marshal. The legislature completed this part of the work by constituting in each county a Board of Commissioners, composed of two persons, associated with the probate judge, whose duty it is to "appoint a county treasurer, coroner, justices of the peace, constables, and *all* other officers provided for by law," and then proceeding to the choice of this very Board, thus delegating and diffusing their usurped power, and tyrannically imposing upon the Territory a crowd of officers in whose appointment the people had no voice, directly or indirectly.

And still the final, inexorable work remained to be done. A legislature renovated in both branches could not assemble until 1858, so that, during this long intermediate period, this whole system must continue in the likeness of law, unless overturned by the National Government, or, in default of such interposition, by the generous uprising of an oppressed people. But it was necessary to guard against possibility of change, even tardily, at a future election; and this was done by two different acts, under the *first* of which all who do not take the oath to support the Fugitive Slave Bill are excluded from the elective franchise, and under the *second* of which all others are entitled to vote who tender a tax of one dollar to the sheriff on the day of election; thus, by provision of Territorial law, disfranchising all opposed to Slavery, and at the same time opening the door to the votes of the invaders; by an unconstitutional shibboleth excluding from the polls the body of actual settlers, and by making the franchise depend upon a petty tax only admitting to the polls the mass of borderers from Missouri. By tyrannical forethought the Usurpation not only fortified all that it did, but assumed a *self-perpetuating* energy.

Thus was the Crime consummated. Slavery stands erect, clanking its chains on the Territory of Kansas, surrounded by a code of death, and trampling upon all cherished liberties, whether of speech, the press, the bar, the trial by jury, or the electoral franchise. And, sir, all this is done, not merely to introduce a wrong which in itself is a denial of all rights, and in dread of which mothers have taken the lives of their offspring,— not merely, as is sometimes said, to protect Slavery in Missouri, since it is futile for this State to complain of Freedom on the side of Kansas when Freedom exists without complaint on the side of Iowa and also on the side of Illinois,— but it is done for the sake of political power, in order to bring two new slaveholding Senators upon this floor, and thus to fortify in the National Government the desperate chances of a waning Oligarchy. As the gallant ship voyaging on pleasant summer seas is assailed by a pirate crew and plundered of its doubloons and dollars, so is this beautiful Territory now assailed in peace and prosperity and robbed of its political power for the sake of Slavery. Even now the black flag of the land pirates from Missouri waves at the mast-head; in their laws you hear the pirate yell and see the flash of the pirate knife; while, incredible to relate, the President, gathering the Slave Power at his back, testifies a pirate sympathy.

Sir, all this was done in the name of Popular Sovereignty. And this is the close of the tragedy. Popular Sovereignty, which, when truly understood, is a fountain of just power, has ended in Popular Slavery,— not in the subjection of the unhappy African race merely, but of this proud Caucasian blood which you boast. The profession with which you began of *All by the People* is lost in the wretched reality of *Nothing for the People*. Popular Sovereignty, in whose deceitful name plighted faith was broken and an ancient Landmark of Freedom overturned, now lifts itself before us like Sin in the terrible picture of Milton, which

> "seemed woman to the waist, and fair,
> But ended foul in many a scaly fold
> Voluminous and vast, a serpent armed
> With mortal sting: about her middle round
> A cry of hell-hounds never ceasing barked
> With wide Cerberean mouths full loud, and rung
> A hideous peal; yet, when they list, would creep,
> If aught disturbed their noise, into her womb,
> And kennel there, yet there still barked and howled
> Within, unseen."

The image is complete at all points; and with this exposure I take my leave of the Crime against Kansas.

The works of Charles Sumner in fifteen volumes contain a vast number of speeches and papers relating to slavery; and, with the unusually full notes which accompany them, these constitute almost a history of the anti-slavery struggle during Sumner's public life. Three of his great anti-slavery speeches in the Senate stand out pre-eminent, and should be read by every student: "Freedom National, Slavery Sectional," Aug. 26, 1852 (Works, vol. iii. 87); "The Crime against Kansas," May 19 and 20, 1856 (iv. 125); and "The Barbarism of Slavery," June 4, 1860 (v. 1). The last is a complete survey of the history and character of slavery, and there is no summary and criticism more complete or powerful. The student should also read the speech "No Property in Man," on the constitutional amendment abolishing slavery, April 8, 1864 (viii. 347); and the eulogy on Abraham Lincoln, June 1, 1865 (ix. 367).

The speech on "The Crime against Kansas," in itself one of the strongest and most influential of Sumner's speeches, possesses the further interest of being the speech which provoked the brutal assault upon Sumner two days after its delivery, by Preston S. Brooks, a representative of South Carolina, which compelled his absence from the Senate for three years, and nearly cost him his life. It is one of the longest of his speeches, discussing: "first, the crime against Kansas, in its origin and extent; second, the apologies for the crime; and, third, the true remedy." The first main section, following the powerful exordium, is given in the present leaflet.

The Memoirs and Letters of Charles Sumner, in four volumes, by Edward L. Pierce, is one of the most thorough biographies which has been written of any American, and one of the most important contributions to the history of the anti-slavery struggle. In Chapters XXXVI., XL., and XLIII. of the third volume will be found the accounts respectively of the circumstances attending the delivery of the three great speeches especially referred to above.

There are brief lives of Sumner by Nason, Chaplin, and Anna L. Dawes. There is also a valuable volume edited by William M. Cornell, containing a memoir by the editor, and the various important eulogies of Sumner after his death, including that by Carl Schurz before the Boston city government, that by George William Curtis before the Massachusetts legislature, and the eulogies in Congress.

PUBLISHED BY

THE DIRECTORS OF THE OLD SOUTH WORK,
Old South Meeting-house, Boston, Mass.

Old South Leaflets.

No. 84.

Words of John Brown.

From his Account of his Childhood.

During the war with England a circumstance occurred that in the end made him a most *determined Abolitionist*: & led him to declare, *or Swear: Eternal war* with Slavery. He was staying for a short time with a very gentlemanly landlord since a United States Marshall who held a slave boy near his own age very active, inteligent and good feeling: and to whom John was under considerable obligation for numerous little acts of kindness. *The master* made a great pet of John: brought him to table with his first company: & friends: called their attention to every little smart thing he *said or did:* & to the fact of his being more than a hundred miles from home with a company of cattle alone; while the *negro boy* (who was fully if not more than his equal) was badly clothed, poorly fed: *and lodged in cold weather; &* beaten before his eyes with Iron Shovels or any other thing that came first to hand. This brought John to reflect on the wretched, hopeless condition, of *Fatherless & Motherless* slave *children:* for such children have neither Fathers or Mothers to protect, & provide for them. He sometimes would raise the question *is God their Father?*

John Brown's Reading and Family Worship, as described by his Daughter.

My dear father's favorite books, of a historical character, were "Rollin's Ancient History," Josephus, Plutarch, "Napoleon and his Marshals," and the Life of Oliver Cromwell. Of religious books, Baxter's "Saints' Rest" (in speaking of which at one time he said he could not see how any person could read it through carefully without becoming a Christian), the "Pilgrim's Progress," and Henry "On Meekness." But above all others, the Bible was his favorite volume; and he had such a perfect knowledge of it, that when any person was reading it, he would correct the least mistake. His favorite passages were these, as near as I can remember:—

"Remember them that are in bonds as bound with them."

"Whoso stoppeth his ear at the cry of the poor, he also shall cry himself, but shall not be heard."

"He that hath a bountiful eye shall be blessed; for he giveth his bread to the poor."

"A good name is rather to be chosen than great riches, and loving favor rather than silver or gold."

"Whoso mocketh the poor, reproacheth his Maker; and he that is glad at calamities, shall not be unpunished."

"He that hath pity upon the poor lendeth to the Lord, and that which he hath given will He pay to him again."

"Give to him that asketh of thee, and from him that would borrow of thee turn not thou away."

"A righteous man regardeth the life of his beast; but the tender mercies of the wicked are cruel."

"Withhold not good from them to whom it is due, when it is in the power of thine hand to do it."

"Except the Lord build the house, they labor in vain that build it; except the Lord keepeth the city, the watchman walketh in vain."

"I hate vain thoughts, but thy law do I love."

The last chapter of Ecclesiastes was a favorite one, and on Fast-days and Thanksgivings he used very often to read the fifty-eighth chapter of Isaiah.

When he would come home at night, tired out with labor, he would, before going to bed, ask some of the family to read chapters (as was his usual course night and morning); and would almost always say, "Read one of David's Psalms."

His favorite hymns (Watts's) were these: "Blow ye the trumpet, blow!" "Sweet is Thy word, my God, my King!" "I'll praise my Maker with my breath"; "Oh, happy is the man who hears!" "Why should we start, and fear to die!" "With songs and honors sounding loud"; "Ah, lovely appearance of death!"

An Early Letter on Slavery.

John Brown to his Brother Frederick.

RANDOLPH, PA., Nov. 21, 1834.

Dear Brother,— As I have had only one letter from Hudson since you left here, and that some weeks since, I begin to get uneasy and apprehensive that all is not well. I had satisfied my mind about it for some time, in expectation of seeing father here, but I begin to give that up for the present. Since you left me I have been trying to devise some means whereby I might do something in a practical way for my poor fellow-men who are in bondage, and having fully consulted the feelings of my wife and my three boys, we have agreed to get at least one negro boy or youth, and bring him up as we do our own,— viz., give him a good English education, learn him what we can about the history of the world, about business, about general subjects, and, above all, try to teach him the fear of God. We think of three ways to obtain one: First, to try to get some Christian slaveholder to release one to us. Second, to get a free one if no one will let us have one that is a slave. Third, if that does not succeed, we have all agreed to submit to considerable privation in order to buy one. This we are now using means in order to effect, in the confident expectation that God is about to bring them all out of the house of bondage.

I will just mention that when this subject was first introduced, Jason had gone to bed; but no sooner did he hear the thing hinted, than his warm heart kindled, and he turned out to have a part in the discussion of a subject of such exceeding interest. I have for years been trying to devise some way to get a school a-going here for blacks, and I think that on many accounts it would be a most favorable location. Children here would have no intercourse with vicious people of their own kind, nor with openly vicious persons of any kind. There would be no powerful opposition influence against such a thing; and should there be any, I believe the settlement might be so effected in future as to have almost the whole influence of the place in favor of such a school. Write me how you would like to join me, and try to get on from Hudson and thereabouts some first-rate abolitionist families with you. I do honestly believe that our united exertions alone might soon, with the good hand of our God upon us, effect it all.

This has been with me a favorite theme of reflection for years. I think that a place which might be in some measure settled with a view to such an object would be much more favorable to such an undertaking than would any such place as Hudson, with all its conflicting interests and feelings; and I do think such advantages ought to be afforded the young blacks, whether they are all to be immediately set free or not. Perhaps we might, under God, in that way do more towards breaking their yoke effectually than in any other. If the young blacks of our country could once become enlightened, it would most assuredly operate on slavery like firing powder confined in rock, and all slaveholders know it well. Witness their heaven-daring laws against teaching blacks. If once the Christians in the free States would set to work in earnest in teaching the blacks, the people of the slaveholding States would find themselves constitutionally driven to set about the work of emancipation immediately. The laws of this State are now such that the inhabitants of any township may raise by a tax in aid of the State school-fund any amount of money they may choose by a vote, for the purpose of common schools, which any child may have access to by application. If you will join me in this undertaking, I will make with you any arrangement of our temporal concerns that shall be fair. Our health is good, and our prospects about business rather brightening. Affectionately yours,

JOHN BROWN.

INSTRUCTIONS TO HIS SPRINGFIELD, MASS., "GILEADITES," AN ORGANIZATION OF COLORED PEOPLE.

WORDS OF ADVICE.

Branch of the United States League of Gileadites. Adopted Jan. 15, 1851, as written and recommended by John Brown.

"UNION IS STRENGTH."

Nothing so charms the American people as personal bravery. Witness the case of Cinques, of everlasting memory, on board the "Amistad." The trial for life of one bold and to some extent successful man, for defending his rights in good earnest, would arouse more sympathy throughout the nation than the accumulated wrongs and sufferings of more than three millions of our submissive colored population. We need not mention the Greeks struggling against the oppressive Turks, the Poles against Russia, nor the Hungarians against Austria and Russia combined, to prove this. *No jury can be found in the Northern States that would convict a man for defending his rights to the last extremity. This is well understood by Southern Congressmen, who insisted that the right of trial by jury should not be granted to the fugitive.* Colored people have ten times the number of fast friends among the whites than they suppose, and would have ten times the number they now have were they but half as much in earnest to secure their dearest rights as they are to ape the follies and extravagances of their white neighbors, and to indulge in idle show, in ease, and in luxury. Just think of the money expended by individuals in your behalf in the past twenty years! Think of the number who have been mobbed and imprisoned on your account! Have any of you seen the Branded Hand? Do you remember the names of Lovejoy and Torrey?

Should one of your number be arrested, you must collect together as quickly as possible, so as to outnumber your adversaries who are taking an active part against you. Let no ablebodied man appear on the ground unequipped, or with his weapons exposed to view: let that be understood beforehand. Your plans must be known only to yourself, and with the understanding that all traitors must die, wherever caught and proven to be guilty. "Whosoever is fearful or afraid, let him return and depart early from Mount Gilead" (Judges vii. 3; Deut. xx. 8). Give all cowards an opportunity to show it on condition of holding their peace. *Do not delay one moment after you are ready: you will lose all your resolution if you do. Let the first blow be the signal for all to engage; and when engaged do not do your work by halves, but make clean work with your enemies,—and be sure you meddle not with any others.* By going about your business quietly, you will get the job disposed of before the number that an uproar would bring together can collect; and you will have the advantage of those who come out against you, for they will be wholly unprepared with either equipments or matured plans; all with them will be confusion and terror. Your enemies will be slow to attack you after you have done up the work nicely; and if they should, they will have to encounter your white friends as well as you; for you may safely calculate on a division of the whites, and may by that means get to an honorable parley.

Be firm, determined, and cool; but let it be understood that you are not to be driven to desperation without making it an awful dear job to others as well as to you. Give them to know distinctly that those who live in wooden houses should not throw fire, and that you are just as able to suffer as your white neighbors. *After effecting a rescue, if you are assailed, go into the houses of your most prominent and influential white friends with your wives; and that will effectually fasten upon them the suspicion of being connected with you, and will compel them to make a common cause with you, whether they would otherwise live up to their profession or not. This would leave them no choice in the matter.* Some would doubtless prove themselves true of their own choice; others would flinch. That would be taking them at their own words. You may make a tumult in the court-room where a trial is going on, by burning gunpowder freely in paper packages, if you cannot think of any better way to create a momentary alarm, and might possibly give one or more of your enemies a hoist. But in such case the prisoner will need to take the hint at once, and bestir himself; and so should his friends improve the opportunity for a general rush.

A lasso might possibly be applied to a slave-catcher for once with good effect. Hold on to your weapons, and never be persuaded to leave them, part with them, or have them far away from you. *Stand by one another and by your friends, while a drop of blood remains; and be hanged, if you must, but tell no tales out of school. Make no confession.*

Union is strength. Without some well-digested arrangements nothing to any good purpose is likely to be done, let the demand be never so great. Witness the case of Hamlet and Long in New York, when there was no well-defined plan of operations or suitable preparation beforehand.

The desired end may be effectually secured by the means proposed; namely, the enjoyment of our inalienable rights.

THE FIGHT OF OSAWATOMIE.

Published in the Newspapers at the Time.

Early in the morning of the 30th of August the enemy's scouts approached to within one mile and a half of the western boundary of the town of Osawatomie. At this place my son

Frederick (who was not attached to my force) had lodged, with some four other young men from Lawrence, and a young man named Garrison, from Middle Creek. The scouts, led by a proslavery preacher named White, shot my son dead in the road, while he — as I have since ascertained — supposed them to be friendly. At the same time they butchered Mr. Garrison, and badly mangled one of the young men from Lawrence, who came with my son, leaving him for dead. This was not far from sunrise. I had stopped during the night about two and one-half miles from them, and nearly one mile from Osawatomie. I had no organized force, but only some twelve or fifteen new recruits, who were ordered to leave their preparations for breakfast and follow me into the town, as soon as this news was brought to me.

As I had no means of learning correctly the force of the enemy, I placed twelve of the recruits in a log-house, hoping we might be able to defend the town. I then gathered some fifteen more men together, whom we armed with guns; and we started in the direction of the enemy. After going a few rods, we could see them approaching the town in line of battle, about half a mile off, upon a hill west of the village. I then gave up all idea of doing more than to annoy, from the timber near the town, into which we were all retreated, and which was filled with a thick growth of underbrush; but I had no time to recall the twelve men in the log-house, and so lost their assistance in the fight. At the point above named I met with Captain Cline, a very active young man, who had with him some twelve or fifteen mounted men, and persuaded him to go with us into the timber, on the southern shore of the Osage, or Marais des Cygnes, a little to the north-west from the village. Here the men, numbering not more than thirty in all, were directed to scatter and secrete themselves as well as they could, and await the approach of the enemy. This was done in full view of them (who must have seen the whole movement), and had to be done in the utmost haste. I believe Captain Cline and some of his men were not even dismounted in the fight, but cannot assert positively. When the left wing of the enemy had approached to within common rifle-shot, we commenced firing, and very soon threw the northern branch of the enemy's line into disorder. This continued some fifteen or twenty minutes, which gave us an uncommon opportunity to annoy them. Captain Cline and his men soon got out of ammunition, and retired across the river.

After the enemy rallied, we kept up our fire, until, by the leaving of one and another, we had but six or seven left. We then retired across the river. We had one man killed — a Mr. Powers, from Captain Cline's company — in the fight. One of my men, a Mr. Partridge, was shot in crossing the river. Two or three of the party who took part in the fight are yet missing, and may be lost or taken prisoners. Two were wounded; namely, Dr. Updegraff and a Mr. Collis. I cannot speak in too high terms of them, and of many others I have not now time to mention.

One of my best men, together with myself, was struck by a partially spent ball from the enemy, in the commencement of the fight, but we were only bruised. The loss I refer to is one of my missing men. The loss of the enemy, as we learn by the different statements of our own as well as their people, was some thirty one or two killed, and from forty to fifty wounded. After burning the town to ashes and killing a Mr. Williams they had taken, whom neither party claimed, they took a hasty leave, carrying their dead and wounded with them. They did not attempt to cross the river, nor to search for us, and have not since returned to look over their work.

I give this in great haste, in the midst of constant interruptions. My second son was with me in the fight, and escaped unharmed. This I mention for the benefit of his friends. Old Preacher White, I hear, boasts of having killed my son. Of course he is a lion.

JOHN BROWN.

LAWRENCE, KANSAS, Sept. 7, 1856.

STATEMENT OF HIS VIRGINIA PLAN TO FREDERICK DOUGLASS IN 1847.

From Douglass's "Life and Times."

Captain Brown cautiously approached the subject which he wished to bring to my attention, for he seemed to apprehend opposition to his views. He denounced slavery in look and language fierce and bitter; thought that slaveholders had forfeited their right to live, and that the slaves had the right to gain their liberty in any way they could; did not believe that "moral suasion" would ever liberate the slave, nor that political action would abolish the system. He had long had a plan which could accomplish this end, and had invited me to his house to lay that plan before me; he had been some time looking for colored men to whom he could safely reveal his secret, and at times he had almost despaired of finding such men; but now he was encouraged, for he saw heads of such rising up in all directions. He had observed my course, at home and abroad, and he wanted my co-operation. His plan, as it then lay in his mind, had much to commend it. It did not, as some suppose, contemplate a general rising among the slaves, and a general slaughter of the slavemasters: an insurrection, he thought, would only defeat the object; but his plan did contemplate the creating of an armed force which should act in the very heart of the South. He was not averse to the shedding of blood, and thought the practice of carrying arms would be a good one for the colored people to adopt, as it would give them a sense of their manhood. No people, he said, could have self-respect, or be respected, who would not fight for their freedom. He called my attention to a map of the United States, and pointed out to me the ranges which stretch away from the borders of New York into the Southern States. "These mountains," he said, "are the basis of my plan. God has given the strength of the hills to freedom; they were placed here for the emancipation of the negro race; they are full of natural forts, where one man for defence will be equal to a hundred for attack; they are full also of good hiding-places, where large numbers of brave men could be concealed, and baffle and elude pursuit for a long time. I know these mountains well, and could take a body of men into them and keep them there, despite of all the efforts of Virginia to dislodge them. The true object to be sought is, first of all, to destroy the money-value of slave property; and that can only be done by rendering such property insecure. My plan, then, is to take at first about twenty-five picked men, and begin on a small scale; supply them arms and ammunition, and post them in squads of five on a line of twenty-five miles. The most persuasive and judicious of them shall then go down to the fields from time to time, as opportunity offers, and induce the slaves to join them, seeking and selecting the most restless and daring."

He saw that in this part of the work the utmost care must be used to avoid treachery and disclosure. Only the most conscientious and skilled should be sent on this perilous duty; with care and enterprise he thought he could soon gather a force of a hundred hardy men, who would be content to lead the free and adventurous life to which he proposed to train them. When these were properly drilled, and each man had found the place for which he was best suited, they would begin work in earnest; they would run off the slaves in large numbers, retain the brave and strong ones in the mountains, and send the weak and timid to the North by the "underground railroad"; his operations would be enlarged with increasing numbers, and would not be confined to one locality.

When I asked him how he would support these men, he said emphatically he would subsist them upon the enemy. Slavery was a state of war, and the slave had a right to anything necessary to his freedom. "But," said I, "suppose you succeed in running off a few slaves, and thus impress the Virginia slaveholders with a sense of insecurity in their slaves,— the effect will only be to make them sell their slaves farther South." "That," said he, "will be first what I want to do; then I would follow them up. If we could drive slavery out of one county, it would be a great gain; it would weaken the system throughout the State." "But they would employ bloodhounds to hunt you out of the mountains." "That they might attempt," said he, "but the chances are we should whip them; and when we should have whipped one squad, they would be careful how they pursued." "But you might be surrounded and cut off from your means of subsistence." He thought that could not be done so they could not cut their way out; but even if the worst came, he could but be killed, and he had no better use for his life than to lay it down in the cause of the slave. When I suggested that we might convert the slaveholders, he became much excited, and said that could never be; "he knew their proud hearts, and that they would never be induced to give up their slaves until they felt a big stick about their heads." He thought I might have noticed the simple manner in which he lived, adding that he had adopted this in order to save money to carry out his purposes. This was said in no boastful tone, for he felt that he had delayed already too long, and had no room to boast either his zeal or his self-denial. Had some men made such display of rigid virtue, I should have rejected it as affected, false, or hypocritical, but in John Brown I felt it to be as real as iron or granite. From this night spent with John Brown in 1847, while I continued to write and speak against slavery, I became all the less hopeful of its peaceful abolition. My utterances became more and more tinged by the color of this man's strong impressions.

Brown's Plan as Explained in Canada in 1858.

Richard Realf's Report.

John Brown stated that for twenty or thirty years the idea had possessed him like a passion of giving liberty to the slaves; that he made a journey to England, during which he made a tour upon the European continent, inspecting all fortifications, and especially all earthwork forts which he could find, with a view of applying the knowledge thus gained, with modifications and inventions of his own, to a mountain warfare in the United States. He stated that he had read all the books upon insurrectionary warfare that he could lay his hands on: the Roman warfare, the successful opposition of the Spanish chieftains during the period when Spain was a Roman province,— how with ten thousand men, divided and subdivided into small companies, acting simultaneously yet separately, they withstood the whole consolidated power of the Roman Empire through a number of years. In addition to this, he had become very familiar with the successful warfare waged by Schamyl, the Circassian chief, against the Russians; he had posted himself in relation to the war of Toussaint L'Ouverture; he had become thoroughly acquainted with the wars in Hayti and the islands round about; and from all these things he had drawn the conclusion,— believing, as he stated there he did believe, and as we all (if I may judge from myself) believed,— that upon the first intimation of a plan formed for the liberation of the slaves, they would immediately rise all over the Southern States. He supposed that they would come into the mountains to join him, where he purposed to work, and that by flocking to his standard they would enable him (making the line of mountains which cuts diagonally through Maryland and Virginia, down through the Southern States into Tennessee and Alabama, the base of his operations) to act upon the plantations on the plains lying on each side of that range of mountains; that we should be able to establish ourselves in the fastnesses. And if any hostile action were taken against us, either by the militia of the States or by the armies of the United States, we purposed to defeat first the militia, and next, if possible, the troops of the United States; and then organize the free blacks under the provisional constitution, which would carve out for the locality of its jurisdiction all that mountainous region in which the blacks were to be established, in which they were to be taught the useful and mechanical arts, and all the business of life. Schools were also to be established, and so on. The negroes were to be his soldiers.

Provisional Constitution and Ordinances for the People of the United States.

[This is the preamble of the constitution drawn up by Brown in 1858 for the government of the slaves whom he proposed to free.]

Preamble.

Whereas slavery, throughout its entire existence in the United States, is none other than a most barbarous, unprovoked, and unjustifiable war of one portion of its citizens upon another portion — the only conditions of which are perpetual imprisonment and hopeless servitude or absolute extermination — in utter disregard and violation of those eternal and self-evident truths set forth in our Declaration of Independence :

Therefore, we, citizens of the United States, and the oppressed people who by a recent decision of the Supreme Court are declared to have no rights which the white man is bound to respect, together with all other people degraded by the laws thereof, do, for the time being, ordain and establish for ourselves the following Provisional Constitution and Ordinances, the better to protect our persons, property, lives, and liberties, and to govern our actions :

Old Brown's Farewell.

To the Plymouth Rocks, Bunker Hill Monuments, Charter Oaks, and Uncle Tom's Cabins.

He has left for Kansas; has been trying since he came out of the Territory to secure an outfit, or, in other words, the means of arming and thoroughly equipping his regular minute-men, who are mixed up with the people of Kansas. And he leaves the States with a feeling of deepest sadness, that after having exhausted his own small means, and with his family and his brave men suffered hunger, cold, nakedness, and some of them sickness, wounds, imprisonment in irons, with extreme cruel treatment, and others death ; that after lying on the ground for months in the most sickly, unwholesome, and uncomfortable places, some of the time with sick and wounded, destitute of any shelter, hunted like wolves, and sustained in part by Indians; that after all this, in order to sustain a cause which every citizen of this "glorious republic" is under equal moral obligation to do, and for the neglect of which he will be held accountable by God,— a cause in which every man, woman, and child of the entire human family has a deep and awful interest,— that when no wages are asked or expected, he cannot secure, amid all the wealth, luxury, and extravagance of this "heaven-exalted" people, even the necessary supplies of the common soldier. "How are the mighty fallen!"

I am destitute of horses, baggage-wagons, tents, harness, saddles, bridles, holsters, spurs, and belts; camp equipage, such as cooking and eating utensils, blankets, knapsacks, intrenching-tools, axes, shovels, spades, mattocks, crowbars; have not a supply of ammunition; have not money sufficient to pay freight and travelling expenses; and left my family poorly supplied with common necessaries.

BOSTON, April, 1857.

JOHN BROWN TO F. B. SANBORN.

PETERBORO, N.Y., Feb. 24, 1858.

My dear Friend,— Mr. Morton has taken the liberty of saying to me that you felt half inclined to make a common cause with me. I greatly rejoice at this; for I believe when you come to look at the ample field I labor in, and the rich harvest which not only this entire country, but the whole world during the present and future generations may reap from its successful cultivation, you will feel that you are out of your element until you find you are in it, an entire unit. What an inconceivable amount of good you might so effect by your counsel, your example, your encouragement, your natural and acquired ability for active service! And, then, how very little we can possibly lose! Certainly the cause is enough to *live* for, if not to —— for. I have only had this one opportunity, in a life of nearly sixty years; and could I be continued ten times as long again, I might not again have another equal opportunity. God has honored but comparatively a very small part of mankind with any possible chance for such mighty and soul-satisfying rewards. But, my dear friend, if you should make up your mind to do so, I trust it will be wholly from the promptings of your own spirit, after having thoroughly counted the cost. I would flatter no man into such a measure, if I could do it ever so easily.

I expect nothing but to "endure hardness"; but I expect to effect a mighty conquest, even though it be like the last victory of Samson. I felt for a number of years, in earlier life. a steady, strong desire to die: but since I saw any prospect of becoming a "reaper" in the great harvest, I have not only felt quite willing to live, but have enjoyed life much; and am now rather anxious to live for a few years more.

Your sincere friend,

JOHN BROWN.

JOHN BROWN TO THEODORE PARKER.

BOSTON, MASS., March 7, 1858.

My dear Sir,— Since you know I have an almost countless brood of poor hungry chickens to "scratch for," you will not reproach me for scratching even on the Sabbath. At any rate, I trust God will not. I want you to undertake to provide a substitute for an address you saw last season, directed to the officers and soldiers of the United States Army. The ideas contained in that address I of course like, for I furnished the skeleton. I never had the ability to clothe those ideas in language at all to satisfy myself; and I was by no means satisfied with the style of that address, and do not know as I can give any correct idea of what I want. I will, however, try.

In the first place it must be short, or it will not be generally read. It must be in the simplest or plainest language, without the least affectation of the scholar about it, and yet be worded with great clearness and power. The anonymous writer must (in the language of the Paddy) be "afther others," and not "afther himself at all, at all." If the spirit that communicated Franklin's Poor Richard (or some other good spirit) would dictate, I think it would be quite as well employed as the "dear sister spirits" have been for some years past. The address should be appropriate, and particularly adapted to the peculiar circumstances we anticipate. and should look to the actual change of service from that of Satan to the service of God. It should be, in short, a most earnest and powerful appeal to men's sense of right and to their feelings of humanity. Soldiers are men, and no man can certainly calculate the value and importance of getting a single "nail into old Captain Kidd's chest." It should be provided beforehand, and be ready in advance to distribute by all persons, male and female, who may be disposed to favor the right.

I also want a similar short address, appropriate to the peculiar circumstances, intended for all persons, old and young, male and female, slaveholding and non-slaveholding, to be sent out broadcast over the entire nation. So by every male and female prisoner on being set at liberty, and to be read by them during confinement. I know that men will listen, and reflect, too, under such circumstances. Persons will hear your antislavery lectures and abolition lectures when they have become virtually slaves themselves. The impressions made on prisoners by kindness and plain dealing, instead of barbarous and cruel treatment, such as they might give, and instead of being slaughtered like wild reptiles, as they might very naturally expect, are not only powerful, but lasting. Females are susceptible of being carried away entirely by the kindness of an intrepid and magnanimous soldier, even when his bare name was but a terror the day previous. Now, dear sir, I have told you about as well as I know how what I am anxious at once to secure. Will you write the tracts, or get them written, so that I may commence colporteur?

Very respectfully your friend,

JOHN BROWN.

BROWN'S WORDS TO GOVERNOR WISE AT HARPER'S FERRY.

Governor, I have from all appearances not more than fifteen or twenty years the start of you in the journey to that eternity of which you kindly warn me; and, whether my time here shall be fifteen months or fifteen days or fifteen hours, I am equally prepared to go. There is an eternity behind and an eternity before; and this little speck in the centre, however long, is but comparatively a minute. The difference between your tenure and mine is trifling, and I therefore tell you to be prepared. I am prepared. You all have a heavy responsibility, and it behooves you to prepare more than it does me.

JOHN BROWN'S LAST SPEECH TO THE COURT (NOV. 2, 1859).

I have, may it please the Court, a few words to say.

In the first place, I deny everything but what I have all along admitted,— the design on my part to free the slaves. I intended certainly to have made a clean thing of that matter, as I did last winter, when I went into Missouri and there took slaves without the snapping of a gun on either side, moved them through the country, and finally left them in Canada. I designed to have done the same thing again, on a larger scale. That was all I intended. I never did intend murder, or treason, or the destruction of property, or to excite or incite slaves to rebellion, or to make insurrection.

I have another objection; and that is, it is unjust that I should suffer such a penalty. Had I interfered in the manner which I admit, and which I admit has been fairly proved (for I admire the truthfulness and candor of the greater portion of the witnesses who have testified in this case),— had I so interfered in behalf of the rich, the powerful, the intelligent, the so-called great, or in behalf of any of their friends,— either father, mother, brother, sister, wife, or children, or any of that class,— and suffered and sacrificed what I have in this interference, it would have been all right; and every man in this court would have deemed it an act worthy of reward rather than punishment.

This court acknowledges, as I suppose, the validity of the law of God. I see a book kissed here which I suppose to be the Bible, or at least the New Testament. That teaches me that all things whatsoever I would that men should do to me, I should do even so to them. It teaches me, further, to "remember them that are in bonds, as bound with them." I endeavored to act up to that instruction. I say, I am yet too young to understand that God is any respecter of persons. I believe that to have interfered as I have done — as I have always freely admitted I have done — in behalf of His despised poor, was not wrong, but right. Now, if it is deemed necessary that I should forfeit my life for the furtherance of the ends of justice, and mingle my blood further with the blood of my children and with the blood of millions in this slave country whose rights are disregarded by wicked, cruel, and unjust enactments,— I submit; so let it be done!

Let me say one word further.

I feel entirely satisfied with the treatment I have received on my trial. Considering all the circumstances, it has been more generous than I expected. But I feel no consciousness of guilt. I have stated from the first what was my intention, and what was not. I never had any design against the life of any person, nor any disposition to commit treason, or excite slaves to rebel, or make any general insurrection. I never encouraged any man to do so, but always discouraged any idea of that kind.

Let me say, also, a word in regard to the statements made by some of those connected with me. I hear it has been stated by some of them that I have induced them to join me. But the contrary is true. I do not say this to injure them, but as regretting their weakness. There is not one of them but joined me of his own accord, and the greater part of them at their own expense. A number of them I never saw, and never had a word of conversation with, till the day they came to me; and that was for the purpose I have stated.

Now I have done.

Prison Letters.

To his Family.

Charlestown, Jefferson County, Va., Oct. 31, 1859.

My dear Wife and Children, every one,— I suppose you have learned before this by the newspapers that two weeks ago to-day we were fighting for our lives at Harper's Ferry; that during the fight Watson was mortally wounded, Oliver killed, William Thompson killed, and Dauphin slightly wounded; that on the following day I was taken prisoner, immediately after which I received several sabre-cuts on my head and bayonet-stabs in my body. As nearly as I can learn, Watson died of his wound on Wednesday, the second — or on Thursday, the third — day after I was taken. Dauphin was killed when I was taken, and Anderson I suppose, also. I have since been tried, and found guilty of treason, etc., and of murder in the first degree. I have not yet received my sentence. No others of the company with whom you were acquainted were, so far as I can learn, either killed or taken. Under all these terrible calamities I feel quite cheerful in the assurance that God reigns and will overrule all for his glory and the best possible good. I feel no consciousness of guilt in the matter, nor even mortification on account of my imprisonment and irons; and I feel perfectly sure that very soon no member of my family will feel any possible disposition to "blush on my account." Already dear friends at a distance, with kindest sympathy, are cheering me with the assurance that posterity, at least, will do me justice. I shall commend you all together, with my beloved but bereaved daughters-in-law, to their sympathies, which I do not doubt will soon reach you. I also commend you all to Him "whose mercy endureth forever,"— to the God of my fathers, "whose I am, and whom I serve." "He will never leave you nor forsake you," unless you forsake Him. Finally, my dearly beloved, be of good comfort. Be sure to remember and follow my advice, and my example, too, so far as it has been consistent with the holy religion of Jesus Christ,— in which I remain a most firm and humble believer. Never forget the poor, nor think anything you bestow on them to be lost to you, even though they may be black as Ebedmelech, the Ethiopian eunuch, who cared for Jeremiah in the pit of the dungeon; or as black as the one to whom Philip preached Christ. Be sure to entertain strangers, for thereby some have — "Remember them that are in bonds as bound with them."

I am in charge of a jailer like the one who took charge of Paul and Silas; and you may rest assured that both kind hearts and kind faces are more or less about me, while thousands are thirsting for my blood. "These light afflictions, which are but for a moment, shall work out for us a far more exceeding and eternal weight of glory." I hope to be able to write you again. Copy this, Ruth, and send it to your sorrow-stricken brothers to comfort them. Write me a few words in regard to the welfare of all. God Almighty bless you all, and make you "joyful in the midst of all your tribulations!" Write to John Brown, Charlestown, Jefferson County, Va., care of Captain John Avis.

Your affectionate husband and father,

JOHN BROWN.

P.S.—Yesterday, November 2, I was sentenced to be hanged on December 2 next. Do not grieve on my account. I am still quite cheerful. God bless you!

Yours ever,

JOHN BROWN.

To Mrs. Child.

MRS. L. MARIA CHILD. OCTOBER 31.

My dear Friend,— such you prove to be, though a stranger, — Your most kind letter has reached me, with the kind offer to come here and take care of me. Allow me to express my gratitude for your great sympathy, and at the same time to propose to you a different course, together with my reasons for wishing it. I should certainly be greatly pleased to become personally acquainted with one so gifted and so kind; but I cannot avoid seeing some objections to it under present circumstances. First, I am in charge of a most humane gentleman, who with his family have rendered me every possible attention I have desired or that could be of the least advantage; and I am so far recovered from my wounds as no longer to require nursing. Then, again, it would subject you to great personal inconvenience and heavy expense, without doing me any good. Allow me to name to you another channel through which you may reach me with your sympathies much more effectually. I have at home a wife and three young daughters, the youngest but little over five years old, the oldest nearly sixteen. I have also two daughters-in-law, whose husbands have both fallen near me here. There is also another widow, Mrs. Thompson, whose husband fell here. Whether she is a mother or not I cannot say. All these, my wife included, live at North Elba, Essex County, N.Y. I have a middle-aged son, who has been in some degree a cripple from his childhood, who would have as much as he could well do to earn a living. He was a most dreadful sufferer in Kansas, and lost all he had laid up. He has not enough to clothe himself for the winter comfortably. I have no living son or son-in-law who did not suffer terribly in Kansas.

Now, dear friend, would you not as soon contribute fifty cents now, and a like sum yearly, for the relief of those very poor and deeply afflicted persons, to enable them to supply themselves and their children with bread and very plain clothing, and to enable the children to receive a common English education? Will you also devote your own energies to induce others to join you in giving a like amount, to constitute a little fund for the purpose named?

I cannot see how your coming here can do me the least good; and I am quite certain you can do me immense good where you are. I am quite cheerful under all my afflicting circumstances and prospects, having, as I humbly trust, "the peace of God, which passeth all understanding," to rule in my heart. You may make such use of this as you see fit. God Almighty bless and reward you a thousand-fold!

Yours in sincerity and truth,

JOHN BROWN.

To his Family.

CHARLESTOWN, JEFFERSON COUNTY, VA., Nov. 8, 1859.

Dear Wife and Children, every one,— I will begin by saying that I have in some degree recovered from my wounds, but that I am quite weak in my back and sore about my left kidney. My appetite has been quite good for most of the time since I was hurt. I am supplied with almost everything I could desire to make me comfortable, and the little I do lack (some articles of clothing which I lost) I may perhaps soon get again. I am, besides, quite cheerful, having (as I trust) "the peace of God, which passeth all understanding," to "rule in my heart," and the testimony (in some degree) of a good conscience that I have not lived altogether in vain. I can trust God with both the time and the manner of my death, believing, as I now do, that for me at this time to seal my testimony for God and humanity with my blood will do vastly more toward advancing the cause I have earnestly endeavored to promote, than all I have done in my life before. I beg of you all meekly and quietly to submit to this, not feeling yourselves in the least *degraded* on that account. Remember, dear wife and children all, that Jesus of Nazareth suffered a most excruciating death on the cross as a felon, under the most aggravating circumstances. Think also of the prophets and apostles and Christians of former days, who went through greater tribulations than you or I, and try to be reconciled. May God Almighty comfort all your hearts, and soon wipe away all tears from your eyes! To him be endless praise! Think, too, of the crushed millions who "have no comforter." I charge you all never in your trials to forget the griefs "of the poor that cry, and of those that have none to help them."

I wrote most earnestly to my dear and afflicted wife not to come on for the present, at any rate. I will now give her my reasons for doing so. First, it would use up all the scanty means she has, or is at all likely to have, to make herself and children comfortable hereafter. For let me tell you that the sympathy that is now aroused in your behalf may not always follow you. There is but little more of the romantic about helping poor widows and their children than there is about trying to relieve poor "niggers." Again, the little comfort it might afford us to meet again would be dearly bought by the pains of a final separation. We must part: and I feel assured for us to meet under such dreadful circumstances would only add to our distress. If she comes on here, she must be only a gazing-stock throughout the whole journey, to be remarked upon in every look, word, and action, and by all sorts of creatures, and by all sorts of papers, throughout the whole country. Again, it is my most decided judgment that in quietly and submissively staying at home vastly more of generous sympathy will reach her, without such dreadful sacrifice of feeling as she must put up with if she comes on. The visits of one or two female friends that have come on here have produced great excitement, which is very annoying; and they cannot possibly do me any good. Oh, Mary! do not come, but patiently wait for the meeting of those who love God and their fellow-men, where no separation must follow. "They shall go no more out forever." I greatly long to hear from some one of you, and to learn anything that in any way affects your welfare. I sent you ten dollars the other day; did you get it? I have also endeavored to stir up Christian friends to visit and write to you in your deep affliction. I have no doubt that some of them, at least, will heed the call. Write to me, care of Captain John Avis, Charlestown, Jefferson County, Virginia.

"Finally, my beloved, be of good comfort." May all your names be "written in the Lamb's book of life!" — may you all have the purifying and sustaining influence of the Christian religion! — is the earnest prayer of

Your affectionate husband and father,
JOHN BROWN.

NOVEMBER 9.

P.S.— I cannot remember a night so dark as to have hindered the coming day, nor a storm so furious or dreadful as to prevent the return of warm sunshine and a cloudless sky. But, beloved ones, do remember that this is not your rest, — that in this world you have no abiding place or continuing city. To God and his infinite mercy I always commend you.

J. B.

From a Letter to his Wife, Nov. 16, 1859.

Now let me say a word about the effort to educate our daughters. I am no longer able to provide means to help towards that object, and it therefore becomes me not to dictate in the matter. I shall gratefully submit the direction of the whole thing to those whose generosity may lead them to undertake in their behalf, while I give anew a little expression of my own choice respecting it. You, my wife, perfectly well know that I have always expressed a decided preference for a very plain but perfectly practical education for both sons and daughters. I do not mean an education so very miserable as that you and I received in early life; nor as some of our children enjoyed.

When I say plain but practical, I mean enough of the learning of the schools to enable them to transact the common business of life comfortably and respectably, together with that thorough training to good business habits which best prepares both men and women to be useful though poor, and to meet the stern realities of life with a good grace. You well know that I always claimed that the music of the broom, wash-tub, needle, spindle, loom, axe, scythe, hoe, flail, etc., should first be learned at all events, and that of the piano, etc., afterwards. I put them in that order as most conducive to health of body and mind; and for the obvious reason, that after a life of some experience and of much observation, I have found ten women as well as ten men who have made their mark in life right, whose early training was of that plain, practical kind, to one who had a more popular and fashionable early training. But enough of that.

To the Rev. —— McFarland.

JAIL, CHARLESTOWN, Wednesday, Nov. 23, 1859.

THE REV. —— MCFARLAND.

Dear Friend,— Although you write to me as a stranger, the spirit you show towards me and the cause for which I am in bonds makes me feel towards you as a dear friend. I would be glad to have you or any of my liberty-loving ministerial friends here, to talk and pray with me. I am not a stranger to the way of salvation by Christ. From my youth I have studied much on that subject, and at one time hoped to be a minister myself; but God had another work for me to do. To me it is given, in behalf of Christ, not only to believe on him, but also to suffer for his sake. But while I trust that I have some experimental and saving knowledge of religion, it would be a great pleasure to me to have some one better qualified than myself to lead my mind in prayer and meditation, now that my time is so near a close. You may wonder, are there no ministers of the gospel here? I answer, no. There are no ministers of Christ here. These ministers who profess to be Christian, and hold slaves or advocate slavery, I cannot abide them. My knees will not bend in prayer with them, while their hands are stained with the blood of souls. The subject you mention as having been preaching on the day before you wrote to me is one which I have often thought of since my imprisonment. I think I feel as happy as Paul did when he lay in prison. He knew if they killed him, it would greatly advance the cause of Christ; that was the reason he rejoiced so. On that same ground "I do rejoice, yea, and will rejoice." Let them hang me; I forgive them, and may God forgive them, for they know not what they do. I have no regret for the transaction for which I am condemned. I went against the laws of men, it is true, but "whether it be right to obey God or men, judge ye." Christ told me to remember them that were in bonds as bound with them, to do towards them as I would wish them to do towards me in similar circumstances. My conscience bade me do that. I tried to do it, but failed. Therefore I have no regret on that score. I have no sorrow either as to the result, only for my poor wife and children. They have suffered much, and it is hard to leave them uncared for. But God will be a husband to the widow and a father to the fatherless.

I have frequently been in Wooster, and if any of my old friends from about Akron are there, you can show them this letter. I have but a few more days, and I feel anxious to be away "where the wicked cease from troubling, and the weary are at rest." Farewell.

Your friend, and the friend of all friends of liberty,

JOHN BROWN.

To Hon. D. R. Tilden.

Hon. D. R. Tilden.

CHARLESTOWN, JEFFERSON COUNTY, VA.,
Monday, Nov. 28, 1859.

My dear Sir,—Your most kind and comforting letter of the 23d inst. is received. I have no language to express the feelings of gratitude and obligation I am under for your kind interest in my behalf ever since my disaster. The great bulk of mankind estimate each other's actions and motives by the measure of success or otherwise that attends them through life. By that rule, I have been one of the worst and one of the best of men. I do not claim to have been one of the latter, and I leave it to an impartial tribunal to decide whether the world has been the worse or the better for my living and dying in it. My present great anxiety is to get as near in readiness for a different field of action as I well can, since being in a good measure relieved from the fear that my poor brokenhearted wife and children would come to immediate want. May God reward a thousand-fold all the kind efforts made in their behalf! I have enjoyed remarkable cheerfulness and composure of mind ever since my confinement; and it is a great comfort to feel assured that I am permitted to die for a cause, — not merely to pay the debt of nature, as all must. I feel myself to be most unworthy of so great distinction. The particular manner of dying assigned to me gives me but very little uneasiness. I wish I had the time and the ability to give you, my dear friend, some little idea of what is daily, and I might almost say hourly, passing within my prison walls; and could my friends but witness only a few of these scenes, just as they occur, I think they would feel very well reconciled to my being here, just what I am, and just as I am. My whole life before had not afforded me one half the opportunity to plead for the right. In this, also, I find much to reconcile me to both my present condition and my immediate prospect. I may be very insane; and I am so, if insane at all. But if that be so, insanity is like a very pleasant dream to me. I am not in the least degree conscious of my ravings, of my fears, or of any terrible visions whatever; but fancy myself entirely composed, and that my sleep, in particular, is as sweet as that of a healthy, joyous little infant. I pray God that he will grant me a continuance of the same calm but delightful dream, until I come to know of those realities which eyes have not seen and which ears have not heard. I have scarce realized that I am in prison or in irons at all. I certainly think I was never more cheerful in my life. . . .

Your friend in truth,

JOHN BROWN.

To Mrs. George L. Stearns.

CHARLESTOWN, JEFFERSON COUNTY. VA., Nov. 29, 1859.

MRS. GEORGE L. STEARNS, Boston, Mass.

My dear Friend,— No letter I have received since my imprisonment here has given me more satisfaction or comfort than yours of the 8th instant. I am quite cheerful, and was never more happy. Have only time to write a word. May God forever reward you and all yours! My love to all who love their neighbors. I have asked to be spared from having any weak or hypocritical prayers made over me when I am publicly murdered, and that my only religious attendants be poor little dirty, ragged, bareheaded and barefooted slave boys and girls, led by some old gray-headed slave mother.

Farewell! Farewell!

Your friend,

JOHN BROWN.

John Brown's Last Letter to his Family.

CHARLESTOWN PRISON, JEFFERSON COUNTY, VA,
Nov. 30, 1859.

My dearly beloved Wife, Sons, and Daughters, every one,— As I now begin probably what is the last letter I shall ever write to any of you, I conclude to write to all at the same time. I will mention some little matters particularly applicable to little property concerns in another place.

I recently received a letter from my wife, from near Philadelphia, dated November 22, by which it would seem that she was about giving up the idea of seeing me again. I had written her to come on if she felt equal to the undertaking, but I do not know that she will get my letter in time. It was on her own account, chiefly, that I asked her to stay back. At first I had a most strong desire to see her again, but there appeared to be very serious objections; and should we never meet in this life, I trust that she will in the end be satisfied it was for the best at least, if not most for her comfort.

I am waiting the hour of my public murder with great composure of mind and cheerfulness; feeling the strong assurance that in no other possible way could I be used to so much advantage to the cause of God and of humanity, and that nothing that either I or all my family have sacrificed or suffered will be lost. The reflection that a wise and merciful as well as just and holy God rules not only the affairs of this world, but of all worlds, is a rock to set our feet upon under all circumstances,—even those more severely trying ones in which our own feelings and wrongs have placed us. I have now no doubt but that our seeming disaster will ultimately result in the most glorious success. So, my dear shattered and broken family, be of good cheer, and believe and trust in God with all your heart and with all your soul; for he doeth all things well. Do not feel ashamed on my account, nor for one moment despair of the cause or grow weary of well-doing. I bless God I never felt stronger confidence in the certain and near approach of a bright morning and glorious day than I have felt, and do now feel, since my confinement here. I am endeavoring to return, like a poor prodigal, as I am, to my Father, against whom I have always sinned, in the hope that he may kindly and forgivingly meet me, though a very great way off.

Oh, my dear wife and children, would to God you could know how I have been travailing in birth for you all, that no one of you may fail of the grace of God through Jesus Christ; that no one of you may be blind to the truth and glorious light of his Word, in which life and immortality are brought to light. I beseech you, every one, to make the Bible your daily and nightly study, with a child-like, honest, candid, teachable spirit of love and respect for your husband and father. And I beseech the God of my fathers to open all your eyes to the discovery of the truth. You cannot imagine how much you may soon need the consolations of the Christian religion. Circumstances like my own for more than a month past have convinced me, beyond all doubt, of my own great need of some theories treasured up, when our prejudices are excited, our vanity worked up to the highest pitch. Oh, do not trust your eternal all upon the boisterous ocean, without even a helm or compass to aid you in steering! I do not ask of you to throw away your reason; I only ask you to make a candid, sober use of your reason.

My dear young children, will you listen to this last poor admonition of one who can only love you? Oh, be determined at once to give your whole heart to God, and let nothing shake or alter that resolution. You need have no fears of regretting it. Do not be vain and thoughtless, but sober-minded; and let me entreat you all to love the whole remnant of our once great family. Try and build up again your broken walls, and to make the utmost of every stone that is left. Nothing can so tend to make life a blessing as the consciousness that your life and example bless and leave others stronger. Still, it is ground of the utmost comfort to my mind to know that so many of you as have had the opportunity have given some proof of your fidelity to the great family of men. Be faithful unto death: from the exercise of habitual love to man it cannot be very hard to love his Maker.

I must yet insert the reason for my firm belief in the divine inspiration of the Bible, notwithstanding I am, perhaps, naturally sceptical,—certainly not credulous. I wish all to consider it most thoroughly when you read that blessed book, and see whether you cannot discover such evidence yourselves. It is the purity of heart, filling our minds as well as work and actions, which is everywhere insisted on, that distinguishes it from all the other teachings, that commends it to my conscience. Whether my heart be willing and obedient or not, the inducement that it holds out is another reason of my conviction of its truth and genuineness; but I do not here omit this, my last argument on the Bible, that eternal life is what my soul is panting after this moment. I mention this as a reason for endeavoring to leave a valuable copy of the Bible, to be carefully preserved in remembrance of me, to so many of my posterity, instead of some other book at equal cost.

I beseech you all to live in habitual contentment with moderate circumstances and gains of worldly store, and earnestly to teach this to your children and children's children after you, by example as well as precept. Be determined to know by experience, as soon as may be, whether Bible instruction is of divine origin or not. Be sure to owe no man anything, but to love one another. John Rogers wrote to his children, "Abhor that arrant whore of Rome." John Brown writes to his children to abhor, with undying hatred also, that sum of all villanies,—slavery. Remember, "he that is slow to anger is better than the mighty," and "he that ruleth his spirit than he that taketh a city." Remember also that "they being wise shall shine, and they that turn many to righteousness, as the stars for ever and ever."

And now, dearly beloved family, to God and the work of his grace I commend you all.

Your affectionate husband and father,

JOHN BROWN.

The Last Paper written by John Brown, handed to One of the Guards on the Morning of his Execution.

CHARLESTOWN, VA., Dec. 2, 1859.

I, John Brown, am now quite *certain* that the crimes of this *guilty land* will never be purged away but with *blood*. I had, as I now think vainly, flattered myself that without very much bloodshed it might be done.

"The Life and Letters of John Brown" by Frank B. Sanborn is the completest and best biography and, written as it was by one so intimate with his work and purposes, is likely to remain the final authoritative word. There are less critical works by Redpath and Webb; and Van Holst's noble essay has been translated and published in a separate volume, with valuable introduction and notes by Mr. Frank L. Stearns. "Echoes of Harper's Ferry" is a collection, edited by Redpath in 1860, of the notable tributes to John Brown by Wendell Phillips, Emerson, Thoreau, Theodore Parker, Victor Hugo and many others.

PUBLISHED BY

THE DIRECTORS OF THE OLD SOUTH WORK,
Old South Meeting-house, Boston, Mass.

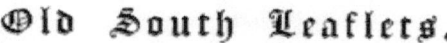

Old South Leaflets.

No. 85.

The First Lincoln and Douglas Debate.

AT OTTAWA, ILL., AUG. 21, 1858.

MR. DOUGLAS'S OPENING SPEECH.

Ladies and Gentlemen,—I appear before you to-day for the purpose of discussing the leading political topics which now agitate the public mind. By an arrangement between Mr. Lincoln and myself, we are present here to-day for the purpose of having a joint discussion, as the representatives of the two great political parties of the State and Union, upon the principles in issue between those parties; and this vast concourse of people shows the deep feeling which pervades the public mind in regard to the questions dividing us.

Prior to 1854, this country was divided into two great political parties, known as the Whig and Democratic parties. Both were national and patriotic, advocating principles that were universal in their application. An old-line Whig could proclaim his principles in Louisiana and Massachusetts alike. Whig principles had no boundary sectional line: they were not limited by the Ohio River, nor by the Potomac, nor by the line of the free and slave States, but applied and were proclaimed wherever the Constitution ruled or the American flag waved over the American soil. So it was and so it is with the great Democratic party, which, from the days of Jefferson until this period, has proven itself to be the historic party of this nation. While the Whig and Democratic parties differed in regard to a bank, the tariff, distribution, the specie circular, and the sub-treasury, they agreed on the great slavery question which now agitates the Union. I say that the Whig party and the Democratic party agreed on the slavery question, while they differed on those matters of expediency to which I have referred. The Whig party and the Democratic party jointly adopted the compromise measures of 1850 as the basis of a proper and just solution of the slavery question in all its forms. Clay was the great leader, with Webster on his right and Cass on his left, and sustained by the patriots in the Whig and Democratic ranks who had devised and enacted the compromise measures of 1850.

In 1851 the Whig party and the Democratic party united in Illinois in adopting resolutions indorsing and approving the principles of the compromise measures of 1850 as the proper adjustment of that question. In 1852, when the Whig party assembled in convention at Baltimore for the purpose of nominating a candidate for the presidency, the first thing it did was to declare the compromise measures of 1850, in substance and in principle, a suitable adjustment of that question. [Here the speaker was interrupted by loud and long-continued applause.] My friends, silence will be more acceptable to me in the discussion of these questions than applause. I desire to address myself to your judgment, your understanding, and your consciences, and not to your passions or your enthusiasm. When the Democratic convention assembled in Baltimore in the same year, for the purpose of nominating a Democratic candidate for the presidency, it also adopted the compromise measures of 1850 as the basis of Democratic action. Thus you see that up to 1853-54 the Whig party and the Democratic party both stood on the same platform with regard to the slavery question. That platform was the right of the people of each State and each Territory to decide their local and domestic institutions for themselves, subject only to the Federal Constitution.

During the session of Congress of 1853-54 I introduced into the Senate of the United States a bill to organize the Territories of Kansas and Nebraska on that principle which had been adopted in the compromise measures of 1850, approved by the Whig party and the Democratic party in Illinois in 1851, and indorsed by the Whig party and the Democratic party in national convention in 1852. In order that there might be no misunderstanding in relation to the principle involved in the Kansas and Nebraska bill, I put forth the true intent and meaning of the act in these words: "It is the true intent and meaning of this act not to legislate slavery into any State or Territory, or to exclude it therefrom, but to leave the people thereof perfectly free to form and regulate their domestic institutions in their own way, subject only to the Federal Constitution." Thus you see that up to 1854, when the Kansas and Nebraska bill was brought into Congress for the purpose of carrying out the principles which both parties had up to that time indorsed and approved, there had been no division in this country in regard to that principle except the opposition of the Abolitionists. In the House of Representatives of the Illinois legislature, upon a resolution asserting that principle, every Whig and every Democrat in the House voted in the affirmative, and only four men voted against it, and those four were old-line Abolitionists.

In 1854 Mr. Abraham Lincoln and Mr. Lyman Trumbull entered into an arrangement, one with the other, and each with his respective friends, to dissolve the old Whig party on the one hand, and to dissolve the old Democratic party on the other, and to connect the members of both into an Abolition party, under the name and disguise of a Republican party. The terms of that arrangement between Lincoln and Trumbull have been published by Lincoln's special friend, James H. Matheny, Esq.; and they were that Lincoln should have General Shields's place in the United States Senate, which was then about to become vacant, and that Trumbull should have my seat when my term expired. Lincoln went to work to Abolitionize the Old Whig party all over the State, pretending that he was then as good a Whig as ever; and Trumbull went to work in his part of the State preaching Abolitionism in its milder and lighter form, and trying to Abolitionize the Democratic party, and bring old Democrats handcuffed and bound hand and foot into the Abolition camp. In pursuance of the arrangement the parties met at Springfield in October, 1854, and proclaimed their new platform. Lincoln was to bring into the Abolition camp the old-line Whigs, and transfer them over to Giddings, Chase, Fred Douglass, and Parson Lovejoy, who were ready to receive them and christen them in their new faith. They laid down on that occasion a platform for their new Republican party, which was thus to be constructed. I have the resolutions of the State convention then held, which was the first mass State convention ever held in Illinois by the Black Republican party; and I now hold them in my hands and will read a part of them, and cause the others to be printed. Here are the most important and material resolutions of this Abolition platform:—

1. *Resolved*, That we believe this truth to be self-evident, that, when parties become subversive of the ends for which they are established, or incapable of restoring the government to the true principles of the Constitution, it is the right and duty of the people to dissolve the political bands by which they may have been connected therewith, and to organize new parties upon such principles and with such views as the circumstances and the exigencies of the nation may demand.

2. *Resolved*, That the times imperatively demand the reorganization of parties, and, repudiating all previous party attachments, names, and predilections, we unite ourselves together in defence of the liberty and Constitution of the country, and will hereafter co-operate as the Republican party, pledged to the accomplishment of the following purposes: to bring the administration of the government back to the control of first principles; to restore Nebraska and Kansas to the position of free Territories; that, as the Constitution of the United States vests in the States, and not in Congress, the power to legislate for the extradition of fugitives from labor, to repeal and entirely abrogate the fugitive-slave law; to restrict slavery to those States in which it exists; to prohibit the admission of any more slave States into the Union; to abolish slavery in the District of Columbia; to exclude slavery from all the Territories over which the general government has exclusive jurisdiction; and to resist the acquirement of any more Territories unless the practice of slavery therein forever shall have been prohibited.

3. *Resolved*, That in furtherance of these principles we will use such constitutional and lawful means as shall seem best adapted to their accomplishment, and that we will support no man for office, under the general or State government, who is not positively and fully committed to the support of these principles, and whose personal character and conduct is not a guarantee that he is reliable, and who shall not have abjured old party allegiance and ties.

Now, gentlemen, your Black Republicans have cheered every one of those propositions; and yet I venture to say that you cannot get Mr. Lincoln to come out and say that he is now in favor of each one of them. That these propositions, one and all, constitute the platform of the Black Republican party of this day, I have no doubt; and, when you were not aware for what purpose I was reading them, your Black Republicans cheered them as good Black Republican doctrines. My object in reading these resolutions was to put the question to Abraham Lincoln this day, whether he now stands and will stand by each article in that creed, and carry it out. I desire to know whether Mr. Lincoln to-day stands as he did in 1854, in favor of the unconditional repeal of the fugitive-slave law. I desire him to answer whether he stands pledged to-day, as he did in 1854, against the admission of any more slave States into the Union, even if the people want them. I want to know whether he stands pledged against the admission of a new State into the Union with such a constitution as the people of that State may see fit to make. I want to know whether he stands to-day pledged to the abolition of slavery in the District of Columbia. I desire him to answer whether he stands pledged to the prohibition of the slave-trade between the different States. I desire to know whether he stands pledged to prohibit slavery in all the Territories of the United States, north as well as south of the Missouri Compromise line. I desire him to answer whether he is opposed to the acquisition of any more territory unless slavery is prohibited therein. I want his answer to these questions. Your affirmative cheers in favor of this Abolition platform are not satisfactory. I ask Abraham Lincoln to answer these questions, in order that, when I trot him down to lower Egypt, I may put the same questions to him. My principles are the same everywhere. I can proclaim them alike in the North, the South, the East, and the West. My principles will apply wherever the Constitution prevails and the American flag waves. I desire to know whether Mr. Lincoln's principles will bear transplanting from Ottawa to Jonesboro? I put these questions to him to-day distinctly, and ask an answer. I have a right to an answer; for I quote from the platform of the Republican party, made by himself and others at the time that party was formed, and the bargain made by Lincoln to dissolve and kill the Old Whig party, and transfer its members, bound hand and foot, to the Abolition party, under the direction of Giddings and Fred Douglass. In the remarks I have made on this platform, and the position of Mr. Lincoln upon it, I mean nothing personally disrespectful or unkind to that gentleman. I have known him for nearly twenty-five years. There were many points of sympathy between us when we first got acquainted. We were both comparatively boys, and both struggling with poverty in a strange land. I was a school-teacher in the town of Winchester, and he a flourishing grocery-keeper in the town of Salem. He was more successful in his occupation than I was in mine, and hence more fortunate in this world's goods. Lincoln is one of those peculiar men who perform with admirable skill everything which they undertake. I made as good a school-teacher as I could, and, when a cabinet-maker, I made a good bedstead and tables, although my old boss said I succeeded better with bureaus and secretaries than with anything else; but I believe that Lincoln was always more successful in business than I, for his business enabled him to get into the legislature. I met him there, however, and had sympathy with him, because of the up-hill struggle we both had in life. He was then just as good at telling an anecdote as now. He could beat any of the boys wrestling or running a foot-race, in pitching quoits or tossing a copper; could ruin more liquor than all the boys of the town together; and the dignity and impartiality with which he presided at a horse-race or fist-fight excited the admiration and won the praise of everybody that was present and participated. I sympathized with him because he was struggling with difficulties, and so was I. Mr. Lincoln served with me in the legislature in 1836, when we both retired; and he subsided or became submerged, and he was lost sight of as a public man for some years. In 1846, when Wilmot introduced his celebrated proviso, and the Abolition tornado swept over the country, Lincoln again turned up as a member of Congress from the Sangamon district. I was then in the Senate of the United States, and was glad to welcome my old friend and companion. Whilst in Congress, he distinguished himself by his opposition to the Mexican war, taking the side of the common enemy against his own country; and, when he returned home, he found that the indignation of the people followed him everywhere, and he was again submerged, or obliged to retire into private life, forgotten by his former friends. He came up again in 1854, just in time to make this Abolition or Black Republican platform, in company with Giddings, Lovejoy, Chase, and Fred Douglass, for the Republican party to stand upon. Trumbull, too, was one of our own contemporaries. He was born and raised in old Connecticut, was bred a Federalist, but, removing to Georgia, turned Nullifier when nullification was popular, and, as soon as he disposed of his clocks and wound up his business, migrated to Illinois, turned politician and lawyer here, and made his appearance in 1841 as a member of the legislature. He became noted as the author of the scheme to repudiate a large portion of the State debt of Illinois, which, if successful, would have brought infamy and disgrace upon the fair escutcheon of our glorious State. The odium attached to that measure consigned him to oblivion for a time. I helped to do it. I walked into a public meeting in the hall of the House of Representatives, and replied to his repudiating speeches, and resolutions were carried over his head denouncing repudiation, and asserting the moral and legal obligation of Illinois to pay every dollar of the debt she owed and every bond that bore her seal. Trumbull's malignity has followed me since I thus defeated his infamous scheme.

These two men, having formed this combination to Abolitionize the Old Whig party and the old Democratic party, and put themselves into the Senate of the United States, in pursuance of their bargain, are now carrying out that arrangement. Matheny states that Trumbull broke faith; that the bargain was that Lincoln should be the senator in Shields's place, and Trumbull was to wait for mine; and the story goes that Trumbull cheated Lincoln, having control of four or five Abolitionized Democrats who were holding over in the Senate. He would not let them vote for Lincoln, which obliged the rest of the Abolitionists to support him in order to secure an Abolition senator. There are a number of authorities for the truth of this besides Matheny, and I suppose that even Mr. Lincoln will not deny it.

Mr. Lincoln demands that he shall have the place intended for Trumbull, as Trumbull cheated him and got his; and Trumbull is stumping the State, traducing me for the purpose of securing the position for Lincoln, in order to quiet him. It was in consequence of this arrangement that the Republican convention was impanelled to instruct for Lincoln and nobody else; and it was on this account that they passed resolutions that he was their first, their last, and their only choice. Archy Williams was nowhere, Browning was nobody, Wentworth was not to be considered; they had no man in the Republican party for the place except Lincoln, for the reason that he demanded that they should carry out the arrangement.

Having formed this new party for the benefit of deserters from Whiggery and deserters from Democracy, and having laid down the Abolition platform which I have read, Lincoln now takes his stand and proclaims his Abolition doctrines. Let me read a part of them. In his speech at Springfield to the convention which nominated him for the Senate he said:—

In my opinion, it will not cease until a crisis shall have been reached and passed. "A house divided against itself cannot stand." I believe this government cannot endure permanently half slave and half free. I do not expect the Union to be dissolved,— I do not expect the house to fall,— but I do expect it will cease to be divided. It will become all one thing or all the other. Either the opponents of slavery will arrest the further spread of it, and place it where the public mind shall rest in the belief that it is in the course of ultimate extinction, or its advocates will push it forward till it shall become alike lawful in all the States,— old as well as new, North as well as South. ["Good," "Good," and cheers.]

I am delighted to hear you Black Republicans say, "Good." I have no doubt that doctrine expresses your sentiments: and I will prove to you now, if you will listen to me, that it is revolutionary and destructive of the existence of this government. Mr. Lincoln, in the extract from which I have read, says that this government cannot endure permanently in the same condition in which it was made by its framers — divided into free and slave States. He says that it has existed for about seventy years thus divided, and yet he tells you that it cannot endure permanently on the same principles and in the same relative condition in which our fathers made it. Why can it not exist divided into free and slave States? Washington, Jefferson, Franklin, Madison, Hamilton, Jay, and the great men of that day made this government divided into free States and slave States, and left each State perfectly free to do as it pleased on the subject of slavery. Why can it not exist on the same principles on which our fathers made it? They knew when they framed the Constitution that in a country as wide and broad as this, with such a variety of climate, production, and interest, the people necessarily required different laws and institutions in different localities. They knew that the laws and regulations which would suit the granite hills of New Hampshire would be unsuited to the rice plantations of South Carolina; and they therefore provided that each State should retain its own legislature and its own sovereignty, with the full and complete power to do as it pleased within its own limits, in all that was local and not national. One of the reserved rights of the States was the right to regulate the relations between master and servant, on the slavery question. At the time the Constitution was framed there were thirteen States in the Union, twelve of which were slaveholding States and one a free State. Suppose this doctrine of uniformity preached by Mr. Lincoln, that the States should all be free or all be slave, had prevailed; and what would have been the result? Of course, the twelve slaveholding States would have overruled the one free State; and slavery would have been fastened by a constitutional provision on every inch of the American republic, instead of being left, as our fathers wisely left it, to each State to decide for itself. Here I assert that uniformity in the local laws and institutions of the different States is neither possible nor desirable. If uniformity had been adopted when the government was established, it must inevitably have been the uniformity of slavery everywhere, or else the uniformity of negro citizenship and negro equality everywhere.

We are told by Lincoln that he is utterly opposed to the Dred Scott decision, and will not submit to it, for the reason that he says it deprives the negro of the rights and privileges of citizenship. That is the first and main reason which he assigns for his warfare on the Supreme Court of the United States and its decision. I ask you, Are you in favor of conferring upon the negro the rights and privileges of citizenship? Do you desire to strike out of our State constitution that clause which keeps slaves and free negroes out of the State, and allow the free negroes to flow in, and cover your prairies with black settlements? Do you desire to turn this beautiful State into a free negro colony, in order that, when Missouri abolishes slavery, she can send one hundred thousand emancipated slaves into Illinois, to become citizens and voters, on an equality with yourselves? If you desire negro citizenship, if you desire to allow them to come into the State and settle with the white man, if you desire them to vote on an equality with yourselves, and to make them eligible to office, to serve on juries, and to adjudge your rights, then support Mr. Lincoln and the Black Republican party, who are in favor of the citizenship of the negro. For one, I am opposed to negro citizenship in any and every form. I believe this government was made on the white basis. I believe it was made by white men, for the benefit of white men and their posterity forever; and I am in favor of confining citizenship to white men, men of European birth and descent, instead of conferring it upon negroes, Indians, and other inferior races.

Mr. Lincoln, following the example and lead of all the little Abolition orators who go around and lecture in the basements of schools and churches, reads from the Declaration of Independence that all men were created equal, and then asks how can you deprive a negro of that equality which God and the Declaration of Independence award to him? He and they maintain that negro equality is guaranteed by the laws of God, and that it is asserted in the Declaration of Independence. If they think so, of course they have a right to say so, and so vote. I do not question Mr. Lincoln's conscientious belief that the negro was made his equal, and hence is his brother; but, for my own part, I do not regard the negro as my equal, and positively deny that he is my brother or any kin to me whatever. Lincoln has evidently learned by heart Parson Lovejoy's catechism. He can repeat it as well as Farnsworth, and he is worthy of a medal from Father Giddings and Fred Douglass for his Abolitionism. He holds that the negro was born his equal and yours, and that he was endowed with equality by the Almighty, and that no human law can deprive him of these rights which were guaranteed to him by the Supreme Ruler of the universe. Now I do not believe that the Almighty ever intended the negro to be the equal of the white man. If he did, he has been a long time demonstrating the fact. For thousands of years the negro has been a race upon the earth; and during all that time, in all latitudes and climates, wherever he has wandered or been taken, he has been inferior to the race which he has there met. He belongs to an inferior race, and must always occupy an inferior position. I do not hold that, because the negro is our inferior, therefore he ought to be a slave. By no means can such a conclusion be drawn from what I have said. On the contrary, I hold that humanity and Christianity both require that the negro shall have and enjoy every right, every privilege, and every immunity consistent with the safety of the society in which he lives. On that point, I presume, there can be no diversity of opinion. You and I are bound to extend to our inferior and dependent beings every right, every privilege, every facility and immunity consistent with the public good. The question then arises, What rights and privileges are consistent with the public good? This is a question which each State and each Territory must decide for itself. Illinois has decided it for herself. We have provided that the negro shall not be a slave; and we have also provided that he shall not be a citizen, but protect him in his civil rights, in his life, his person, and his property, only depriving him of all political rights whatsoever, and refusing to put him on an equality with the white man. That policy of Illinois is satisfactory to the Democratic party and to me, and, if it were to the Republicans, there would then be no question upon the subject; but the Republicans say that he ought to be made a citizen, and, when he becomes a citizen, he becomes your equal, with all your rights and privileges. They assert the Dred Scott decision to be monstrous because it denies that the negro is or can be a citizen under the Constitution.

Now I hold that Illinois had a right to abolish and prohibit slavery as she did, and I hold that Kentucky has the same right to continue and protect slavery that Illinois had to abolish it. I hold that New York had as much right to abolish slavery as Virginia has to continue it, and that each and every State of this Union is a sovereign power, with the right to do as it pleases upon this question of slavery and upon all its domestic institutions. Slavery is not the only question which comes up in this controversy. There is a far more important one to you; and that is, What shall be done with the free negro? We have settled the slavery question as far as we are concerned: we have prohibited it in Illinois forever, and, in doing so, I think we have done wisely, and there is no man in the State who would be more strenuous in his opposition to the introduction of slavery than I would; but, when we settled it for ourselves, we exhausted all our power over that subject. We have done our whole duty, and can do no more. We must leave each and every other State to decide for itself the same question. In relation to the policy to be pursued toward the free negroes, we have said that they shall not vote; whilst Maine, on the other hand, has said that they shall vote. Maine is a sovereign State, and has the power to regulate the qualifications of voters within her limits. I would never consent to confer the right of voting and of citizenship upon a negro, but still I am not going to quarrel with Maine for differing from me in opinion. Let Maine take care of her own negroes, and fix the qualifications of her own voters to suit herself, without interfering with Illinois; and Illinois will not interfere with Maine. So with the State of New York. She allows the negro to vote provided he owns two hundred and fifty dollars' worth of property, but not otherwise. While I would not make any distinction whatever between a negro who held property and one who did not, yet, if the sovereign State of New York chooses to make that distinction, it is her business, and not mine; and I will not quarrel with her for it. She can do as she pleases on this question if she minds her own business, and we will do the same thing. Now, my friends, if we will only act conscientiously and rigidly upon this great principle of popular sovereignty, which guarantees to each State and Territory the right to do as it pleases on all things local and domestic, instead of Congress interfering, we will continue at peace one with another. Why should Illinois be at war with Missouri, or Kentucky with Ohio, or Virginia with New York, merely because their institutions differ? Our fathers intended that our institutions should differ. They knew that the North and the South, having different climates, productions, and interests, required different institutions. This doctrine of Mr. Lincoln, of uniformity among the institutions of the different States, is a new doctrine, never dreamed of by Washington, Madison, or the framers of this government. Mr. Lincoln and the Republican party set themselves up as wiser than these men who made this government, which has flourished for seventy years under the principle of popular sovereignty, recognizing the right of each State to do as it pleased. Under that principle, we have grown from a nation of three or four millions to a nation of about thirty millions of people. We have crossed the Alleghany mountains and filled up the whole Northwest, turning the prairie into a garden, and building up churches and schools, thus spreading civilization and Christianity where before there was nothing but savage barbarism. Under that principle we have become, from a feeble nation, the most powerful on the face of the earth; and, if we only adhere to that principle, we can go forward increasing in territory, in power, in strength, and in glory until the Republic of America shall be the north star that shall guide the friends of freedom throughout the civilized world. And why can we not adhere to the great principle of self-government upon which our institutions were originally based? I believe that this new doctrine preached by Mr. Lincoln and his party will dissolve the Union if it succeeds. They are trying to array all the Northern States in one body against the South, to excite a sectional war between the free States and the slave States, in order that the one or the other may be driven to the wall.

Mr. Lincoln's Reply.

My Fellow-citizens,— When a man hears himself somewhat misrepresented, it provokes him,— at least, I find it so with myself; but, when misrepresentation become very gross and palpable, it is more apt to amuse him. The first thing I see fit to notice is the fact that Judge Douglas alleges, after running through the history of the old Democratic and the old Whig parties, that Judge Trumbull and myself made an arrangement in 1854 by which I was to have the place of General Shields in the United States Senate, and Judge Trumbull was to have the place of Judge Douglas. Now all I have to say upon that subject is that I think no man — not even Judge Douglas — can prove it, because it is not true. I have no doubt he is "conscientious" in saying it. As to those resolutions that he took such a length of time to read, as being the platform of the Republican party in 1854, I say I never had anything to do with them; and I think Trumbull never had. Judge Douglas cannot show that either of us ever did have anything to do with them. I believe this is true about those resolutions. There was a call for a convention to form a Republican party at Springfield; and I think that my friend Mr. Lovejoy, who is here upon this stand, had a hand in it. I think this is true; and I think, if he will remember accurately, he will be able to recollect that he tried to get me into it, and I would not go in. I believe it is also true that I went away from Springfield, when the convention was in session, to attend court in Tazewell County. It is true they did place my name, though without authority, upon the committee, and afterward wrote me to attend the meeting of the committee; but I refused to do so, and I never had anything to do with that organization. This is the plain truth about all that matter of the resolutions.

Now, about this story that Judge Douglas tells of Trumbull bargaining to sell out the old Democratic party, and Lincoln agreeing to sell out the Old Whig party, I have the means of knowing about that: Judge Douglas cannot have; and I know there is no substance to it whatever. Yet I have no doubt he is "conscientious" about it. I know that, after Mr. Lovejoy got into the legislature that winter, he complained of me that I had told all the Old Whigs of his district that the Old Whig party was good enough for them, and some of them voted against him because I told them so. Now I have no means of totally disproving such charges as this which the judge makes. A man cannot prove a negative; but he has a right to claim that, when a man makes an affirmative charge, he must offer some proof to show the truth of what he says. I certainly cannot introduce testimony to show the negative about things; but I have a right to claim that, if a man says he knows a thing, then he must show how he knows it. I always have a right to claim this, and it is not satisfactory to me that he may be "conscientious" on the subject.

Now, gentlemen, I hate to waste my time on such things, but in regard to that general Abolition tilt that Judge Douglas makes when he says that I was engaged at that time in selling out and Abolitionizing the Old Whig party, I hope you will permit me to read a part of a printed speech that I made then at Peoria, which will show altogether a different view of the position I took in that contest of 1854. [Voice: "Put on your specs."] Yes, sir, I am obliged to do so. I am no longer a young man.

This is the repeal of the Missouri Compromise. The foregoing history may not be precisely accurate in every particular; but I am sure it is sufficiently so for all the uses I shall attempt to make of it, and in it we have before us the chief materials enabling us to correctly judge whether the repeal of the Missouri Compromise is right or wrong.

I think, and shall try to show, that it is wrong,—wrong in its direct effect, —letting slavery into Kansas and Nebraska,— and wrong in its prospective principle,—allowing it to spread to every other part of the wide world where men can be found inclined to take it.

This declared indifference, but, as I must think, covert real zeal for the spread of slavery, I cannot but hate. I hate it because of the monstrous injustice of slavery itself. I hate it because it deprives our republican example of its just influence in the world; enables the enemies of free institutions, with plausibility, to taunt us as hypocrites; causes the real friends of freedom to doubt our sincerity, and especially because it forces so many really good men amongst ourselves into an open war with the very fundamental principles of civil liberty,— criticising the Declaration of Independence, and insisting that there is no right principle of action but self-interest.

Before proceeding, let me say I think I have no prejudice against the Southern people. They are just what we would be in their situation. If slavery did not now exist among them, they would not introduce it. If it did now exist among us, we should not instantly give it up. This I believe of the masses North and South. Doubtless there are individuals on both sides who would not hold slaves under any circumstances; and others who would gladly introduce slavery anew, if it were out of existence. We know that some Southern men do free their slaves, go North, and become tip-top

Abolitionists; while some Northern ones go South, and become most cruel slave-masters.

When Southern people tell us they are no more responsible for the origin of slavery than we, I acknowledge the fact. When it is said that the institution exists, and that it is very difficult to get rid of it in any satisfactory way, I can understand and appreciate the saying. I surely will not blame them for not doing what I should not know how to do myself. If all earthly power were given me, I should not know what to do as to the existing institution. My first impulse would be to free all the slaves, and send them to Liberia,— to their own native land. But a moment's reflection would convince me that, whatever of high hope (as I think there is) there may be in this in the long run, its sudden execution is impossible. If they were all landed there in a day, they would all perish in the next ten days; and there are not surplus shipping and surplus money enough in the world to carry them there in many times ten days. What then? Free them all, and keep them among us as underlings? Is it quite certain that this betters their condition? I think I would not hold one in slavery, at any rate; yet the point is not clear enough to me to denounce people upon. What next? Free them, and make them politically and socially our equals? My own feelings will not admit of this; and, if mine would, we well know that those of the great mass of white people will not. Whether this feeling accords with justice and sound judgment is not the sole question, if, indeed, it is any part of it. A universal feeling, whether well or ill founded, cannot be safely disregarded. We cannot make them equals. It does seem to me that systems of gradual emancipation might be adopted; but, for their tardiness in this, I will not undertake to judge our brethren of the South.

When they remind us of their constitutional rights, I acknowledge them, not grudgingly, but fully and fairly; and I would give them any legislation for the reclaiming of their fugitives which should not, in its stringency, be more likely to carry a free man into slavery than our ordinary criminal laws are to hang an innocent one.

But all this, to my judgment, furnishes no more excuse for permitting slavery to go into our own free territory than it would for reviving the African slave-trade by law. The law which forbids the bringing of slaves from Africa, and that which has so long forbidden the taking of them to Nebraska, can hardly be distinguished on any moral principle; and the repeal of the former could find quite as plausible excuses as that of the latter.

I have reason to know that Judge Douglas knows that I said this. I think he has the answer here to one of the questions he put to me. I do not mean to allow him to catechise me unless he pays back for it in kind. I will not answer questions one after another, unless he reciprocates: but as he has made this inquiry, and I have answered it before, he has got it without my getting anything in return. He has got my answer on the fugitive-slave law.

Now, gentlemen, I don't want to read at any great length: but this is the true complexion of all I have ever said in regard to the institution of slavery and the black race. This is the whole of it; and anything that argues me into his idea of perfect social and political equality with the negro is but a specious and fantastic arrangement of words, by which a man can prove a horse-chestnut to be a chestnut horse. I will say here, while upon this subject, that I have no purpose, either directly or indirectly, to interfere with the institution of slavery in the States where it exists. I believe I have no lawful right to do so, and I have no inclination to do so. I have no purpose to introduce political and social equality between the white and the black races. There is a physical difference between the two, which, in my judgment, will probably forever forbid their living together upon the footing of perfect equality; and, inasmuch as it becomes a necessity that there must be a difference, I, as well as Judge Douglas, am in favor of the race to which I belong having the superior position. I have never said anything to the contrary, but I hold that, notwithstanding all this, there is no reason in the world why the negro is not entitled to all the natural rights enumerated in the Declaration of Independence,—the right to life, liberty, and the pursuit of happiness. I hold that he is as much entitled to these as the white man. I agree with Judge Douglas he is not my equal in many respects,—certainly not in color, perhaps not in moral or intellectual endowment. But in the right to eat the bread, without the leave of anybody else, which his own hand earns, he is my equal and the equal of Judge Douglas, and the equal of every living man.

Now I pass on to consider one or two more of these little follies. The judge is wofully at fault about his early friend Lincoln being a "grocery-keeper." I don't think that it would be a great sin if I had been; but he is mistaken. Lincoln never kept a grocery anywhere in the world. It is true that Lincoln did work the latter part of one winter in a little still-house up at the head of a hollow. And so I think my friend, the judge, is equally at fault when he charges me at the time when I was in Congress of having opposed our soldiers who were fighting in the Mexican war. The judge did not make his charge very distinctly: but I tell you what he can prove, by referring to the record. You remember I was an Old Whig; and, whenever the Democratic party tried to get me to vote that the war had been righteously begun by the President, I would not do it. But, whenever they asked for any money or land-warrants or anything to pay the soldiers there, during all that time, I gave the same vote that Judge Douglas did. You can think as you please as to whether that was consistent. Such is the truth; and the judge has the right to make all he can out of it. But when he, by a general charge, conveys the idea that I withheld supplies from the soldiers who were fighting in the Mexican war, or did anything else to hinder the soldiers, he is, to say the least, grossly and altogether mistaken, as a consultation of the records will prove to him.

As I have not used up so much of my time as I had supposed, I will dwell a little longer upon one or two of these minor topics upon which the judge has spoken. He has read from my speech in Springfield in which I say that "a house divided against itself cannot stand." Does the judge say it can stand? I don't know whether he does or not. The judge does not seem to be attending to me just now, but I would like to know if it is his opinion that a house divided against itself can stand. If he does, then there is a question of veracity, not between him and me, but between the judge and an authority of a somewhat higher character.

Now, my friends, I ask your attention to this matter for the purpose of saying something seriously. I know that the judge may readily enough agree with me that the maxim which was put forth by the Saviour is true, but he may allege that I misapply it; and the judge has a right to urge that in my application I do misapply it, and then I have a right to show that I do not misapply it. When he undertakes to say that because I think this nation, so far as the question of slavery is concerned, will all become one thing or all the other, I am in favor of bringing about a dead uniformity in the various States in all their institutions, he argues erroneously. The great variety of the local institutions in the States, springing from differences in the soil, differences in the face of the country, and in the climate, are bonds of union. They do not make "a house divided against itself," but they make a house united. If they produce in one section of the country what is called for by the wants of another section, and this other section can supply the wants of the first, they are not matters of discord, but bonds of union,—true bonds of union. But can this question of slavery be considered as among these varieties in the institutions of the country? I leave it to you to say whether, in the history of our government, this institution of slavery has not always failed to be a bond of union, and, on the contrary, been an apple of discord and an element of division in the house. I ask you to consider whether, so long as the moral constitution of men's minds shall continue to be the same, after this generation and assemblage shall sink into the grave, and another race shall arise with the same moral and intellectual development we have,— whether, if that institution is standing in the same irritating position in which it now is, it will not continue an element of division?

If so, then I have a right to say that, in regard to this question, the Union is a house divided against itself; and when the judge reminds me that I have often said to him that the institution of slavery has existed for eighty years in some States, and yet it does not exist in some others, I agree to the fact, and I account for it by looking at the position in which our fathers originally placed it,— restricting it from the new Territories where it had not gone, and legislating to cut off its source by the abrogation of the slave-trade, thus putting the seal of legislation against its spread. The public mind did rest in the belief that it was in the course of ultimate extinction. But lately, I think,— and in this I charge nothing on the judge's motives,— lately, I think that he, and those acting with him, have placed that institution on a new basis, which looks to the perpetuity and nationalization of slavery. And, while it is placed upon this new basis, I say, and I have said, that I believe we shall not have peace upon the question until the opponents of slavery arrest the further spread of it, and place it where the public mind shall rest in the belief that it is in the course of ultimate extinction; or, on the other hand, that its advocates will push it forward until it shall become alike lawful in all the States, old as well as new, North as well as South. Now I believe, if we could arrest the spread, and place it where Washington and Jefferson and Madison placed it, it would be in the course of ultimate extinction, and the public mind would, as for eighty years past, believe that it was in the course of ultimate extinction. The crisis would be past, and the institution might be let alone for a hundred years — if it should live so long — in the States where it exists, yet it would be going out of existence in the way best for both the black and the white races. [A voice: "Then do you repudiate popular sovereignty?"] Well, then, let us talk about popular sovereignty! What is popular sovereignty? Is it the right of the people to have slavery or not have it, as they see fit, in the Territories? I will state — and I have an able man to watch me — my understanding is that popular sovereignty, as now applied to the question of slavery, does allow the people of a Territory to have slavery if they want to, but does not allow them not to have it if they do not want it. I do not mean that, if this vast concourse of people were in a Territory of the United States, any one of them would be obliged to have a slave if he did not want one; but I do say that, as I understand the Dred Scott decision, if any one man wants slaves, all the rest have no way of keeping that one man from holding them.

When I made my speech at Springfield, of which the judge complains, and from which he quotes, I really was not thinking of the things which he ascribes to me at all. I had no thought in the world that I was doing anything to bring about a war between the free and slave States. I had no thought in the world that I was doing anything to bring about a political and social equality of the black and white races. It never occurred to me that I was doing anything or favoring anything to reduce to a dead uniformity all the local institutions of the various States. But I must say; in all fairness to him, if he thinks I am doing something which leads to these bad results, it is none the better that I did not mean it. It is just as fatal to the country, if I have any influence in producing it, whether I intend it or not. But can it be true that placing this institution upon the original basis — the basis upon which our fathers placed it — can have any tendency to set the Northern and the Southern States at war with one another, or that it can have any tendency to make the people of Vermont raise sugarcane because they raise it in Louisiana, or that it can compel the people of Illinois to cut pine logs on the Grand prairie, where they will not grow, because they cut pine logs in Maine, where they do grow? The judge says this is a new principle started in regard to this question. Does the judge claim that he is working on the plan of the founders of the government? I think he says in some of his speeches — indeed, I have one here now — that he saw evidence of a policy to allow slavery to be south of a certain line, while north of it it should be excluded; and he saw an indisposition on the part of the country to stand upon that policy, and therefore he set about studying the subject upon original principles, and upon original principles he got up the Nebraska bill! I am fighting it upon these "original principles,"—fighting it in the Jeffersonian, Washingtonian, and Madisonian fashion.

Now, my friends, I wish you to attend for a little while to one or two other things in that Springfield speech. My main object was to show, so far as my humble ability was capable of showing to the people of this country, what I believed was the truth,—that there was a tendency, if not a conspiracy, among those who have engineered this slavery question for the last four or five years, to make slavery perpetual and universal in this nation. Having made that speech principally for that object, after arranging the evidences that I thought tended to prove my proposition, I concluded with this bit of comment:—

> We cannot absolutely know that these exact adaptations are the result of pre-concert; but, when we see a lot of framed timbers, different portions of which we know have been gotten out at different times and places, and by different workmen,—Stephen, Franklin, Roger, and James, for instance, —and when we see these timbers joined together, and see they exactly make the frame of a house or a mill, all the tenons and mortises exactly fitting, and all the lengths and proportions of the different pieces exactly adapted to their respective places, and not a piece too many or too few,—not omitting even the scaffolding,—or if a single piece be lacking, we see the place in the frame exactly fitted and prepared to yet bring such piece in, —in such a case we feel it impossible not to believe that Stephen and Franklin, and Roger and James, all understood one another from the beginning, and all worked upon a common plan or draft drawn before the first blow was struck.

When my friend, Judge Douglas, came to Chicago on the 9th of July, this speech having been delivered on the 16th of June, he made an harangue there in which he took hold of this speech of mine, showing that he had carefully read it; and, while he paid no attention to this matter at all, but complimented me as being a "kind, amiable, and intelligent gentleman," notwithstanding I had said this, he goes on and deduces, or draws out, from my speech this tendency of mine to set the States at war with one another, to make all the institutions uniform, and set the niggers and white people to marry together. Then, as the judge had complimented me with these pleasant titles (I must confess to my weakness), I was a little "taken"; for it came from a great man. I was not very much accustomed to flattery, and it came the sweeter to me. I was rather like the Hoosier with the gingerbread, when he said he reckoned he loved it better than any other man, and got less of it. As the judge had so flattered me, I could not make up my mind that he meant to deal unfairly with me. So I went to work to show him that he misunderstood the whole scope of my speech, and that I really never intended to set the people at war with one another. As an illustration, the next time I met him, which was at Springfield, I used this expression, that I claimed no right under the Constitution, nor had I any inclination, to enter into the slave States and interfere with the institutions of slavery. He says upon that, Lincoln will not enter into the slave States, but will go to the banks of the Ohio, on this side, and shoot over! He runs on, step by step, in the horse-chestnut style of argument, until in the Springfield speech he says, "Unless he shall be successful in firing his batteries until he shall have extinguished slavery in all the States, the Union shall be dissolved." Now I don't think that was exactly the way to treat "a kind, amiable, intelligent gentleman." I know, if I had asked the judge to show when or where it was I had said that, if I didn't succeed in firing into the slave States until slavery should be extinguished, the Union should be dissolved, he could not have shown it. I understand what he would do. He would say, "I don't mean to quote from you, but this was the result of what you say." But I have the right to ask, and I do ask now, Did you not put it in such a form that an ordinary reader or listener would take it as an expression from me?

In a speech at Springfield, on the night of the 17th, I thought I might as well attend to my business a little; and I recalled his attention as well as I could to this charge of conspiracy to nationalize slavery. I called his attention to the fact that he had acknowledged in my hearing twice that he had carefully read the speech; and, in the language of the lawyers, as he had twice read the speech, and still had put in no plea or answer, I took a default on him. I insisted that I had a right then to renew that charge of conspiracy. Ten days afterward I met the judge at Clinton,—that is to say, I was on the ground, but not in the discussion,—and heard him make a speech. Then he comes in with his plea to this charge, for the first time; and his plea when put in, as well as I can recollect it, amounted to this: that he never had any talk with Judge Taney or the President of the United States with regard to the Dred Scott decision before it was made; I (Lincoln) ought to know that the man who makes a charge without knowing it to be true falsifies as much as he who knowingly tells a falsehood; and, lastly, that he would pronounce the whole thing a falsehood; but he would make no personal application of the charge of falsehood, not because of any regard for the "kind, amiable, intelligent gentleman," but because of his own personal self-respect! I have understood since then (but [turning to Judge Douglas] will not hold the judge to it if he is not willing) that he has broken through the "self-respect," and has got to saying the thing out. The judge nods to me that it is so. It is fortunate for me that I can keep as good-humored as I do, when the judge acknowledges that he has been trying to make a question of veracity with me. I know the judge is a great man, while I am only a small man; but I feel that I have got him. I demur to that plea. I waive all objections that it was not filed till after default was taken, and demur to it upon the merits. What if Judge Douglas never did talk with Chief Justice Taney and the President before the Dred Scott decision was made: does it follow that he could not have had as perfect an understanding without talking as with it? I am not disposed to stand upon my legal advantage. I am disposed to take his denial as being like an answer in chancery, that he neither had any knowledge, information, nor belief in the existence of such a conspiracy. I am disposed to take his answer as being as broad as though he had put it in these words. And now, I ask, even if he had done so, have not I a right to prove it on him, and to offer the evidence of more than two witnesses, by whom to prove it; and, if the evidence proves the existence of the conspiracy, does his broad answer, denying all knowledge, information, or belief, disturb the fact? It can only show that he was used by conspirators, and was not a leader of them.

Now in regard to his reminding me of the moral rule that persons who tell what they do not know to be true falsify as much as those who knowingly tell falsehoods. I remember the rule, and it must be borne in mind that in what I have read to you I do not say that I know such a conspiracy to exist. To that I reply, I believe it. If the judge says that I do not believe it, then he says what he does not know, and falls within his own rule that he who asserts a thing which he does not know to be true falsifies as much as he who knowingly tells a falsehood. I want to call your attention to a little discussion on that branch of the case, and the evidence which brought my mind to the conclusion which I expressed as my belief. If, in arraying that evidence, I had stated anything which was false or erroneous, it needed but that Judge Douglas should point it out, and I would have taken it back with all the kindness in the world. I do not deal in that way. If I have brought forward anything not a fact, if he will point it out, it will not even ruffle me to take it back. But, if he will not point out anything erroneous in the evidence, is it not rather for him to show by a comparison of the evidence that I have reasoned falsely than to call the "kind, amiable, intelligent gentleman" a liar? If I have reasoned to a false conclusion, it is the vocation of an able debater to show by argument that I have wandered to an erroneous conclusion. I want to ask your attention to a portion of the Nebraska bill which Judge Douglas has quoted: "it being the true intent and meaning of this act not to legislate slavery into any Territory or State, nor to exclude it therefrom, but to leave the people thereof perfectly free to form and regulate their domestic institutions in their own way, subject only to the Constitution of the United States." Thereupon Judge Douglas and others began to argue in favor of "popular sovereignty,"— the right of the people to have slaves if they wanted them, and to exclude slavery if they did not want them. "But," said, in substance, a senator from Ohio (Mr. Chase, I believe), "we more than suspect that you do not mean to allow the people to exclude slavery if they wish to; and, if you do mean it, accept an amendment which I propose expressly authorizing the people to exclude slavery." I believe I have the amendment here before me, which was offered, and under which the people of the Territory, through their proper representatives, might, if they saw fit, prohibit the existence of slavery therein. And now I state it as a fact, to be taken back if there is any mistake about it, that Judge Douglas and those acting with him voted that amendment down. I now think that those men who voted it down had a real reason for doing so. They know what that reason was. It looks to us, since we have seen the Dred Scott decision pronounced, holding that, "under the Constitution," the people cannot exclude slavery,— I say it looks to outsiders, poor, simple, "amiable, intelligent gentlemen," as though the niche was left as a place to put that Dred Scott decision in,— a niche which would have been spoiled by adopting the amendment.

And now I say again, if this was not the reason, it will avail the judge much more to calmly and good-humoredly point out to these people what that other reason was for voting the amendment down than swelling himself up to vociferate that he may be provoked to call somebody a liar.

Again, there is in that same quotation from the Nebraska bill this clause: "it being the true intent and meaning of this bill not to legislate slavery into any Territory or State." I have always been puzzled to know what business the word "State" had in that connection. Judge Douglas knows. He put it there. He knows what he put it there for. We outsiders cannot say what he put it there for. The law they were passing was not about States, and was not making provision for States. What was it placed there for? After seeing the Dred Scott decision, which holds that the people cannot exclude slavery from a Territory, if another Dred Scott decision shall come, holding that they cannot exclude it from a State, we shall discover that, when the word was originally put there, it was in view of something which was to come in due time. we shall see that it was the other half of something. I now say again, if there is any different reason for putting it there, Judge Douglas, in a good-humored way, without calling anybody a liar, can tell what the reason was.

When the judge spoke at Clinton, he came very near making a charge of falsehood against me. He used, as I found it printed in a newspaper, which, I remember, was very nearly like the real speech, the following language:—

> I did not answer the charge [of conspiracy] before for the reason that I did not suppose there was a man in America with a heart so corrupt as to believe such a charge could be true. I have too much respect for Mr. Lincoln to suppose he is serious in making the charge.

I confess this is rather a curious view, that out of respect for me he should consider I was making what I deemed rather a grave charge in fun. I confess it strikes me rather strangely. But I let it pass. As the judge did not for a moment believe that there was a man in America whose heart was so "corrupt" as to make such a charge, and as he places me among the "men in America" who have hearts base enough to make such a charge, I hope he will excuse me if I hunt out another charge very like this; and, if it should turn out that in hunting I should find that other, and it should turn out to be Judge Douglas himself who made it, I hope he will reconsider this question of the deep corruption of heart he has thought fit to ascribe to me. In Judge Douglas's speech of March 22, 1858, which I hold in my hand, he says: —

In this connection there is another topic to which I desire to allude. I seldom refer to the course of newspapers or notice the articles which they publish in regard to myself; but the course of the Washington *Union* has been so extraordinary for the last two or three months that I think it well enough to make some allusion to it. It has read me out of the Democratic party every other day, at least for two or three months, and keeps reading me out, and, as if it had not succeeded, still continues to read me out, using such terms as "traitor," "renegade," "deserter," and other kind and polite epithets of that nature. Sir, I have no vindication to make of my Democracy against the Washington *Union*, or any other newspaper. I am willing to allow my history and actions for the last twenty years to speak for themselves as to my political principles and my fidelity to political obligations. The Washington *Union* has a personal grievance. When the editor was nominated for public printer, I declined to vote for him, and stated that at some time I might give my reasons for doing so. Since I declined to give that vote, this scurrilous abuse, these vindictive and constant attacks, have been repeated almost daily on me. Will my friend from Michigan read the article to which I allude?

This is a part of the speech. You must excuse me from reading the entire article of the Washington *Union*, as Mr. Stuart read it for Mr. Douglas. The judge goes on and sums up, as I think, correctly: —

Mr. President, you here find several distinct propositions advanced boldly by the Washington *Union* editorially, and apparently authoritatively; and any man who questions any of them is denounced as an Abolitionist, a Free-soiler, a fanatic. The propositions are, first, that the primary object of all government at its original institution is the protection of person and property; second, that the Constitution of the United States declares that the citizens of each State shall be entitled to all the privileges and immunities of citizens in the several States; and that, therefore, thirdly, all State laws, whether organic or otherwise, which prohibit the citizens of one State from settling in another with their slave property, and especially declaring it forfeited, are direct violations of the original intention of the government and Constitution of the United States; and, fourth, that the emancipation of the slaves of the Northern States was a gross outrage on the rights of property, inasmuch as it was involuntarily done on the part of the owner.

Remember that this article was published in the *Union* on the 17th of November, and on the 18th appeared the first article giving the adhesion of the *Union* to the Lecompton constitution. It was in these words: —

"KANSAS AND HER CONSTITUTION. The vexed question is settled. The problem is solved. The dead point of danger is passed. All serious trouble to Kansas affairs is over and gone."

And a column nearly of the same sort. Then, when you come to look into the Lecompton constitution, you find the same doctrine incorporated in it which was put forth editorially in the *Union*. What is it?

"ARTICLE 7, *Section* 1. The right of property is before and higher than any constitutional sanction; and the right of the owner of a slave to such slave and its increase is the same and as inviolable as the right of the owner of any property whatever."

Then in the schedule is a provision that the constitution may be amended after 1864 by a two-thirds vote.

"But no alteration shall be made to affect the right of property in the ownership of slaves."

It will be seen by these clauses in the Lecompton constitution that they are identical in spirit with the *authoritative* article in the Washington *Union* of the day previous to its indorsement of this constitution.

I pass over some portions of the speech, and I hope that any one who feels interested in this matter will read the entire section of the speech, and see whether I do the judge an injustice. He proceeds:—

When I saw that article in the *Union* of the 17th of November, followed by the glorification of the Lecompton constitution on the 18th of November, and this clause in the constitution asserting the doctrine that a State has no right to prohibit slavery within its limits, I saw that there was a fatal blow being struck at the sovereignty of the States of this Union.

I stop the quotation there, again requesting that it may all be read. I have read all of the portion I desire to comment upon. What is this charge that the judge thinks I must have a very corrupt heart to make? It was a purpose on the part of certain high functionaries to make it impossible for the people of one State to prohibit the people of any other State from entering it with their "property," so called, and making it a slave State. In other words, it was a charge implying a design to make the institution of slavery national. And now I ask your attention to what Judge Douglas has himself done here. I know that he made that part of the speech as a reason why he had refused to vote for a certain man for public printer; but, when we get at it, the charge itself is the very one I made against him, that he thinks I am so corrupt for uttering. Now whom does he make that charge against? Does he make it against that newspaper editor merely? No: he says it is identical in spirit with the Lecompton constitution, and so the framers of that constitution are brought in with the editor of the newspaper in that "fatal blow being struck." He did not call it a "conspiracy." In his language it is a "fatal blow being struck." And, if the words carry the meaning better when changed from a "conspiracy" into a "fatal blow being struck," I will change my expression, and call it "fatal blow being struck." We see the charge made not merely against the editor of the *Union*, but all the framers of the Lecompton constitution; and not only so, but the article was an authoritative article. By whose authority? Is there any question but that he means it was by the authority of the President and his cabinet,— the administration? Is there any sort of question but that he means to make that charge? Then there are the editors of the *Union*, the framers of the Lecompton constitution, the President of the United States and his cabinet, and all the supporters of the Lecompton constitution, in Congress and out of Congress, who are all involved in this "fatal blow being struck." I commend to Judge Douglas's consideration the question of how corrupt a man's heart must be to make such a charge!

Now, my friends, I have but one branch of the subject, in the little time I have left, to which to call your attention; and, as I shall come to a close at the end of that branch, it is probable that I shall not occupy quite all the time allotted to me. Although on these questions I would like to talk twice as long as I have, I could not enter upon another head and discuss it properly without running over my time. I ask the attention of the people here assembled and elsewhere to the course that Judge Douglas is pursuing every day as bearing upon this question of making slavery national. Not going back to the records, but taking the speeches he makes, the speeches he made yesterday and day before, and makes constantly all over the country.— I ask your attention to them. In the first place, what is necessary to make the institution national? Not war. There is no danger that the people of Kentucky will shoulder their muskets, and, with a young nigger stuck on every bayonet, march into Illinois and force them upon us. There is no danger of our going over there and making war upon them. Then what is necessary for the nationalization of slavery? It is simply the next Dred Scott decision. It is merely for the Supreme Court to decide that no State under the Constitution can exclude it, just as they have already decided that under the Constitution neither Congress nor the Territorial legislature can do it. When that is decided and acquiesced in, the whole thing is done. This being true, and this being the way, as I think, that slavery is to be made national, let us consider what Judge Douglas is doing every day to that end. In the first place, let us see what influence he is exerting on public sentiment. In this and like communities, public sentiment is everything. With public sentiment, nothing can fail; without it, nothing can succeed. Consequently, he who moulds public sentiment goes deeper than he who enacts statutes or pronounces decisions. He makes statutes and decisions possible or impossible to be executed. This must be borne in mind, as also the additional fact that Judge Douglas is a man of vast influence, so great that it is enough for many men to profess to believe anything when they once find out that Judge Douglas professes to believe it. Consider also the attitude he occupies at the head of a large party,— a party, which he claims has a majority of all the voters in the country.

This man sticks to a decision which forbids the people of a Territory to exclude slavery, and he does so not because he says it is right in itself,— he does not give any opinion on that, — but because it has been decided by the court; and, being decided by the court, he is, and you are, bound to take it in your political action as law,— not that he judges at all of its merits, but because a decision of the court is to him a "Thus saith the Lord." He places it on that ground alone, and you will bear in mind that thus committing himself unreservedly to this decision commits him to the next one just as firmly as to this. He did not commit himself on account of the merit or demerit of the decision, but it is a "Thus saith the Lord." The next decision, as much as this, will be a "Thus saith the Lord." There is nothing that can divert or turn him away from this decision. It is nothing that I point out to him that his great prototype, General Jackson, did not believe in the binding force of decisions. It is nothing to him that Jefferson did not so believe. I have said that I have often heard him approve of Jackson's course in disregarding the decision of the Supreme Court pronouncing a national bank constitutional. He says I did not hear him say so. He denies the accuracy of my recollection. I say he ought to know better than I; but I will make no question about this thing, though it still seems to me that I heard him say it twenty times. I will tell him, though, that he now claims to stand on the Cincinnati platform, which affirms that Congress cannot charter a national bank, in the teeth of that old standing decision that Congress can charter a bank. And I remind him of another piece of history on the question of respect for judicial decisions, and it is a piece of Illinois history, belonging to a time when a large party to which Judge Douglas belonged were displeased with a decision of the Supreme Court of Illinois, because they had decided that a governor could not remove a secretary of state. You will find the whole story in Ford's History of Illinois, and I know that Judge Douglas will not deny that he was then in favor of overslaughing that decision by the mode of adding five new judges, so as to vote down the four old ones. Not only so, but it ended in the judge's sitting down on the very bench as one of the five new judges to break down the four old ones. It was in this way precisely that he got his title of judge. Now, when the judge tells me that men appointed conditionally to sit as members of a court will have to be catechised beforehand upon some subject, I say, " You know, judge: you have tried it." When he says a court of this kind will lose the confidence of all men, will be prostituted and disgraced by such a proceeding, I say, "You know best, judge: you have been through the mill."

But I cannot shake Judge Douglas's teeth loose from the Dred Scott decision. Like some obstinate animal (I mean no disrespect) that will hang on when he has once got his teeth fixed,— you may cut off a leg or you may tear away an arm, still he will not relax his hold. And so I may point out to the judge, and say that he is bespattered all over, from the beginning of his political life to the present time, with attacks upon judicial decisions.— I may cut off limb after limb of his public record, and strive to wrench from him a single dictum of the court, yet I cannot divert him from it. He hangs to the last to the Dred Scott decision. These things show there is a purpose strong as death and eternity for which he adheres to this decision, and for which he will adhere to all other decisions of the same court. [A Hibernian: "Give us something besides Drid Scott."] Yes; no doubt you want to hear something that don't hurt. Now, having spoken of the Dred Scott decision, one more word, and I am done. Henry Clay, my beau-ideal of a statesman, the man for whom I fought all my humble life,— Henry Clay once said of a class of men who would repress all tendencies to liberty and ultimate emancipation that they must, if they would do this, go back to the era of our independence, and muzzle the cannon which thunders its annual joyous return; they must blow out the moral lights around us; they must penetrate the human soul, and eradicate there the love of liberty; and then, and not till then, could they perpetuate slavery in this country! To my thinking, Judge Douglas is, by his example and vast influence, doing that very thing in this community when he says that the negro has nothing in the Declaration of Independence. Henry Clay plainly understood the contrary. Judge Douglas is going back to the era of our Revolution, and to the extent of his ability muzzling the cannon which thunders its annual joyous return. When he invites any people, willing to have slavery, to establish it, he is blowing out the moral lights around us. When he says he "cares not whether slavery is voted down or voted up," — that it is a sacred right of self-government,— he is, in my judgment, penetrating the human soul, and eradicating the light of reason and the love of liberty in this American people. And now I will only say that when, by all these means and appliances, Judge Douglas shall succeed in bringing public sentiment to an exact accordance with his own views,— when these vast assemblages shall echo back all these sentiments,— when they shall come to repeat his views and to avow his principles, and to say all that he says on these mighty questions,— then it needs only the formality of the second Dred Scott decision, which he indorses in advance, to make slavery alike lawful in all the States,— old as well as new, North as well as South.

LINCOLN'S FAREWELL ADDRESS AT SPRINGFIELD, ILL., AS HE WAS LEAVING FOR WASHINGTON, FEBRUARY 11, 1861.

My Friends,— No one, not in my situation, can appreciate my feeling of sadness at this parting. To this place, and the kindness of this people, I owe everything. Here I have lived a quarter of a century, and have passed from a young to an old man. Here my children have been born, and one is buried. I now leave, not knowing when or whether ever I may return, with a task before me greater than that which rested upon Washington. Without the assistance of that Divine Being who ever attended him, I cannot succeed. With that assistance, I cannot fail. Trusting in Him who can go with me, and remain with you, and be everywhere for good, let us confidently hope that all will yet be well. To His care commending you, as I hope in your prayers you will commend me, I bid you an affectionate farewell.

Abraham Lincoln was nominated for the United States Senate by the Republican State Convention at Springfield, Ill., June 17, 1858, and accepted the nomination in a remarkable speech before the convention, sharply defining the national issues of the time. Senator Douglas, then a candidate for re-election, reviewed this speech in an address at Chicago, July 9, Mr. Lincoln being present; and the next evening Mr. Lincoln made a speech in reply. After various other speeches by both candidates a series of seven joint debates was arranged, which took place at Ottawa, Freeport, Jonesboro, Charleston, Galesburg, Quincy, and Alton, Ill., the first on August 21, the last on October 15, 1858. The first speaker in each debate occupied an hour, an hour and a half was given for the reply, and then the first speaker had a half-hour to close the debate. Mr. Douglas's closing word at Ottawa is not given in the present leaflet, as it related to personalities and not to the general political issues. A complete report of all of the debates is given in the first volume of Lincoln's Works, edited by Nicolay and Hay. In the same volume will be found Lincoln's great speech at the Cooper Institute, New York, February 27, 1860, which did more than anything else save the debates with Douglas to bring him prominently before the country at large, and insure his nomination for the presidency later in the same year.

Nicolay and Hay's "Abraham Lincoln, A History," in ten volumes, is more than a biography of Lincoln: it is a comprehensive history as well of the anti-slavery struggle and the civil war. There are many briefer lives of Lincoln,— by Arnold, Holland, Morse, Raymond, and others. The Life by Herndon has special interest as the work of one who was Lincoln's law partner and intimate friend for many years. The essay on Lincoln by Carl Schurz is a magnificent critical estimate. "Reminiscences of Lincoln by Distinguished Men of his Time," edited by Rice, is a book of great value. The Life of Lincoln by Charles Carleton Coffin is an admirable work for young people. Lincoln's two Inaugural Addresses and the Emancipation Proclamation are published in Old South Leaflet No. 11.

www.ingramcontent.com/pod-product-compliance
Lightning Source LLC
Chambersburg PA
CBHW020926230426
43666CB00008B/1590